50 Jackson Hole Photography Hotspots

A Guide for Photographers and Wildlife Enthusiasts

2nd Edition

by
Aaron Linsdau

Additional Photography:
Beth Holmes
Randy Isaacson
Loren Nelson

Sastrugi Press
Jackson, WY

Copyright © 2022 by Aaron Linsdau

All rights reserved. No part of this book may be reproduced or transmitted in any form or by any means, electronic or mechanical, including photocopying, recording, or by any information storage and retrieval system without the written permission of the author, except where permitted by law.

Sastrugi Press / Published by arrangement with the author

50 Jackson Hole Photography Hotspots, 2nd Edition: A Guide for Photographers and Wildlife Enthusiasts

The author has made every effort to accurately describe the locations contained in this work. Travel to some locations in this book may be hazardous. The publisher has no control over and does not assume any responsibility for author or third-party websites or their content describing these locations, how to travel there, nor how to do it safely. Sketch maps provided are approximate. Refer to official government maps.

Any person exploring to these locations is personally responsible for checking local conditions prior to departure. You are responsible for your own actions and decisions. The information contained in this work is based solely on the author's research at the time of publication and may not be accurate. Neither the publisher nor the author assumes any liability for anyone exploring, visiting, or traveling the locations described in this work.

Sastrugi Press
PO Box 1297, Jackson, WY 83001, United States
www.sastrugipress.com

Quantity sales: Special discounts are available on quantity purchases by corporations, associations, and others. For details, contact the publisher at the address above.

Library of Congress Cataloging-in-Publication Data Available

Names: Linsdau, Aaron, author.
Title: 50 Jackson Hole photography hotspots, 2nd Edition: A guide for photographers and wildlife enthusiasts / by Aaron Linsdau ; additional photography, Beth Holmes, Randy Isaacson, Loren Nelson.
Other titles: Fifty Jackson Hole photography hotspots
Description: Jackson, WY : Sastrugi Press, [2022] | Series: 50 photography hotspots
Subjects: LCSH: Outdoor photography--Wyoming--Jackson Hole. | Jackson Hole (Wyo.)--Guidebooks.
Classification: LCC TR659.5 .L56 2022 (print) | LCC TR659.5 (ebook) | DDC 778.7/1097872--dc23/eng/20220511

Summary: Discover the best photography locations in Jackson Hole, Wyoming and Grand Teton National Park.

ISBN-13: 978-1-64922-250-3 (paperback)

ISBN-13: 978-1-64922-249-7 (hardback)

778.7—dc23

All photography, maps and artwork by the author, except as noted.
10 9 8 7 6 5

Cover image © Aaron Linsdau
Back cover images: © Aaron Linsdau, © Beth Holmes, © Randy Isaacson, © Loren Nelson

Dedicated to my dad, Tim Linsdau, who gave my first camera, instilled the love of photography, and created a passion for the outdoors through the Scouting program.

CONTENTS

Jackson Area Map	5
Introduction	7
Travel	8
Environment	9
Subjects	11
Cameras & Lenses	12
Techniques & Timing	15

MAP #1   JACKSON LAKE — 19

Cattleman's Bridge	20
Colter Bay Area	23
Fire Smoke In Jackson Hole	26
Grand View Point	29
Jackson Lake Lodge	32
Oxbow Bend	35
Signal Mountain	38
Snake River Overlook	40
Willow Flats Turnout	43

MAP #2   JENNY LAKE — 45

Bar BC Ranch	46
Beaver Ponds	49
Blacktail Ponds Overlook	52
Chapel of the Transfiguration	54
Delta Lake	57
Hidden Falls / Inspiration Point	60
Jenny Lake Overlook on the One Way	63
Jenny Lake Trail	66
Lucas-Fabian Homestead	70
Menors Ferry	73
Patriarch Tree	75
Phelps Lake	78
Schwabacher Landing	81
String Lake	85
Taggart Lake	88

MAP #3   CENTRAL JACKSON — 91

Miller House	92
National Elk Refuge	95
National Wildlife Museum	98
Park Sign North of the Fish Hatchery	100
Snow King Overlook	102

MAP #4   GROSS VENTRE NORTH — 104

Cunningham Cabin	105
Shadow Mountain	108
The Observatory	110
Togwotee Overlook	112
Toppings Lake Ridge	114
Triangle X Ranch Meadow	117
Wolff Ranch Road / Elk Ranch Flats	119

MAP #5   GROSS VENTRE SOUTH — 121

Antelope Flats Road	122
Gros Ventre Road	124
Kelly Warm Springs	127
Mormon Row	129
Moulton Barn	131
Pink House and John Moulton Barn	134
Red and Lavender Hills	137
Shane Cabins	139
Sleeping Indian	141
Teton Science School	143
Wedding Tree	145

MAP #6   TETON VALLEY — 149

Pine Creek Pass	150
Teton Canyon Idaho	152
Teton Valley	154

About the Author	157
Additional Photographer Biographies	158
Other Books by the Author	159

Jackson Hole Area Map

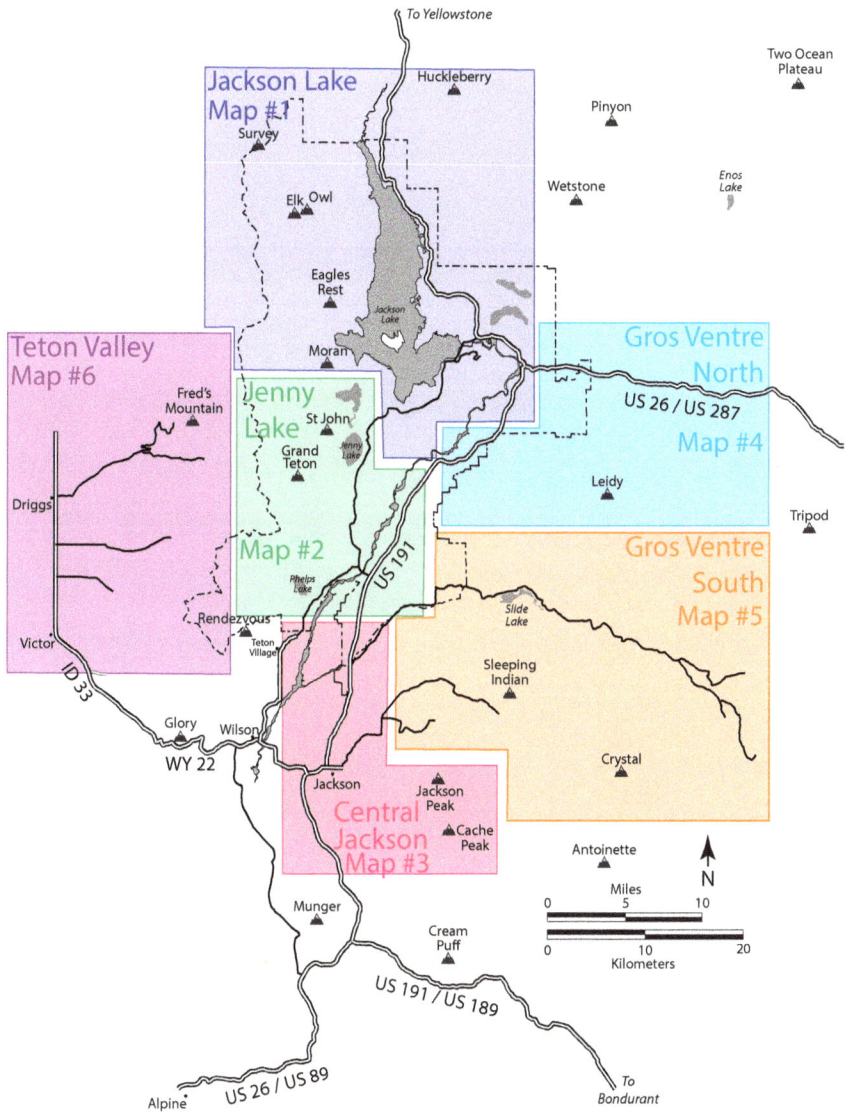

Note: The GPS coordinates in this book use the WGS84 (World Geodetic System) projection. Miles are statute miles.

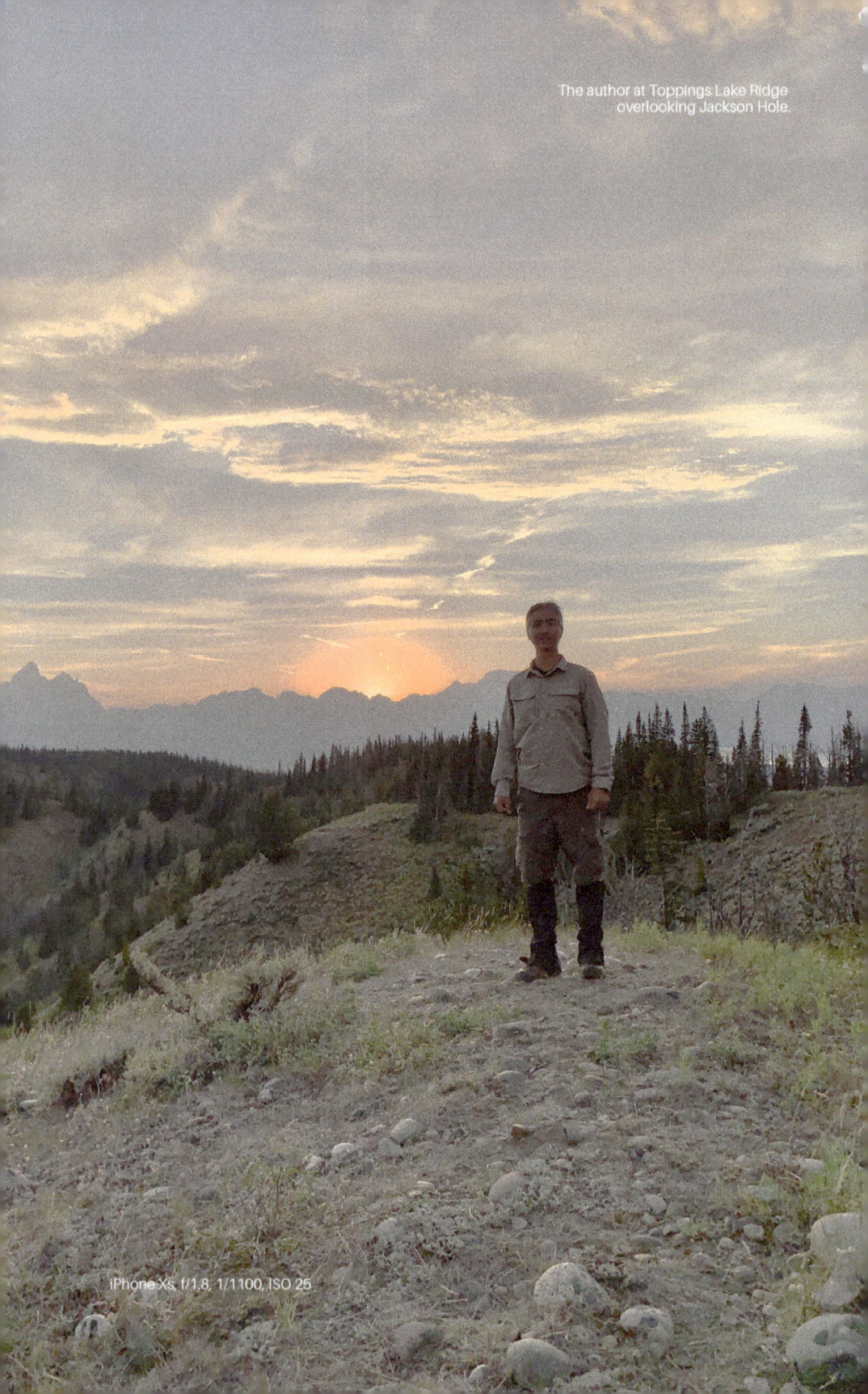

The author at Toppings Lake Ridge overlooking Jackson Hole.

iPhone Xs, f/1.8, 1/1100, ISO 25

INTRODUCTION

Photography in Jackson Hole is one of the most popular activities in the region. It is, perhaps, only overshadowed by hiking and skiing. People travel from all around the world for the landscapes and animals of Jackson Hole. The views are unmatched in the Lower 48 United States. There is nothing else in the United States like this small corner of northwest Wyoming and eastern Idaho.

As virtually every adult has a smartphone capable of taking photos, it is easier than ever to visit Jackson Hole and take stunning photographs. The biggest challenge is knowing where to go. The enterprising photographer can spend hours scouring the Internet, combing social media sites, and asking friends. Though this is educational, the time yield is not as good. That is where this book comes in.

Contained in the text and the photos are the most photogenic spots in all of Jackson Hole. Some are well known while others are not. Time again, well-known photographers have asked for a copy of this book because they weren't familiar with some of the sites contained inside. The collection of locations is garnered from two decades of photography, videography, hiking, backpacking, camping, and climbing experience from a Jackson Hole native.

Each hotspot contains a short description of what is to be expected at each location. The birds and animals tend to be most active in the early morning and late in the day. During the heat of the day, animals tend to stay under tree cover. For best photography and viewing, the best hours are at dawn and the few hours before dusk.

This book is broken into six areas: Central Jackson, Gros Ventre North, Gros Ventre South, Jackson Lake, Jenny Lake, and Teton Valley. Each of these areas is unique and well worth visiting. The desire to drive right up to the mountains and photograph them is understandable. However, by inspecting each section of hotspots in this book, the reader will discover that the viewpoints at unexpected places will yield surprising results.

SAFETY

Hiking during a warm summer day in Jackson Hole is an exquisite experience. Travelers from all over the world visit to enjoy the landscape, animals, and plant life. However, there are some dangers visitors must be aware of. For virtually all hikers, a walk will go exactly as planned. It's the seemingly minor stumble, overestimation of ability, or unexpected weather that changes a pleasant walk into an ordeal.

Exercise caution when you are viewing and photographing wildlife. The animals of Jackson Hole are not tame. They will defend themselves if they feel threatened with unexpected ferocity. Your actions may seem benign but to a threatened animal, they may feel they are in mortal danger.

Jackson Hole has its share of crime. Exercise caution with camera equipment and other valuables. Most thieves are opportunists. Although the town of Jackson is

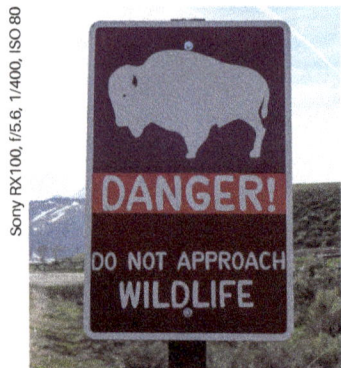

Wildlife need their space. Follow park regulations regarding minimum distances from wildlife to avoid stressing them and creating a negative encounter.

small, the police blotter in the News and Guide is regularly filled with petty crimes. Avoid leaving valubles in vehicles, especially when those valuable are visible. Do your best to prevent becoming an unwitting crime victim.

Be prepared for dramatic weather changes. One day can be incredibly warm while the next can be below freezing. Snow is not uncommon in July and August. Be prepared with some extra clothing just in case.

Each of the following sections will help the first-time visiting photographer better understand Jackson Hole. As with any area, there are nuances and a local photographic language.

TRAVEL

FLYING INTO JACKSON

The Jackson Hole Airport is the only major commercial airport in a national park in America. The normal flight pattern is north to south. If possible, sit on the right-hand side (starboard) of the plane to have an incredible view of the Tetons while flying in. The mountains appear incredibly close and are worth being prepared for a photo. The Cathedral Group is 9.5 miles (15.2 km) northeast of the airport on a bearing of 339º. The airport does not have jetways. Be prepared for windy, cold, and snowy conditions when arriving in winter.

HISTORIC SITES AND TOWN PHOTOGRAPHY

Jackson and Jackson Hole are peppered with historic and unique sites to photograph. A visit to the Wort Hotel and Silver Dollar Bar is necessary to gain a historic perspective of Jackson. The hallways of the restaurant, bar, and hotel have unique and historic images to provide photographic inspiration and ideas.

The original Silver Dollar Bar has 2,032 uncirculated Morgan silver dollars, all from 1921. Children are allowed in the bar until 6pm. Artwork, often from the September Fall Arts Festival, adorns the hotel's lobby. Walls along the hotel's hallway are covered in historical memorabilia, photographs, and also information about the August 5, 1980 fire that defined Jackson's downtown. The hotel was a home for illegal gambling in the "Snake Pit" until the 1950s.

Jackson's Million Dollar Cowboy Bar is well worth a visit as well. This famous and historic bar has horse saddles for barstools and a silver dollar bar top. The posts holding up the building are made of knobbled pine, themselves well worth a few photographs. There is always something going on for adult visitors after the light has faded from the sky. The Mangy Moose Bar at Teton Village (Jackson Hole Mountain Resort) is also a good historic interior photography location. 3295 Village Dr., Teton Village, WY (307-733-4913).

Elk antler arches adorn the town square and are a visitor favorite. These antlers are collected by the Boy Scouts on the National Elk Refuge after they have fallen off the bull elk. The town square is the perfect starting point for exploring the many photography and art galleries.

The Jackson Hole Historical Society Museum, located at 225 N Cache Street in Jackson, (307-733-2414), is a good resource for historic photography. The Jackson Hole Playhouse, located at 145 West Deloney Avenue (307-733-6994) has a photogenic historic lobby. The actors also put on America's longest-running shoot-out show at the corner of East Deloney Avenue and Center Street at 6pm from Labor Day to Memorial Day. This is a perfect time to take photos of actors in period costumes and pose with them for selfies and portraits.

ENVIRONMENT

ATMOSPHERIC SCINTILLATION

When photographing objects far away from the overheated ground, the air can significantly distort an image. This is due to the air being heated by the ground. As this hot air rises in the sky, it slightly deflects light. Over long distances, this scintillation effect can blur objects. At long distances, the shimmer caused by this effect can render objects unrecognizable.

For long-distance photography, the morning is a much better choice, as the sun has not heated the ground. Once the sun heats the ground, the distortion can last well into the afternoon, even after the sun has fallen behind the mountains.

BLUE BIRD SKIES

When skies are clear, this is referred to by locals as "bluebird sky days." They are the most desirable for hiking and travel. However, they yield uninteresting skies. A blank blue sky photographed in color has little drama. Watch the weather forecast and head out, when safe, for more compelling and dramatic images. Some of the worst weather days yield the best photographs.

The Cathedral Group includes the Grand Teton, Mount Owen, Middle Teton, South Teton, Teewinot Mountain, Teepe Pillar, Cloudveil Dome, Nez Perce Peak, and Buck

Mountain, most of which are over 12,000 feet (3,700 m) above sea level and represent eight of the ten highest summits in the Teton Range. Some of the best views of the group are from the north Jenny Lake / String Lake turn-off from the inner park road.

FOREST FIRE SMOKE

At first, smoke from forest fires will seem to eliminate photographic opportunities. However, the interplay between the light and mountain shapes can create far more dramatic images. The views might not be what is expected, but that does not mean all is lost for photography.

HAZY SKIES

Bluebird skies often yield weak imagery with no texture in the sky and blue haze. The high altitude of Jackson Hole means ultraviolet (UV) light and dust particle scatter often negatively affects images. Often, mid-day photographs yield high-contrast, unattractive landscape images. Local photographers use the middle of the day to scout, plan, hike, and rest for the afternoon photographic opportunities.

SEASONAL PHOTOGRAPHY

Photography during the late spring and summer is generally easy. The skies are clear in the morning and develop clouds in the afternoon in July and August. Weather is uncommon during the summer. The northern latitude of the region makes days long a month before and after.

The sky is overcast through much of winter. This makes capturing contrasting scenes easier than when the sky is clear. The temperatures regularly fall below 0ºF (-18ºC) in Jackson Hole. Managing cold and being safe in these conditions can be a real challenge.

Snow comes early to Jackson Hole. The mountains often receive their first dusting of snow in early September. Be prepared for this. Snowfall often catches unwary visitors by surprise. The latitude and elevation of the Greater Yellowstone Ecosystem cause the area to be much colder than the surrounding region.

Colder temperatures bring fall colors. Most of the time the deciduous trees like aspens and cottonwood will change color starting in late August. Once the night air temperature drops below freezing with a reduced amount of daylight, tree leaves will begin changing. This transition from strong greens to vibrant yellow, orange, and red leaves happens quickly here.

Often, the first fall storm with winds will knock leaves off the trees. The optimal window for leaf photography is often only a week long. Locations like Oxbow Bend, Schwabacher, and the Chapel of Transfiguration will have large crowds. Show up an hour or more before sunrise to secure the best position. Scout out your location a day in advance to be prepared for setting up in the dark.

Sun and Moon Path

The sun and moon travel in a diagonal line across the Tetons during sunset. This is due to the northerly latitude of northwest Wyoming. When deciding where to plan for the sun or moon to contact the mountains, expect that either will not transit the sky vertically. Instead, these celestial bodies will sweep across the range from the south. This effect is more pronounced in winter, as the sun sets much further south.

Weather

The temperature over the year is wildly variable. Even from day to day the park can be hot one day and below freezing the next. Respect lightning conditions - many people have been killed over the years climbing and in trails in storms.

The toughest danger from the weather in Grand Teton is the weather and clouds usually arrive from the west. The storms and fast-moving storm cells are impossible to see until they crest over the Teton Range. The sky can be clear all morning and then, in mid-afternoon, lightning can appear seemingly out of nowhere.

During July and August, be aware of the monsoonal action in the mountains. Although the weather is technically not monsoon-driven, the result is the same. Clear morning, clouds by noon, and then random thundershowers and roaring lightning in the afternoon. Do not underestimate the danger weather poses in the region. Your life and the lives of your companions depend on your ability to check the weather beforehand.

SUBJECTS

Animals

Animals in Jackson Hole are powerful and wild. They are a prime reason why many come to visit. However, be aware that even the most docile-looking moose can be aggressive if they feel threatened. This 1,000-pound (453-kg) animal can destroy a car or flip someone high into the air without straining themselves. Many visitors underestimate the power wild animals have. This is especially true of grizzly bears, bison, and moose.

Follow the current Park Service regulations of staying well away from these majestic creatures. Their life is difficult, especially in the winter. If they spend energy trying to escape an overaggressive photographer, they may be injured or even die. Negative visitor and animal incidents have become all too common.

Always maintain a safe distance from wolves and bears of at least 100 yards (100 meters). Maintain 25 yards (25 meters) of distance from all other animals. This is as much for their safety as yours.

CATHEDRAL GROUP

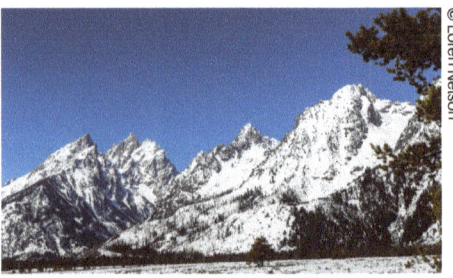

The Cathedral Group in perpetual winter.

The group of summits known as the Cathedral Group is a collection of the tallest mountains in Grand Teton. The summits are: Grand Teton (13,776 feet / 4,198m), Mount Owen (12,928 feet / 3940m), Middle Teton (12,804 feet / 3,902m), South Teton (12,514 feet / 3,814m), Teewinot Mountain (12,325 feet / 3756m), Teepe Pillar (12,266 feet / 3,738 m), Cloudveil Dome (12,026 feet / 3,665 m), and Buck Mountain (11,938 feet / 3,638 m). Buck Mountain is at the southern end and Teewinot is at the northern end of the group.

WATER FALLS

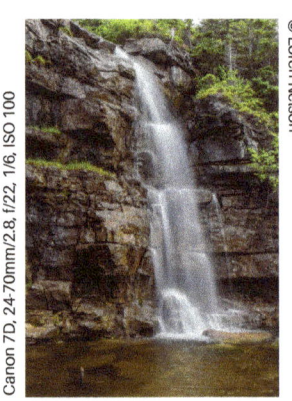

The best shutter speed is determined by the flow of the water and the amount of softening you prefer. Generally, ¼ to 1 second is a good place to start. Always avoid the "lethal" waterfall shutter speed between 1/30 and about 1/100 that will neither "freeze" the water movement nor smooth and soften it.

This shot is a different Hidden Falls outside the park but is included to capture the "softening" of the water flow using a tripod, neutral density filter, and a long 1/6 second shutter speed.

CAMERAS & LENSES

CAMERA SETTINGS

Modern digital cameras are complex devices. However, they only have three fundamental settings that need to be managed for good photography. These settings are ISO, shutter speed, and aperture. For the clearest images, use the lowest ISO possible. To achieve the largest depth of field, use a higher aperture number such as f/11 or higher. When using a stable tripod, most any shutter speed above 1/60 second will suffice for wide-angle up to short telephoto lenses as a general rule.

There are countless details involved in choosing these three settings. The above rules are guidelines to guide the beginning photographer into landscape photography. Many factors affect the selection of ISO, shutter speed, and aperture. These factors include wind, sensor size, lens focal length, desire to freeze or blur motion, and many others. An introductory text or course on photography is well worth the time to take the best photographs possible.

CIRCULAR POLARIZING FILTERS

Circular polarizing filters create the unique effect of cutting off glare and also darkening skies when used correctly. These filters selectively filter random vector light and allow only a specific vector direction light to pass. Since light reflected from wet surfaces is polarized, it is possible to reduce or even eliminate glare off wet rocks and water. Circular polarizers are most popular for darkening the sky. Polarizers are also used as a low-power neutral density filter.

The optimal angle for sky darkening is 90° off the sun's axis relative to the camera's viewpoint. For wide angles, the polarization of the sky will not be consistent across the entire field of view. This can create sky nonuniformity that is difficult to see on a screen or in a viewfinder in the field. They can also shift the color balance of an image. Make sure to test the filter before traveling into the field.

Variable polarizers can create odd-looking cross shapes at their maximum polarization setting. Shoot and view images at large magnification to ensure no odd polarization effects have affected your image.

There is no true digital equivalent to a circular polarizer. Though some software attempts to simulate this effect, a real optical polarizer has no substitute. If you are to bring one filter, the circular polarizer is the one to own.

DYNAMIC RANGE

Each digital camera (and piece of film) has a maximum number of shades of gray that it can record. If the difference between the darkest and brightest parts of an image exceeds a camera's dynamic range, parts of the image will turn completely black or white. The bigger a camera's dynamic range, the more shadow detail it can retain. Considering this is important when photographing in bright daylight with dark shadows in the trees.

LENS ANGLES

Depending on the size of the camera sensor or film, lens width is a relative measure. All lens angles in this book are relative to a full-frame sensor. A full-frame sensor is equivalent to the traditional 35mm film size (24x36mm, known as FX on the Nikon platform). Smaller sensors such as APS-C, Super-35, 1 inch, etc., crop a full-frame lens image. This produces a narrower angle of view.

Below is a list of 35mm full-frame focal lengths and their descriptions used in this book. As there are multiple sensor sizes used in digital photography, camera companies use the classic 35mm film format as the basis for these categories.

Lens angle: Focal Length
Macro: Usually 40-200mm, designed for 1:2 or 1:1 reproduction of small objects
Fisheye: Determined by the lens, usually 6-10mm
Wide-angle: 12mm-35mm
Normal: 45mm-60mm
Telephoto: 80mm-200mm
Extra-long telephoto: 200mm+

MACRO

Macro lenses are specifically designed to magnify small objects to a 1-to-1 subject to image size ratio. For instance, standard lenses cannot focus close enough to allow for a large capture of a single bee on a flower. However, macro lenses excel at this exact job. They are sharp and can be used as general landscape lenses in their focal range, too. Macro lenses are highly versatile because of this.

NEUTRAL DENSITY FILTERS

Neutral density filters, known as ND filters, reduce the light entering a camera lens. These allow the photographer to take long exposures, over 30 seconds, in the middle of the day. The goal of using these filters is to allow objects in motion to blur out, creating an image that would not be possible with a low ISO and a completely closed down lens aperture. The most common use for ND filters is to blur water motion, especially in waterfalls. They are also useful for smoothing flowing water in creeks or waves on a lake. Variable ND filters are also handy to reduce the number of filters necessary. However, at strong darkening levels, these filters can create non-uniformity in the image. Test and learn about them before setting out in the field.

RAW AND JPG FORMATS

There are two common file formats available on most cameras. The first and most common is the JPG format. This compressed file structure is excellent at capturing images while keeping file sizes manageable. Make sure to set your camera to the best JPG setting possible, commonly called: extremely fine, optimal file quality, best, and the like. Most cameras default to a mid-level quality to increase the number of photos the camera holds.

Cameras often have an option for consistent file size or optimal quality. Unless you have a particular need for consistent file sizes in JPG format, choose optimal quality. Often the consistent file size is selected by default by camera companies. This provides a better market description for sales but does little to improve the quality of the images the camera produces.

For the absolute best quality out of your camera, photograph in raw format. If there is an option, such as with Nikon professional cameras, select 14-bit rather than 12-bit raw capture. The dynamic range of raw is many times better than JPG. JPG can capture 256 shades of each color of red, green, and blue; 12-bit raw format can capture 2,048 shades of color; 14-bit raw format holds 16,384 shades of color.

Raw file formats usually require more post-processing in a photo editing program than JPG images. The trade-off for the extra work is the ability to extract the most from your camera. These files allow for the adjustment of the white balance after capture. Adjusting white balance in JPG format is much more difficult.

SPLIT GRADIENT FILTERS

These specialized filters allow the photographer to darken a sky while allowing the shadow detail in the foreground to become more visible. One of the biggest challenges with using a gradient filter is the steep jagged edges of the Teton range. These peaks tend to fall into the darkening zone of even the softest 3-stop gradient filter. Other parts of the valley work well with this style of filters, though.

Thoroughly test and review your images before moving on from a location. Fixing overly darkened summits and trees in post-processing is a time-consuming and difficult process. Many local photographers shoot with 12- or 14-bit raw and apply local gradients in their post-processing software.

TECHNIQUES & TIMING

ALPENGLOW

Alpenglow is the red and pink hue that sometimes colors snow and glaciers on mountain peaks. This coloration is from the penumbra of the Earth's shadow. Once full sunlight strikes the snow surface, the light turns yellow. Alpenglow does not always happen. It is highly atmospheric-dependent. This effect usually lasts at most ten minutes, then the light turns yellow. Usually, the best color of the alpenglow lasts three to five minutes. To capture this effect, be prepared well in advance. Also, photograph in raw format to color correct later.

ASTRONOMICAL SUNRISE CHALLENGES

When the sunset happens, Tetons from the Jackson Hole side will be in silhouette. The same thing happens from Teton Valley during sunrise. To capture the rock, glacial snow, and trees during sunset, use your camera's raw image mode to capture the entire dynamic range. Utilizing 14-bit images will provide the best chance of post-production recovery of color and texture during these unexpectedly challenging photographic times.

ASTROPHOTOGRAPHY

Depending on the time of year and weather, Jackson Hole can provide the opportunity for stunning landscape astrophotography. The biggest challenge is the weather and cloud cover during the winter months.

Since the sky is cloudy in Jackson Hole much of the winter, astrophotography can be a real challenge. This makes for excellent skiing but these conditions are not ideal for capturing the Milky Way over the Tetons. However, when the sky clears out after a storm, this region has some of the best skies in the country. The high altitude and lack of large-city pollution translate to a perfect location for viewing stars.

One of the big challenges is viewing the skies inside the town limits of Jackson. The increase in light pollution from large home landscape lighting and scattered street lighting from in town has seriously impacted night sky clarity in the town limits. Driving a few miles out of town makes a stunning difference in how many stars are visible.

Wyoming Stargazing (www.wyomingstargazing.org) is working with the town of Jackson and the International Dark Sky Association to improve the area's sky clarity. Their observatory on Snow King takes advantage of the high altitude and clear skies to make astronomy available to the public. To learn more about quality night photography, Wyoming Stargazing is an excellent resource to connect with for astrophotography in Jackson Hole.

COLD CAMERA MANAGEMENT

Sub-freezing temperatures are common in Jackson Hole for half the year. This presents a challenge to photographers, as camera gear does not work as well in the cold.

Batteries will die much quicker in the cold. Expect a battery to last half as long or less compared with summer temperatures. Carry all spare batteries in a pocket inside of a jacket. An outside jacket pocket will not keep batteries warm enough to prevent them from running out of power.

Condensation is a serious issue here. When entering a warm building after being in the cold, water condensation can soak a lens, sensor, LCD screen, and viewfinder. Place your camera and lenses in a sealed plastic bag before entering a building or warm car. Allow the camera to warm up before removing it from the bag. Following this process will protect the camera from moisture damage.

COLOR CORRECTION

Capturing the correct and true color of a landscape is more difficult than it might seem. Each camera manufacturer has different color biases in their camera sensor array. This is true of color films, too. Nikon, Canon, Sony, and their kin each have different colors they emphasize.

To capture the true color of a landscape, a color chip calibration card must be used. A white balance card is also handy for quickly correcting out color casts in post-production editing. If one takes the time to photograph a calibrated white card in each particular scene, countless avoidable fiddling hours can be saved with two or three mouse clicks with a calibrated white balance card.

The experienced landscape photographer will know when to deviate from "calibrated color" for something more artistic and pleasing. For beginners, try capturing the most accurate

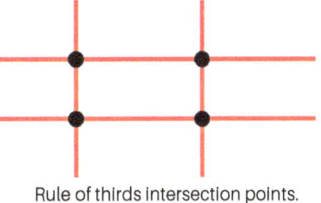
Rule of thirds intersection points.

image possible. This makes later artistic interpretation easier. If an image is captured with "baked in" color in a JPG or other non-adjustable format, color correction becomes exponentially more time-consuming.

COMPOSITION

The artistic rendition of a photograph is at least as important as the technical aspect. Ansel Adams, the famous black and white photographer, is quoted as saying, "There is nothing worse than a sharp image of a fuzzy concept." Beginning photographers often center the subject in the middle of the frame. Sometimes this works but often is not an attractive composition.

The two most useful artistic rendition rules are known as the Golden Ratio and the Rule of Thirds. The golden ratio is based on the Greek mathematical concept of design. Some cameras have viewfinders that show the golden ratio on a grid. A simplified version of the golden ratio is the Rule of Thirds. This easier-to-understand composition suggests placing the most important object into one of four intersection points created by this grid.

These rules are not to be used as absolute rules. Rather, they are suggested as a good starting point to make more compelling images. Study artistic design and photo composition and apply them to get the most out of your efforts in Jackson Hole.

DRONE PHOTOGRAPHY

Drones are a wonderful tool for capturing images otherwise unavailable to the ground-based photographer. They are also useful for scouting out locations, video work, and can provide an aerial perspective that can make your images stand out from the rest.

The use of drones is currently banned in national parks as of the writing of this guidebook. Many sites, such as Flat Creek, where the trumpeter swans reside, have signs restricting drone use as well. Be mindful of the noise impact on animals and people.

FOCUS STACKING

Focus stacking is a very useful technique in macro and close-up photography. It can artificially increase the depth of focus in an image beyond what is possible with most lenses. Multiple images are exposed with focus set to different distances in the frame. The set of images is then blended in post-production software that selects the sharpest exposure from each frame. The technique can work very well in a landscape image. The technique allows the image to have sharp focus on a close foreground element and far away backgrounds simultaneously.

HDR (High Dynamic Range)

High dynamic range photography is a technique where multiple images of different exposures are combined together to create a single image that shows more dynamic range in the highlights and shadows. Originally, the technique had a bad reputation in the early days of digital photography because it was excessively processed. Modern use of HDR allows details in shadows and highlights to become clear and details exaggerated. It can be fun and often creates compelling saturated colors that are enjoyed by many photograph buyers.

Light Painting

Light painting is the method of using a light source to illuminate an object at night. Instead of using a camera strobe, the photographer locks the shutter open. Then, a flashlight or big spotlight is used to illuminate the object in interesting ways. This technique is highly effective at capturing ground objects while still retaining the overhead stars.

Check with the latest park regulations on light painting in Grand Teton at www.nps.gov/grte/.

Telephoto Compression

One of the most underutilized landscape photography techniques in Jackson Hole is the use of a longer lens for landscape. Typically, wildlife photographers will use 400-600mm lenses for animal portraiture or to capture skittish mammals like wolves. So often first-time visitors use their long lenses to capture the mountains up close with sub-optimal results due to the regular atmospheric haze.

However, an 80-200mm range lens will uniquely capture landscape features. Most often photographers will use a 24-70mm f/2.8 lens. This is an excellent, if limiting, choice. By using a mid-range telephoto lens, it is possible to create much more dramatic images. Using a wide to normal lens will render the Tetons minute and unimpressive in the image.

Stop by the Grand Teton Park sign 5 miles (8 km) north of town and watch where all visitors stand. Invariably, people will end up with a photo of themselves with the park sign. The Cathedral Group will appear as a sad afterthought, nearly invisible.

Instead, choose a focal length of around 180mm and march off into the sagebrush. Changing the proportion of the distance from the primary subject to the background will result in an image with impact.

JACKSON LAKE
COVERING HOTSPOTS #1-9

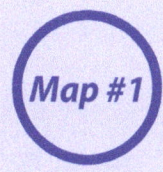

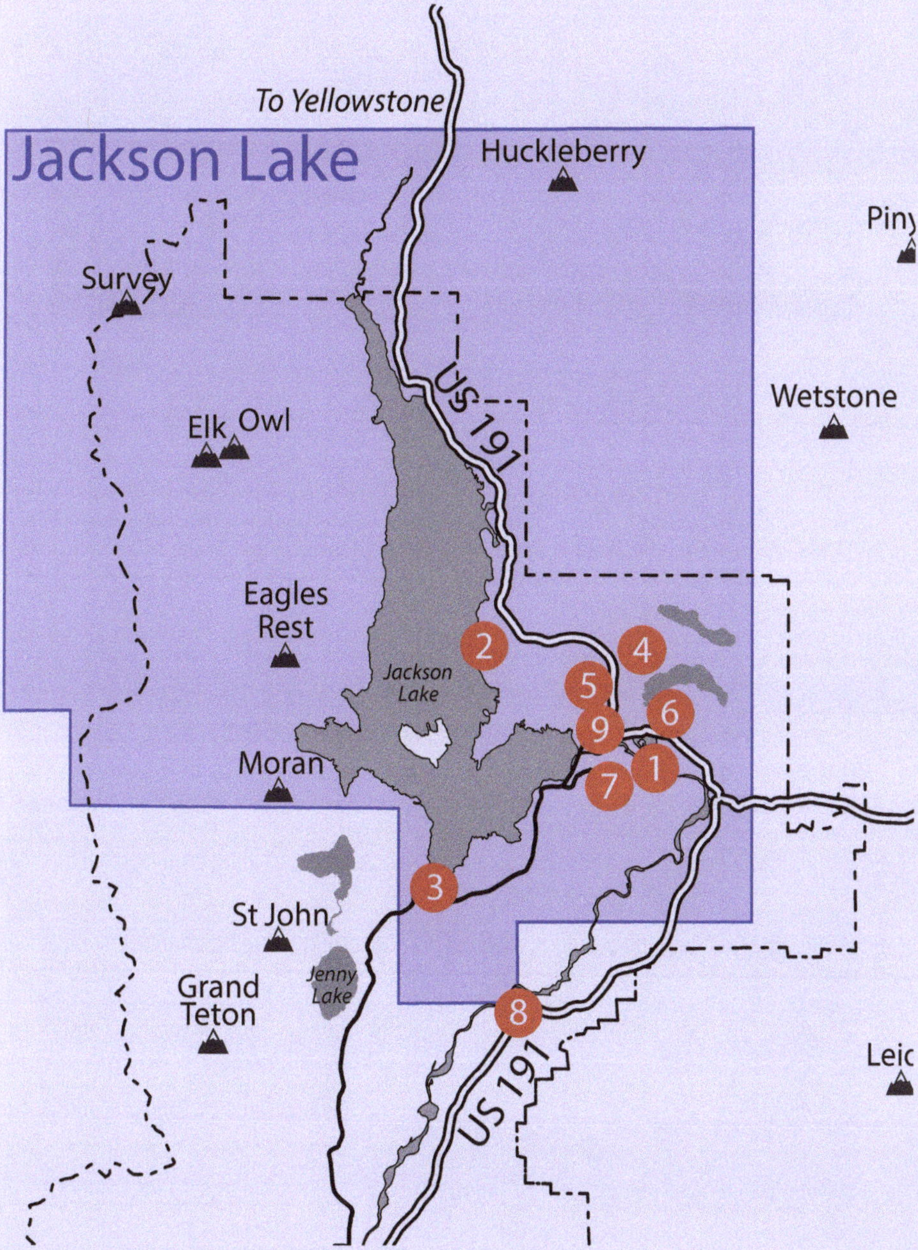

HOTSPOT #1

Cattleman's Bridge

MAP 1

GPS coordinates

43.85663, -110.55328
/ 43°51'24"N, 110°33'1
2"W 12T 0535902E 48
56046N

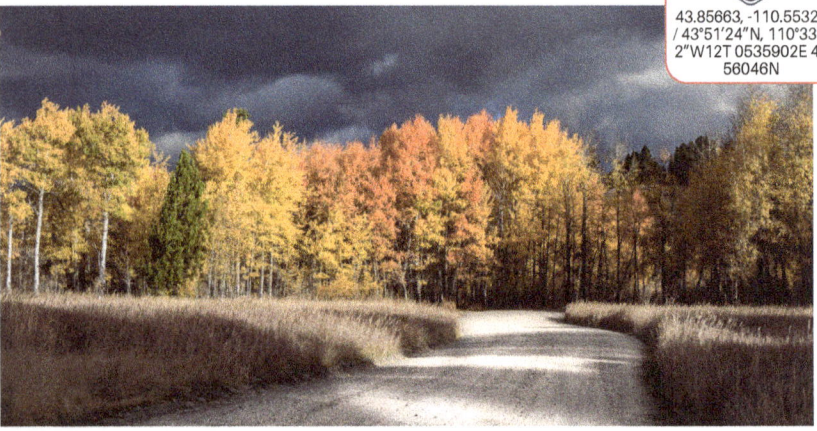

Nikon D810, 24-120mm f/4, f/8, 1/800, ISO 400

DESCRIPTION:

Cattleman's Bridge is at the end of a poorly marked turn-off 1.2 miles (1.9 km) west of Oxbow Bend. The original, narrow plank bridge was used from the 1950s to move cattle across the Snake River. The bridge later collapsed and was removed in 2001. The historic sign provides context and photographic inspiration for the site.

The site is a must stop for photographers pursuing wildflowers in spring and summer. It has great views of the mountains and river. Birds and mammals are common at this site, providing multiple photo opportunities.

This dirt road is a 1-mile (1.6-km) dusty track that is passable by passenger car when it is graded. However, this lightly used road can be rough and muddy after a heavy rain. It is best to avoid it after a rain and 4-wheel drive is necessary.

Nikon D810, 70-200mm f/2.8, f/5, 1/1000, ISO 400

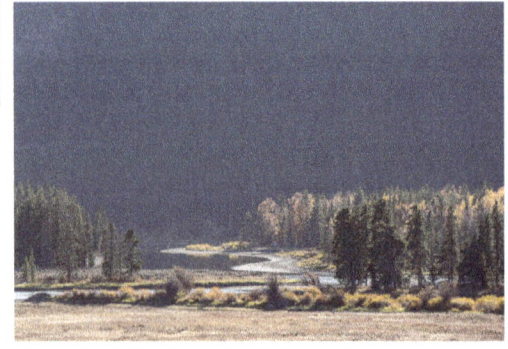

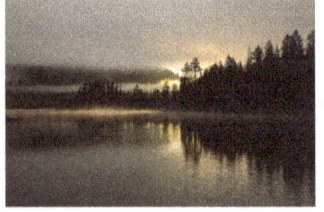

Cattleman's Bridge is one of the best hidden gems of Grand Teton National Park. Easily accessible when there is no snow, this hideaway is the perfect place to enjoy photography.

HOTSPOT #1

DIRECTIONS

Distance from Town Square

Drive north from Jackson on US 191 for 30.3 miles (48.8 km). Turn left (west) at Moran Junction. Continue for 3.4 miles (5.5 km) and turn left (south) on the unmarked dirt road. Continue 1 mile (1.6 km) to the parking lot.

MAP 1

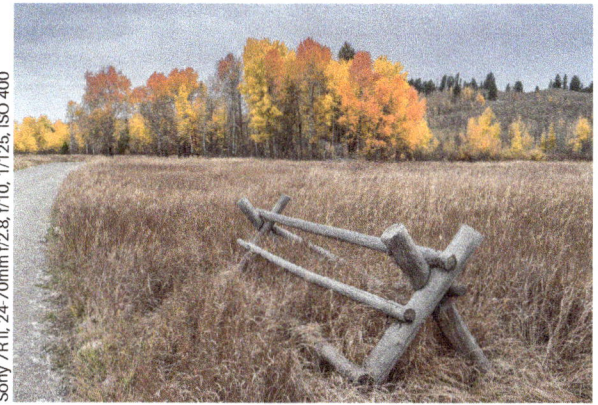

Fall colors and a segment of buck rail fence. The character of the meadow changes markedly from the opening of the road in late May or early June to its closure in late October.

An isolated tree on a foggy, overcast autumn day.

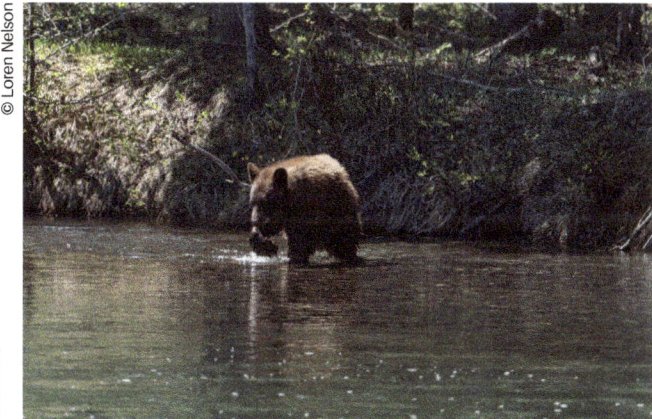

Don't be surprised to find both black and grizzly bears along the road or even in the Snake River.

📷 Site Specific Photography Tips

There are a variety of photographic options at Cattleman's Bridge. For landscapes and river images, a wide angle to normal lens is a good choice. A zoom lens covering these focal lengths is the most desirable for the greatest flexibility.

A moderate telephoto lens will be useful for the chance encounter with wildlife. This lens length is also good to compress the abundant cottonwood trees against the Cathedral Group 15 miles (24 km) southwest of the old bridge site.

HOTSPOT #1

Site Specifics:

Parking: The dirt parking lot is moderately sized. There is usually enough space for standard-sized vehicles to fit here. The dirt road can be rough and difficult to travel during the spring runoff or during rainy conditions.

Access: The site is easy to drive and walk around. The signs at the parking lot will note any seasonal restrictions and rules.

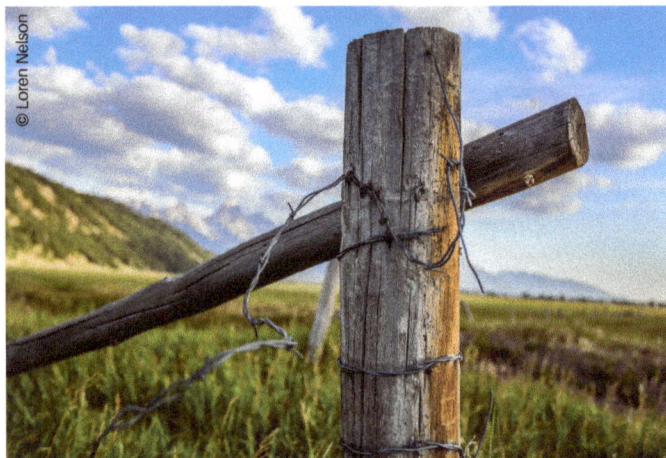

Old and unused fences and other artifacts make interesting foreground elements.

Human activity can add interest and story to your landscape photography.

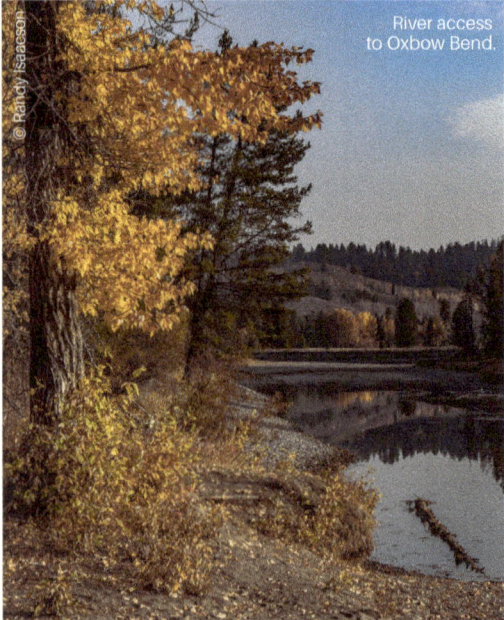

River access to Oxbow Bend.

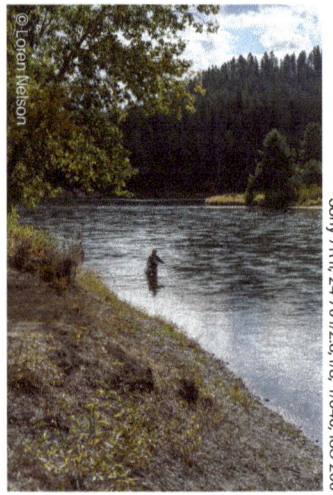

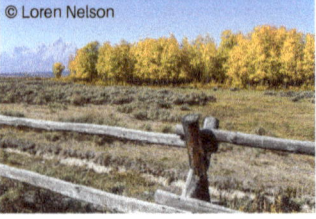

Spring and summer make the road to Cattleman's spectacular and the fall colors of the aspen add to your mountain shots.

*HOT*SPOT #2

Colter Bay area

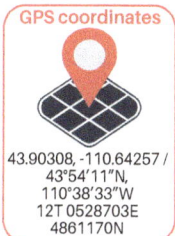

GPS coordinates

43.90308, -110.64257 /
43°54'11"N,
110°38'33"W
12T 0528703E
4861170N

MAP 1

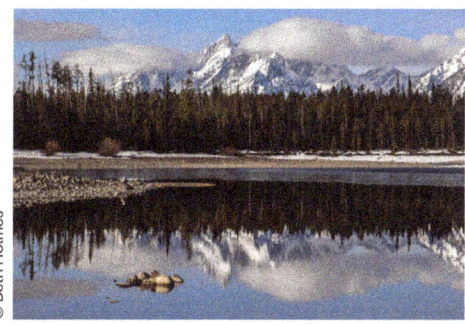

Nikon D810, 24-120mm f/4, f/11, 1/500, ISO 200

DESCRIPTION:

The visitor services, hiking trails, boating, and camping make the Colter Bay area second only to Jenny Lake in visitor popularity. Although there can be a large number of cars, the area is so large that it does not feel crowded. Specific points like the general store, beach, and gas station can be busy. But elsewhere, the park can feel quite empty.

The road and parking areas are plowed in the winter for four-season access. There is even the only heated bathroom in the park available in winter. Multiple trails lead through the area, including one to Hermitage Point. This loop hike is 9.6 miles (15.4 km) gains little elevation but covers significant ground.

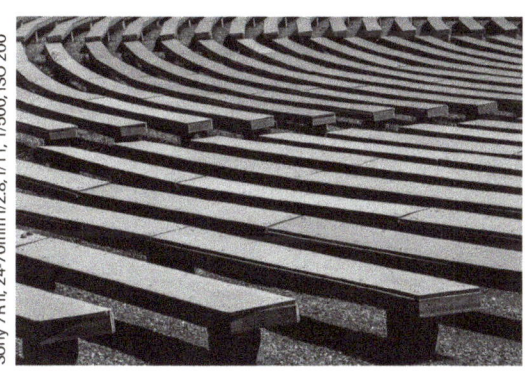

Sony 7R II, 24-70mm f/2.8, f/11, 1/500, ISO 200

© Loren Nelson

An abstract, monochrome view of the Colter Bay amphitheater shot in early December before any snowfall. The buildings in the Colter Bay area are historic and can be interesting subjects in all four seasons. This shot was rendered in Lightroom.

DIRECTIONS

Distance from Town Square

Drive north from Jackson on US 191 for 30.3 miles (48.8 km). Turn left (west) at Moran Junction. Drive 9.3 miles (14.9 km) and turn left at the Colter Bay Junction. Drive to the end of the road, turn left (S) and park near the visitor center.

HOTSPOT #2

MAP 1

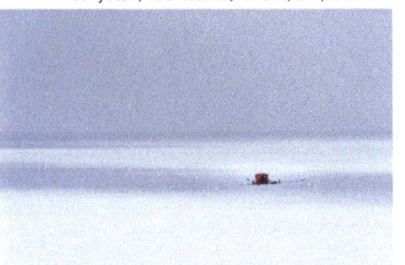

Sony A9 II, 100-400mm, 1/1000, f/11, ISO 100

Minimalism can be interesting. This is a shot of an ice-fisherman in Jackson Lake in mid-winter. It was shot in late afternoon on a cloudy, overcast, cold winter day. The Tetons are in the background but you would never know it.

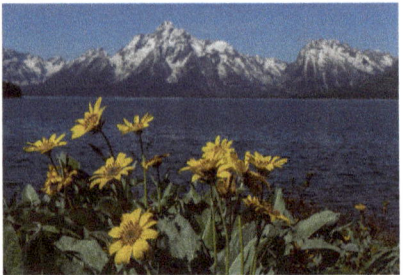

© Loren Nelson

Sony A9 II, 24-70/2.8, 1/400, f/13, ISO 200

Springtime is one of the best times in the Colter Bay area. There are short walks from the parking areas near the beach picnic ground that put the arrowleaf balsamroot flowers above the photographer so you can use them as bright foreground elements with Jackson Lake and the Tetons in the background. This was shot with a wide zoom lens at f/13 to achieve a broad depth of field.

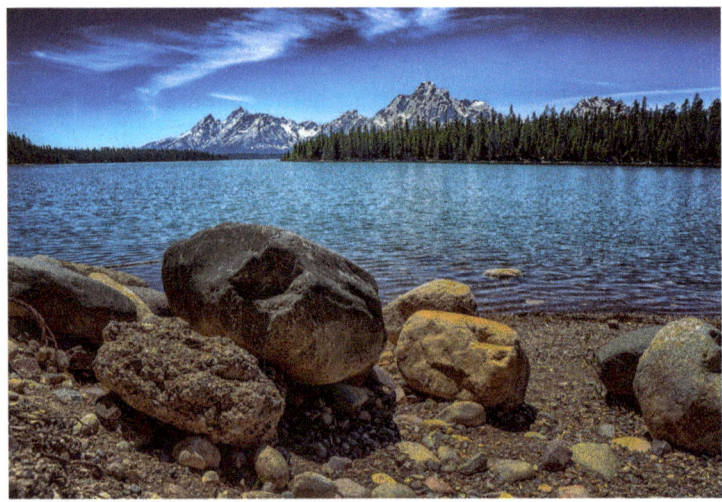

Sony 7R II, 24-70mm f/2.8, f/8, 1/800, ISO 200

The north end of Jackson Lake is often over-looked by visitors because no services are available. A steep walk down to the bank of the lake provides the photographer with some colorful foreground elements. Just remember the climb back up to the highway is steep with loose dirt and rocks.

📷 Site Specific Photography Tips

The areas around Colter Bay provide a wide variety of photographic opportunities. As with other flexible areas, an 18-105mm or 24-70mm lens is handy here. If you enjoy photographing landscapes with trees, a lake, and the mountains as a backdrop, Colter Bay is an excellent place to visit.

Swan Lake and Heron Pond are excellent bird photography spots. These lily-covered lakes attract birds of all types. Bald eagles and osprey nests are common in this area. The hikes to them are mild. Swan Lake is 0.5 mile (0.8 km) from the parking lot. Heron Pond is 1 mile (1.6 km) from the parking lot.

HOTSPOT #2

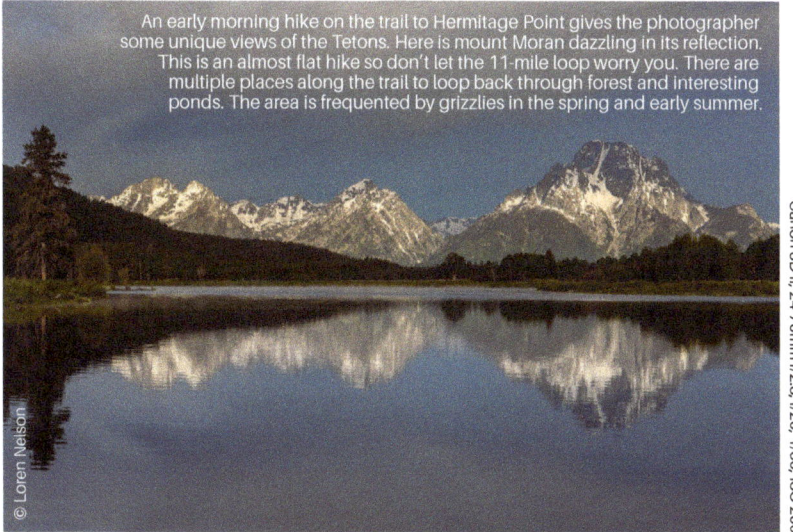

An early morning hike on the trail to Hermitage Point gives the photographer some unique views of the Tetons. Here is mount Moran dazzling in its reflection. This is an almost flat hike so don't let the 11-mile loop worry you. There are multiple places along the trail to loop back through forest and interesting ponds. The area is frequented by grizzlies in the spring and early summer.

Canon 5D II, 24-70mm f/2.8, f/20, 1/60, ISO 200

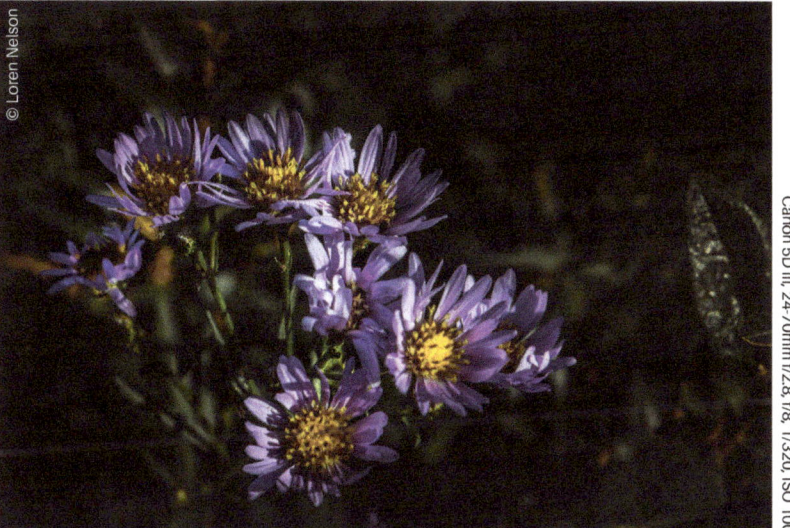

Walking through a dense evergreen forest is not most landscape photographers' idea of a perfect setting but when you look around, small patches of sunlight reveal local beauty.

Canon 5D III, 24-70mm f/2.8, f/8, 1/320, ISO 100

Site Specifics:

Parking: The parking lot at Colter Bay is huge. The spaces closer to the attractions can fill up. When arriving in the middle of the day, tour the farther parking lot for a space and plan to walk. The parking turnover is high at this site, so the chance of finding a good spot is high.

Access: The main points of Colter Bay are accessible by a short hike. There are no significant elevation gains in this area, making it easy to reach nearly any point.

HOTSPOT #2

HOTSPOT #3

Fire smoke in Jackson Hole

MAP 1

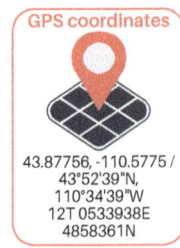

GPS coordinates

43.87756, -110.5775 /
43°52'39"N,
110°34'39"W
12T 0533938E
4858361N

DESCRIPTION:

The mountain west has been plagued with frequent wildfires during the long western drought. Fires from California, Nevada, Oregon, Idaho, and Wyoming send smoke over the Tetons. At times, these massive spires are completely invisible from the valley.

For the budding photographer, this can seem like a complete loss. However, there are locations in the valley where smoke can generate stunning images. At the north end of the valley, sunsets with light beams streaming through the smoke are dramatic. Views from the south end of the valley in smoky conditions are not as easy to capture, as the mountains are not visible on the highway south of the park sign.

A photographer can be disappointed with forest fire smoke. Or, with creative vision, the same photographer can capture images with interesting, unique results. Although first-time visitors want the classic views, the fire season smoke has been a persistent challenge. Using the smoke to create something different than what other photographers have can differentiate your images.

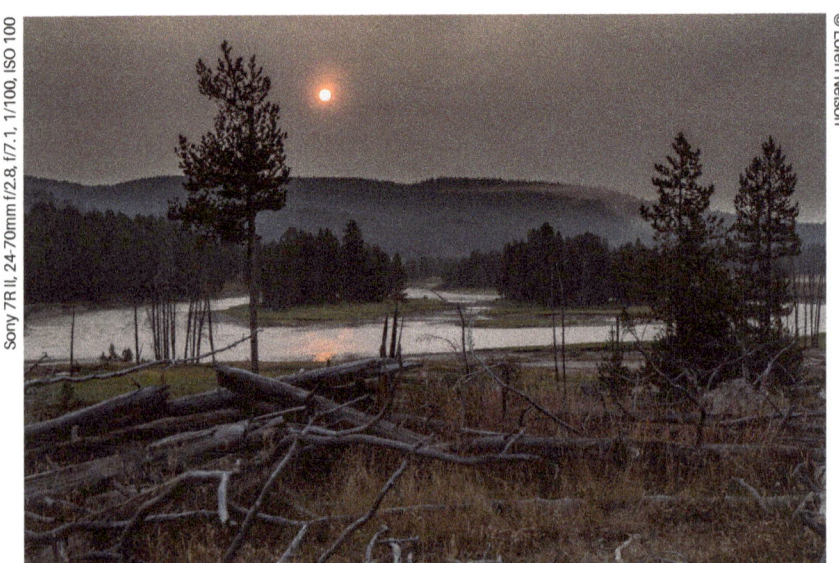

Dense smoke can ruin the vistas of the mountains so the photographer must consider nearer subjects. Full sunlight is blocked in this long exposure shot of deadfall and the meandering river.

HOTSPOT #3

DIRECTIONS

Distance from Town Square

Drive north on Highway 89 early in the afternoon to stake a spot out with views of the Cathedral Group spires. The best position from the north is at Spalding Bay Road and Jackson Lake Lodge (Hotspot 5). The best southern site is at Phelps Lake (Hotspot 21).

To reach Spalding Bay Road, drive north from Jackson on US 191 for 12.3 miles (19.8 km) to Moose Junction and turn left on Teton Park Road. Continue past the entrance station for a total of 12.1 miles (19.5 km) to the Spalding Bay Road junction.

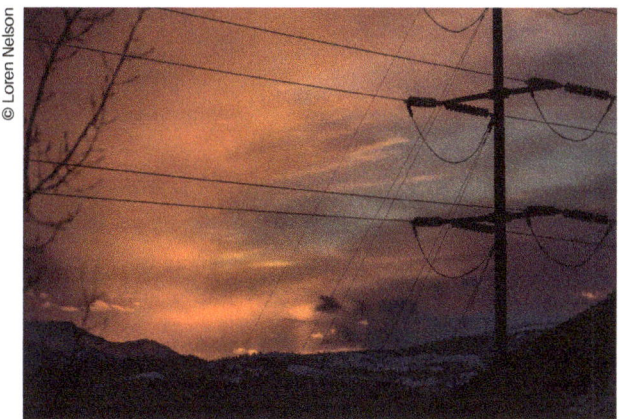

Timing is everything in this smoky sunset shot from a back deck in Jackson. Smoke can create dramatic color or just flat lighting—keep your camera handy.

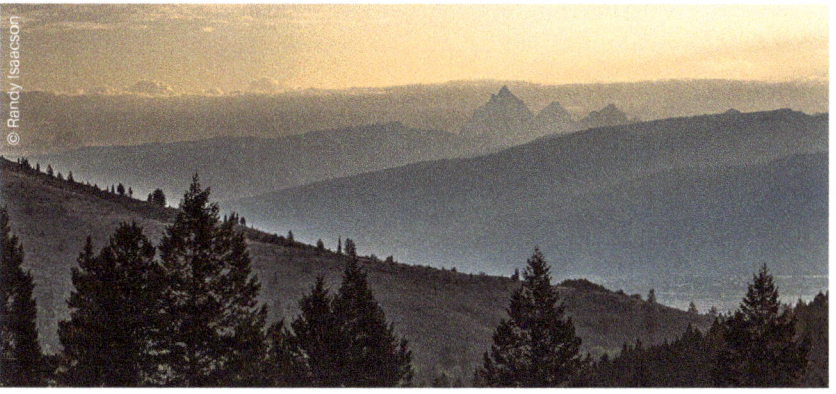

Smoke in Teton Valley can create a dramatic image.

Site Specifics:

Parking: Park along the first dirt loop on Spalding Bay Road, right after the pavement turns to dirt. Other points along the main highway are determined by the conditions and time of day.

Access: The first section of Spalding Bay Road is accessible by passenger car.

MAP 1

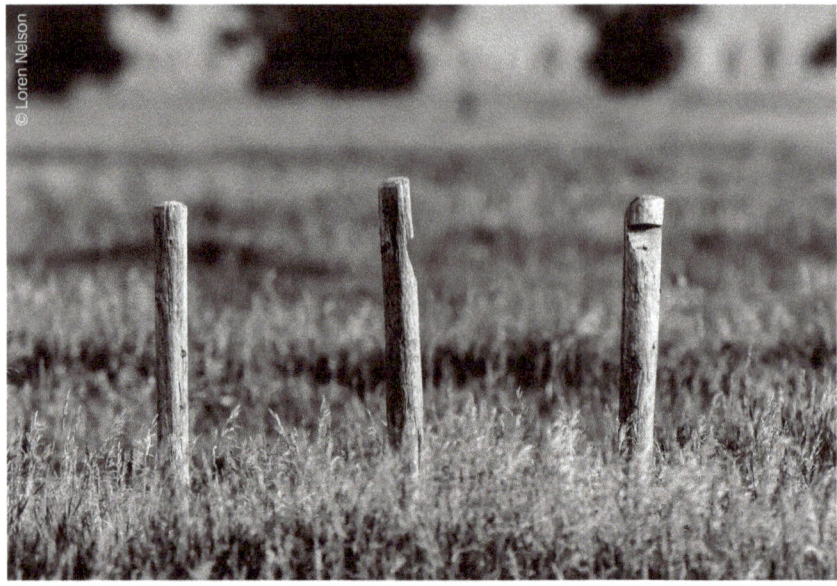

Canon 5D III, 600mm f/4, f/9, 1/640, ISO 400

Colors are severely muted on smoky days but the lack of harsh light is an opportunity to shoot all day long. Consider monochrome processing, closer subjects, and using a de-haze filter when post-processing your images.

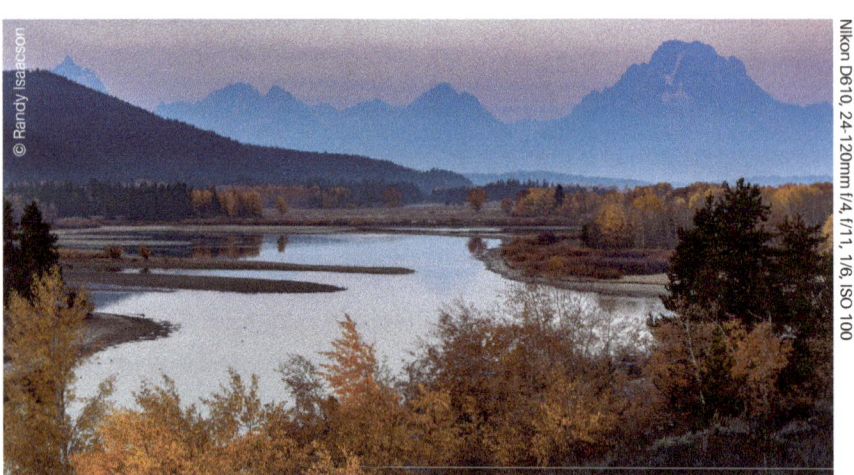

Nikon D610, 24-120mm f/4, f/11, 1/6, ISO 100

Smoke at Oxbow Bend in the fall.

📷 Site Specific Photography Tips

If the smoke isn't too dense, the sunset light beams create incredible images. The glow from sunlight in the smoke can overwhelm a camera sensor, leaving a featureless blob. You may need to underexpose the image several stops to capture all of the dynamic range in smoky conditions.

HOTSPOT #3

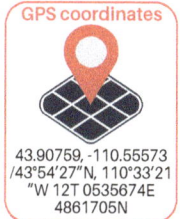

GPS coordinates
43.90759, -110.55573
/43°54'27"N, 110°33'21"W
12T 0535674E 4861705N

HOTSPOT #4

Grand View Point

DESCRIPTION:

The Grand View trail is one of the best-named trails in Grand Teton. The moderate 3.6-mile (5.8 km) out and back hike gains 719 feet (219 m). It is well maintained and accessible north of Jackson Lake Lodge junction on the east side of Highway 89. It can also be reached by hiking from Two Oceans Lake.

There is a short but sometimes rough dirt road to a large parking area. The trail leads to Grand View Point with side trails to Two Oceans and Emma Matilda Lakes. The hike can be very buggy in the spring so take insect repellent.

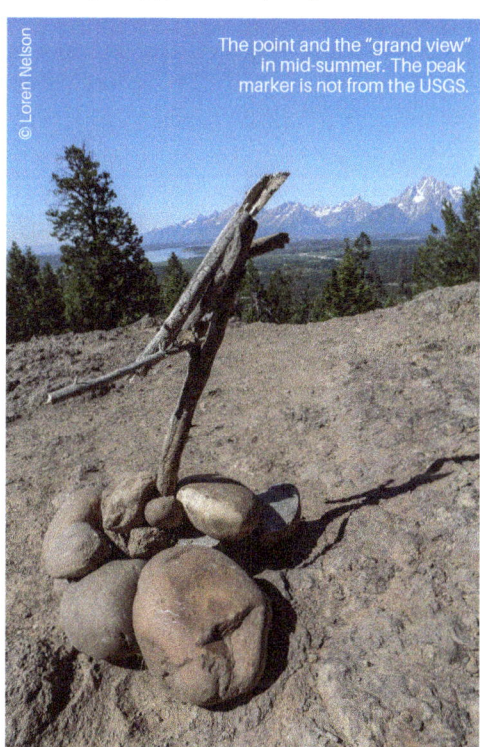

The point and the "grand view" in mid-summer. The peak marker is not from the USGS.
© Loren Nelson
Canon 5D III, 24-70mm f/2.8, f/14, 1/80, ISO 100

DIRECTIONS

Distance from Town Square

Drive north from Jackson on US 191 for 30.3 miles (48.8 km). Turn left (west) at Moran Junction. Drive 5.8 miles (9.3 km) and turn right on an unsigned road. This turnoff is 0.9 mile (1.5 km) north of the Jackson Lake Lodge turnoff. Continue 0.15 mile (0.24 km) and park in the dirt lot.

MAP 1

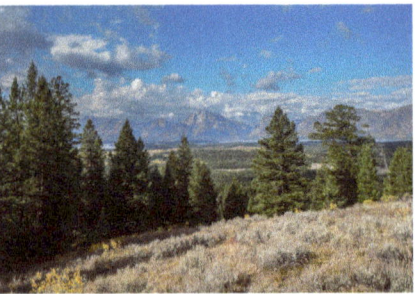

Grand View Point gives a 360-degree view of the central park and the Teton Range. It also gives access to several excellent lake views where the summer crowds are thin.

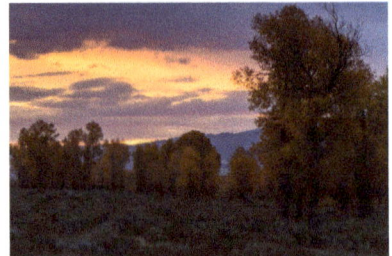

Canon 7D, 24-70mm f/2.8, f/5, 1/60, ISO 800

The view from hiking down from the point near sunset in the early autumn.

Two Oceans Lake is accessible via a long hike from the Grand View Trail or a moderately rough (at times) dirt road drive starting near the east end of the Pacific Creek Road just west of the Moran entrance to Grand Teton National Park. The road is drivable in good weather most of the summer into early autumn until it is closed to access. Grizzly bears are common in this area. Their presence can trigger road and area closures. Hiking in the area is best done with others. Always carry bear spray to help reduce the chance of a negative bear encounter.

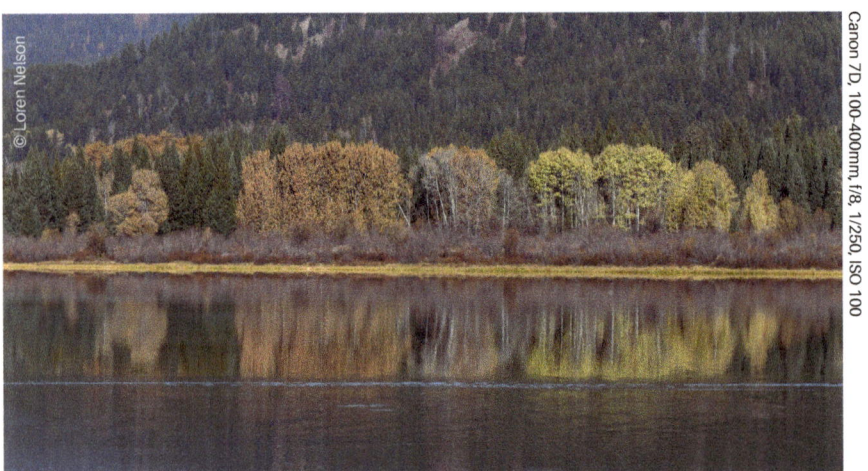

Canon 7D, 100-400mm, f/8, 1/250, ISO 100

This is a reflection shot of aspens and cottonwoods changing to their fall colors.

HIKING DIRECTIONS

Start hiking at the steel gate with the large two-track trail headed northeast. The two-track reduces to a single-track and crosses a road at 0.67 mile (1.1 km) that leads to a visible remote measurement station. There is a trail sign indicating which direction to walk.

In another 0.25 mile (0.4 km), the trail connects with the Emma Matilda Lake Trail. Turn left (north) and walk 0.7 mile (1.1 km) to Grand View Point.

HOTSPOT #4

📷 Site Specific Photography Tips

The views are unparalleled at Grand View Point. To the south, broad swaths of Jackson Lake and the Tetons are visible. To the east, Two Ocean and Matilda Lakes are visible. The steep, rugged mountains of the north Jackson Hole are visible, too.

The best choices for lenses are normal to moderate telephotos. A wide-angle is a good choice to capture the nearby rocks and trees. However, wide-angle lenses will make the mountains look small in the distance.

MAP 1

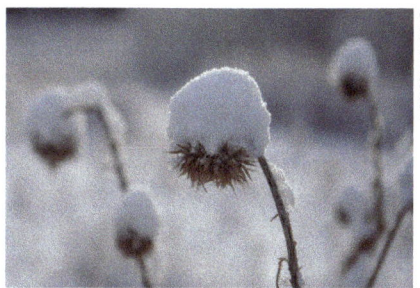

If you are lucky, you might get up Two Oceans Road after an early fall snow shower. These Canadian thistles made nice macro/close-up subjects.

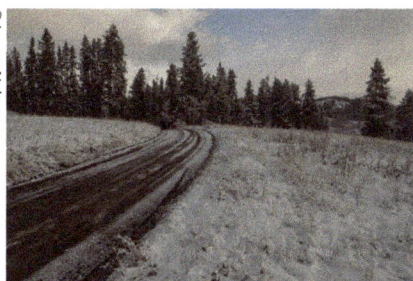

Two Oceans Road often opens in late May or early June and is usually passable in a passenger car when the road is dry. This shot was in October, just before it closed for the winter.

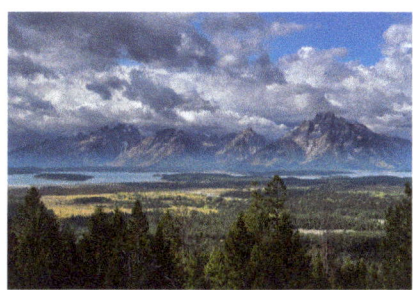

Changing weather and a cloudy day create drama in the Teton Range.

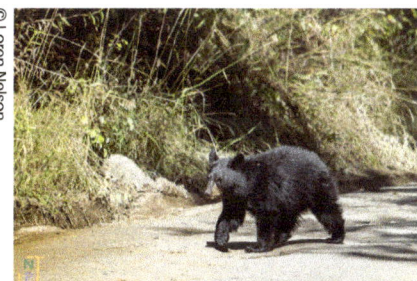

Expect and prepare for wildlife in the Two Oceans area. This black bear was part of a family foraging on last summer berries.

Site Specifics:

Parking: The parking lot is large and is often nearly empty.

Access: This viewpoint requires hiking on a moderately steep trail in bear country. Bring bear spray, a map, and navigation devices. Let someone responsible know where you are going and when to expect you back.

HOTSPOT #4

*HOT*SPOT **#5**

Jackson Lake Lodge

DESCRIPTION:

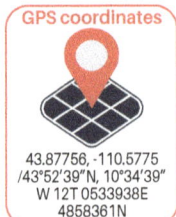

GPS coordinates
43.87756, -110.5775
/43°52'39"N, 10°34'39"
W 12T 0533938E
4858361N

Jackson Lake Lodge is the largest lodge in Grand Teton. This beautiful building has an impressive glass window overlooking the north end of Willow Flats. The restaurants, bars, rooms, and displays are all worth exploring.

The walkway and buck rail fence outside the main window draw large crowds of visitors. The view is unmatched. Jackson Lake, the Cathedral Group, and central Jackson Hole are all visible from this site.

Stroll through the lodge to discover and photograph some of the historic artifacts. There is a mezzanine level above the main hall which provides an elevated view of the main hall.

To gain a viewpoint at Jackson Lake Lodge, take a walk to Lunch Tree Hill. This short hike on a minor hill to the north of the lodge is worthwhile. Elevated views of and the northern section of Willow Flats are unmatched in the area.

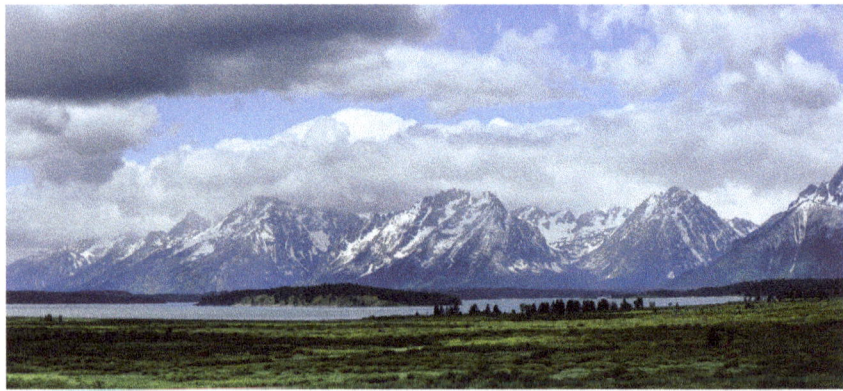

Nikon D800, 85mm f/1.4, f/11, 1/320, ISO 100

DIRECTIONS

Distance from Town Square

Drive north from Jackson on US 191 for 30.3 miles (48.8 km). Turn left (west) at Moran Junction. Continue for 4.9 miles (7.8 km) and turn left (west) into Jackson Lake Lodge.

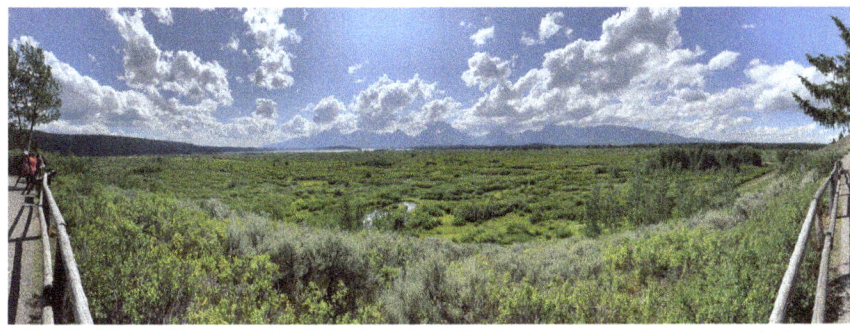

Broad and expansive views from the outside deck at Jackson Lake Lodge allow for impressive panoramic images.

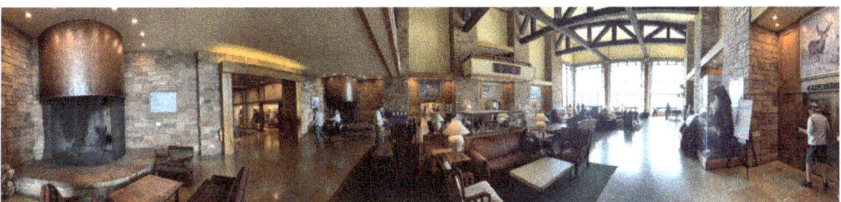

The huge fire places and high ceilings give visitors a feel of being in a large outdoor space.

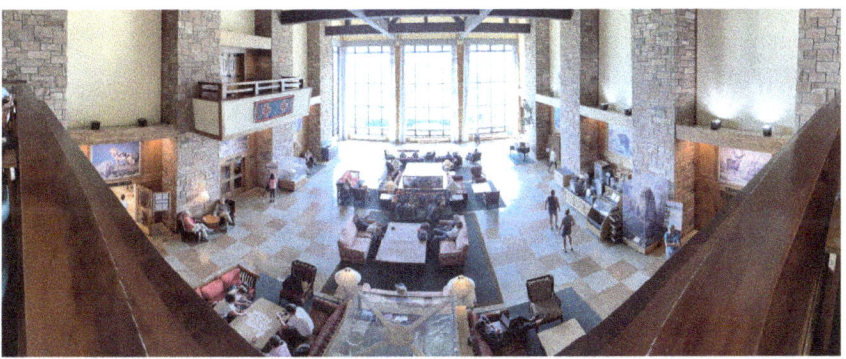

The main hall viewed from the upper floor. Few visitors wander to the upper floor, so it can be a quiet place of refuge.

📷 Site Specific Photography Tips

The lodge features are generally photographed with wide-angle to normal lenses. The inside of the lodge is quite dark compared to the outside. Capturing both presents significant challenges for any camera. Using the HDR technique is the best way to successfully capture the wide dynamic range on the balcony.

Using a tripod is generally not tolerated inside. Check with the staff for the current rules. Use a higher ISO to capture the darker interiors.

HOTSPOT #5

MAP 1

Nikon D810, 70-200mm f/2.8, f/9, 1/3200, ISO 1000

© Beth Holmes

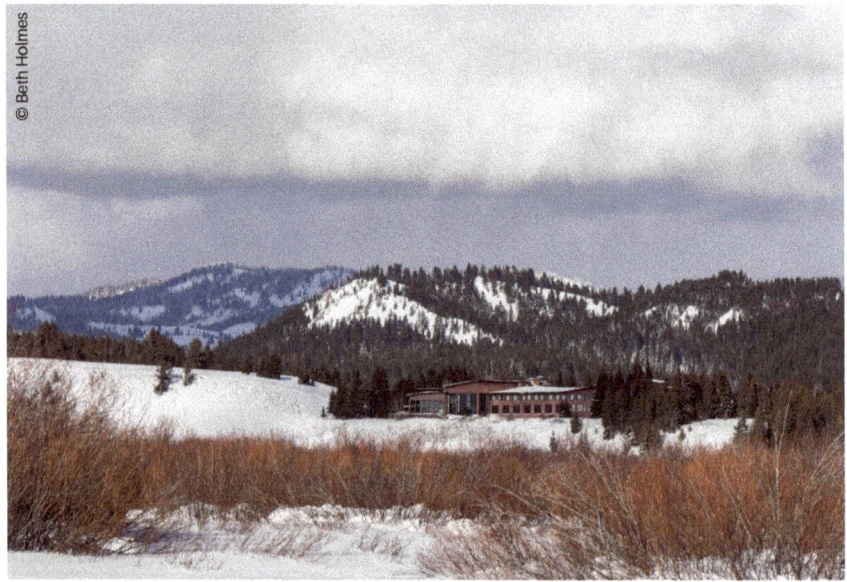

Viewed from a distance during winter, the lodge gently blends into the landscape.

iPhone Xs, f/1.8, 1/60, ISO 1000

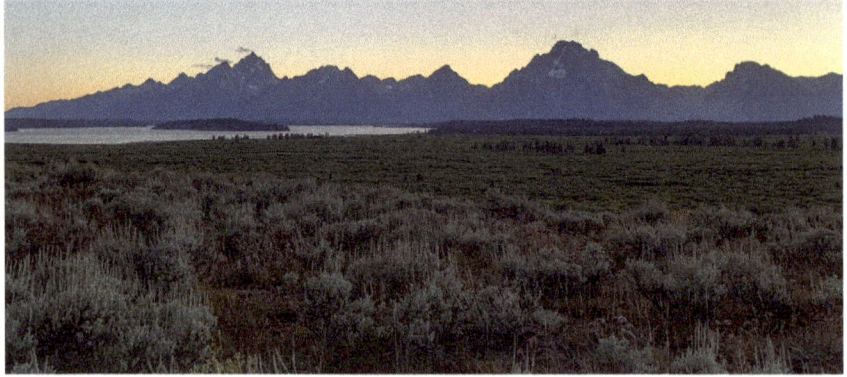

The trail to Lunch Tree Hill is an easy walk and a pleasant escape from the crowds at the lodge.

Site Specifics:

Parking: There is a large parking lot at the lodge. During the summer, the lot can fill up. However, there is enough visitor turnover to make finding a parking space easy.

Access: When the lodge is open in the summer, it is an easy walk inside. There are elevators for disabled access.

HOTSPOT #5

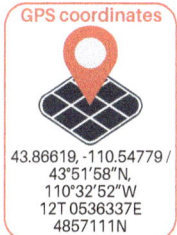

GPS coordinates
43.86619, -110.54779 /
43°51'58"N,
110°32'52"W
12T 0536337E
4857111N

HOT SPOT #6
Oxbow Bend

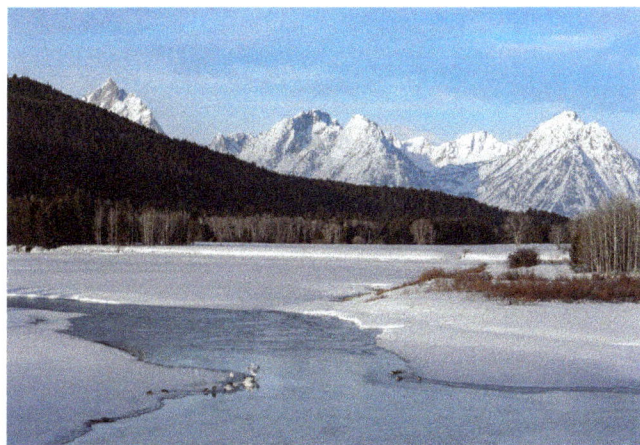

Nikon D810, 85mm f/1.4, f/7.1, 1/1250, ISO 250

DESCRIPTION:

Oxbow Bend is the iconic location on the Snake River just north of the Moran Junction entrance to Grand Teton National Park. It is the site of the famous Ansel Adams photo taken in the 1940s. At first glance, the site is simply another turn-off inside the park. However, this is one of the premier photography hotspot locations in this book.

Mount Moran is 11.6 miles (18.6 km) away and 5,848 feet (1,782 m) above the viewpoint. The view from the turnout has a near-perfect angle above the water to capture Moran's reflection. Bear, moose, eagles, and other animals are often seen here.

During the fall, the aspen leaves on the shore directly west from the viewpoint turn color. This is by far the most popular and ideal time for photography. Thistles often grow along the shore, affording composition opportunities.

Site Specifics:

Parking: The parking lot is sizable and accommodates larger vehicles. However, during busy summer or fall days, the parking lot can be completely full. In the fall, cars are parked bumper to bumper before sunrise.

Access: The site is accessible year-round. During the summer, the parking lot will be busy and can overflow. Be prepared for cold, windy conditions during the winter.

MAP 1

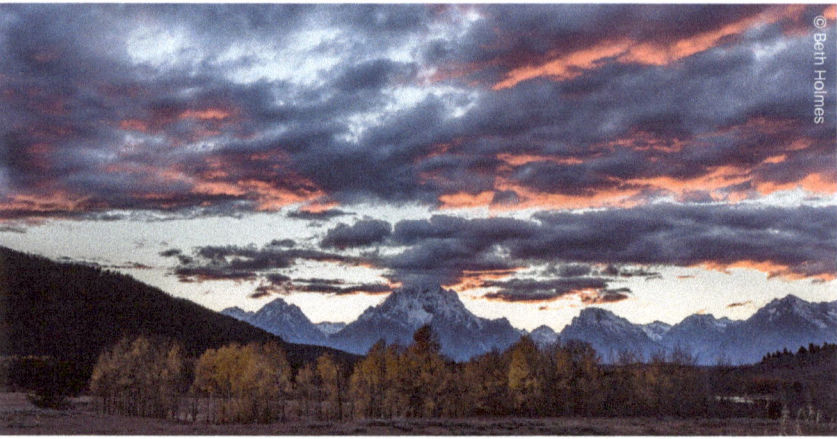

Nikon 810, 24-120mm f/4, f/8, 1/6, ISO 125

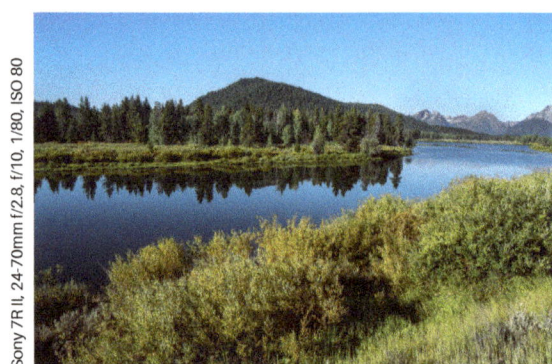

Sony 7R II, 24-70mm f/2.8, f/10, 1/80, ISO 80

A lush summer afternoon on the Oxbow.

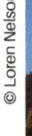

By late October the fall colors are gone but the Tetons are dressed in a layer of snow.

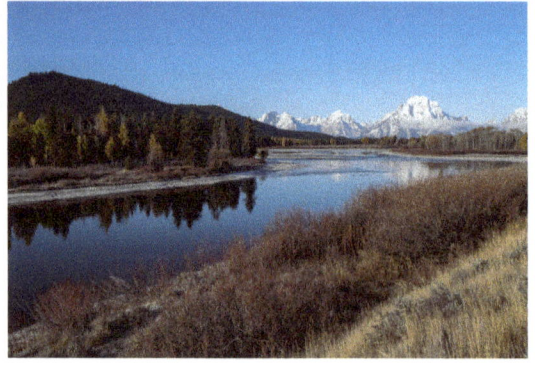

Sony 7R II, 24-70mm f/2.8, f/10, ISO 64

DIRECTIONS   Distance from Town Square

Drive north from Jackson on US 191 for 30.3 miles (48.8 km). Turn left (west) at Moran Junction. Drive 3 miles (4.8 km) to the Oxbow Bend parking lot.

HOTSPOT #6

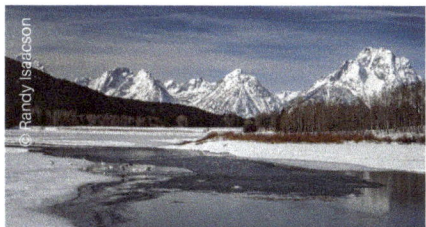
Winter Trumpeter Swans at Oxbow Bend.

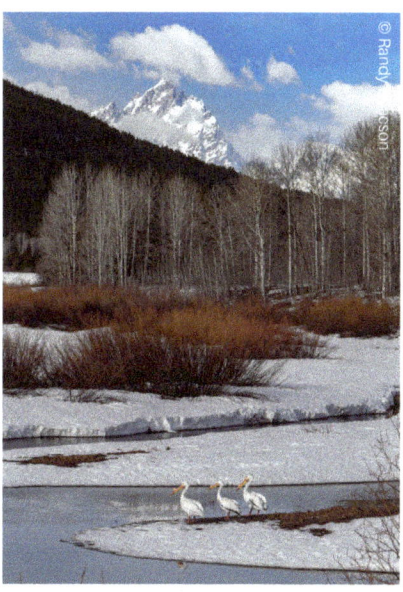

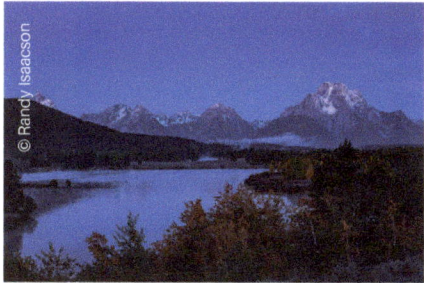
Just before sunrise at Oxbow Bend.

Pelicans at Oxbow Bend preparing for winter.

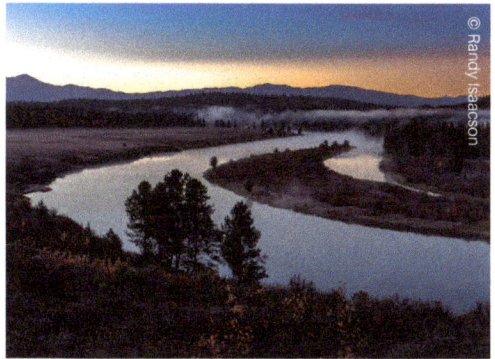
Looking east at Oxbow Bend at sunrise.

📷 Site Specific Photography Tips

The main view from the metal sign is a near-perfect location to take the classic Oxbow Bend photograph. There is a trail that leads to the water's edge to allow for different compositions. For a unique image, climb partly up Lozier Hill (the hill directly east of the turnout). Very few visitors or photographers do this and the views are just as incredible as the turnout.

Fall is the most popular time to photograph Oxbow Bend. Many photographers will show up in the dark, more than an hour before sunrise. Expect that cars will be parked bumper to bumper during this key photography time. The trees typically turn color in early September. The leaves changing color is dependent on nighttime temperatures and how much sunlight is available. Once the night temperature dips below freezing (32°F / 0° C), the leaves will begin changing. Watch the weather forecast for this to happen.

HOTSPOT #7

Signal Mountain

GPS coordinates
43.84904, -110.56745 /
43°50'57"N,
110°34'03"W
12T 0534767E
4855197N

DESCRIPTION:

More than one visitor has been overheard on their phone, telling family back home, "This place looks like *Dances With Wolves*," referencing the 1990 Kevin Costner movie. The eastern view from Signal Mountain is particularly unique because it offers a broad mid-valley view accessible by car. Most other buttes and hills in the center of Jackson Hole are only accessible on foot.

Signal Mountain is far more than the communications hub for the park. It is a site with short trails leading to wildlife, ponds, and accessible forests. A longer hike can take hikers to Signal Mountain Lodge and Jackson Lake.

Views from the north of Jackson Hole and west to the Tetons are worth the short drive or moderate hike to the summit. Be aware the drive to the summit takes longer than one would expect given the distance. The road is winding and narrow.

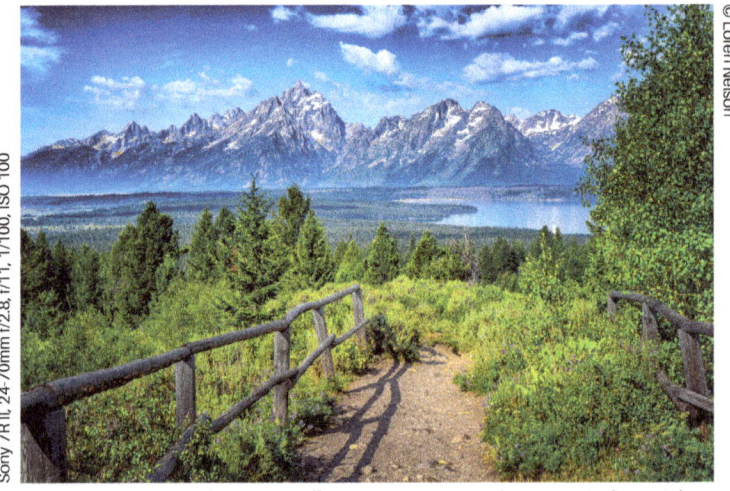

Signal Mountain offers a prime photography spot in Jackson Hole.

DIRECTIONS
Distance from Town Square

Drive north from Jackson on US 191 for 12.3 miles (19.8 km) to Moose Junction and turn left on Teton Park Road. Continue past the entrance station for a total of 16.7 miles (26.9 km) to the Signal Mountain Summit sign. Turn right (E) and continue 4.8 miles (7.7 km) to the summit parking lot.

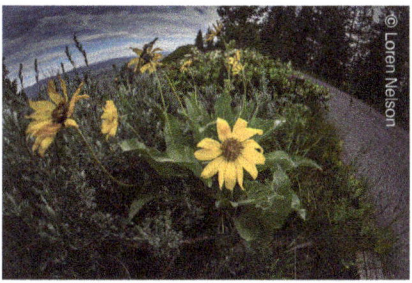
Canon 5D, 8mm fisheye, 1/200, ISO 400

Capturing spring flowers and the landscape of Signal Mountain.

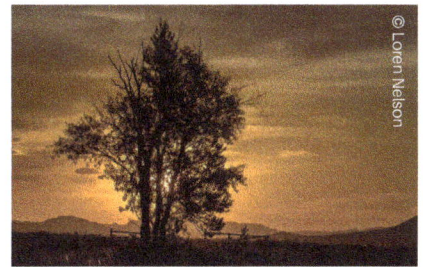
Canon 7D, 70-200mm f/2.8, f/9, 1/3200, ISO 1000

Sunset is a perfect time to find yourself alone in the forest.

Site Specifics:

Parking: Parking at the lower viewpoint and summit can be crowded during the middle of summer. Although there are many parking spaces, they fill up. Typically most visitors stay for thirty minutes or less, making finding a parking space not too much of a challenge.

Access: Both the summit and lower viewpoint are accessed by a short trail. They are both easy walks but may be challenging for the mobility challenged. The summit path has handrails.

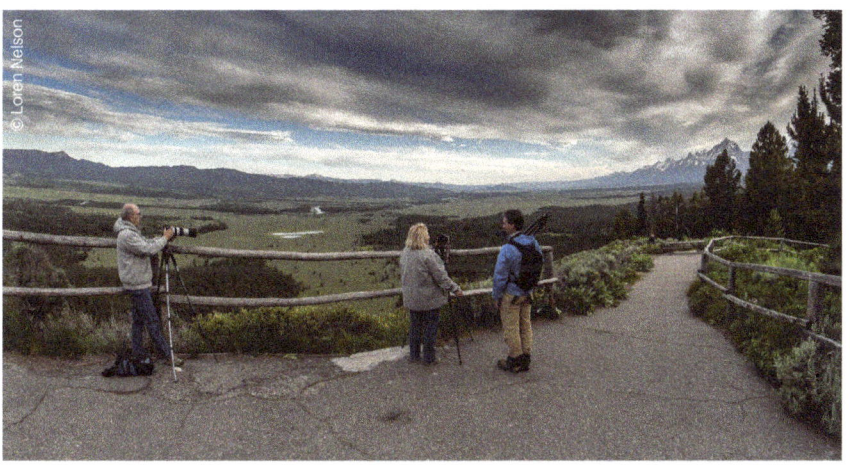
Canon 5D III, 8mm fisheye, 1/320, ISO 400

The author at a Teton Photography Club outing on Signal Mountain.

Site Specific Photography Tips

There are two different overlooks near and at the summit. The lower overlook point allows better views of the west. The views from the summit are partly blocked by tall conifers. The views to the east can be captured with a variety of lenses.

Signal Mountain and the Cathedral Group will cast long shadows during summer evenings. The high contrast can pose dynamic range challenges.

HOTSPOT #7

HOT SPOT #8

Snake River Overlook

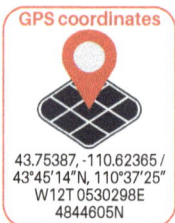

GPS coordinates
43.75387, -110.62365 /
43°45'14"N, 110°37'25"
W12T 0530298E
4844605N

DESCRIPTION:

The Snake River Overlook is the iconic image location of Grand Teton. It is in the same class as Schwabacher and Oxbow Bend. This site is not to be missed.

It was made famous by Ansel Adams when he was on his famous National Parks photography trip. As the trees have grown up since Adams took his photo, it is impossible to reproduce his exact image. As remote aircraft are banned in national parks, achieving a higher vantage point can only be achieved with a large pole with a remote release.

Although the Snake River overlook pullout is on the main highway through the park, it is often overlooked by photographers. Many often drive by if there are no other vehicles in the parking lot because the view is not obvious from the highway.

In the spring it is a great site for long telephoto wildlife images and sometimes wildflowers.

In the winter, the ice and snow on the trees create majestic Arctic conditions. If the winter is particularly cold, the Snake River will freeze partly creating an ice channel. Sometimes the whole surface of the river freezes during prolonged sub-zero (-18°C) conditions.

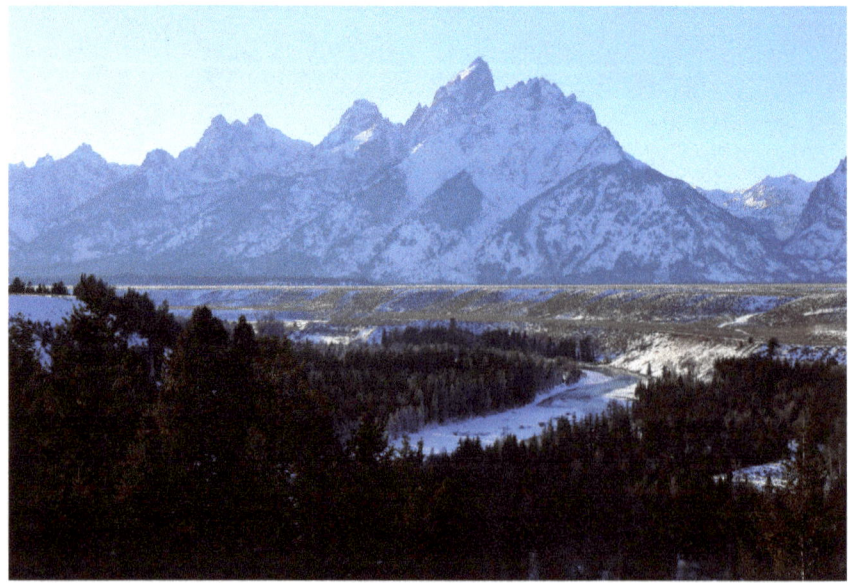

Nikon D300s, 18-105mm, f/9, 1/400, ISO 200

Snake River Overlook.

DIRECTIONS

Distance from Town Square

Drive north from Jackson on US 191 for 20.7 miles (33.3 km). Turn left (west) at the Snake River Overlook parking lot.

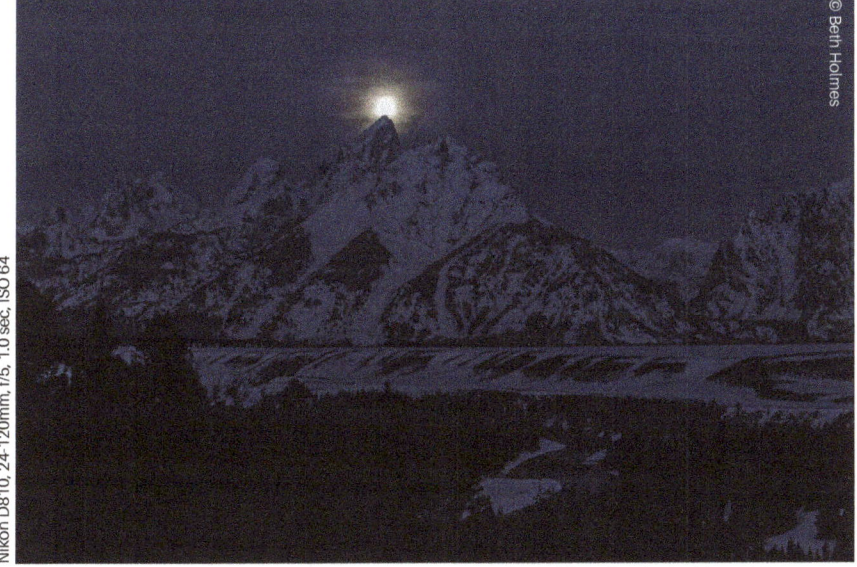

Nikon D810, 24-120mm, f/5, 1.0 sec, ISO 64

Snake River Overlook with a setting moon.

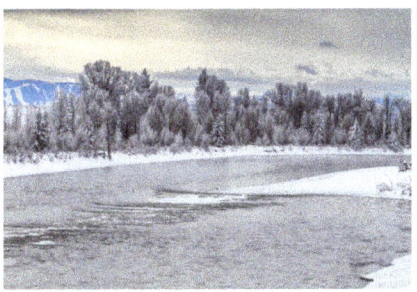

The Snake on a frigid January afternoon.

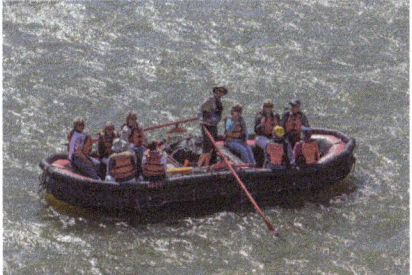

In summer the Snake is full of rafters seeking the deep beauty of the river.

📷 Site Specific Photography Tips

The best viewpoint is at the northern portion of the walkway along the stone wall. Several signs contain interesting park information, including a printed image of one of Adams's images. Partly cloudy skies make the most interesting photographs at this location.

There is no protection from the weather at this location. Be prepared for chilly conditions in the evening, as a breeze often blows over the viewpoint.

HOTSPOT #8

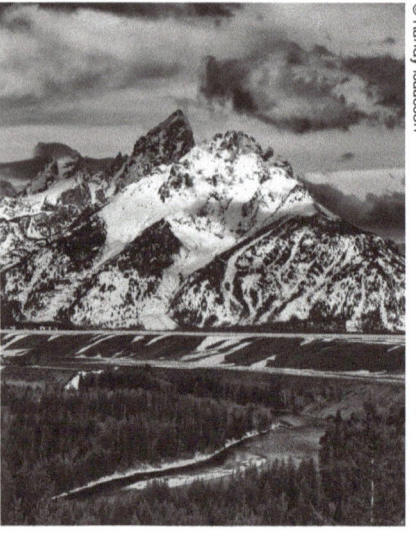
A B&W conversion of Snake River Overlook.

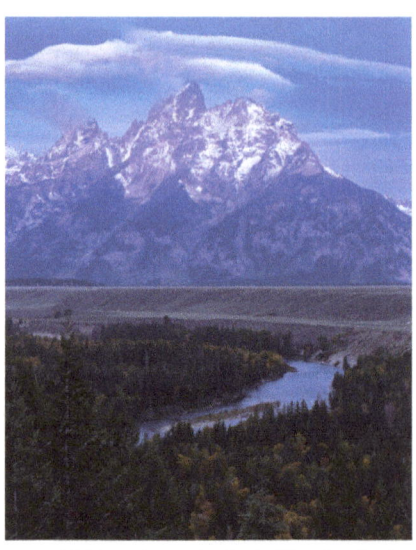
A fall morning at the Snake River Overlook.

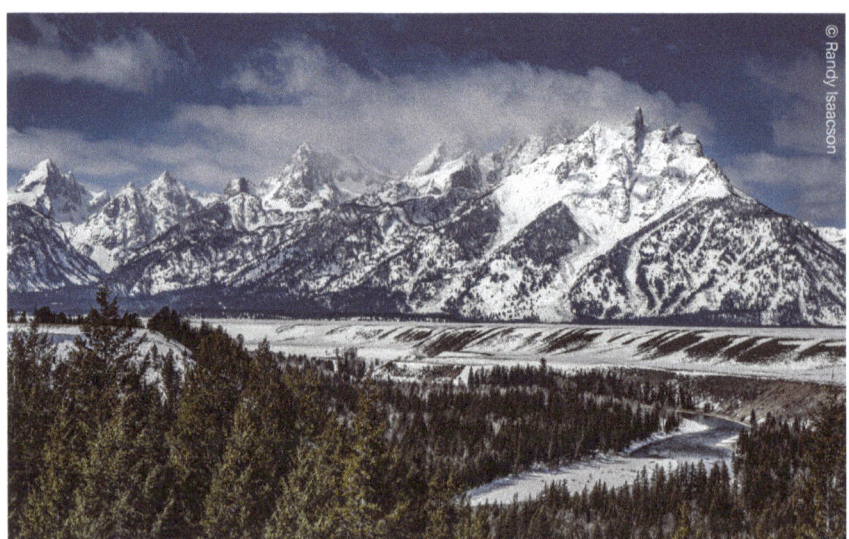
Winter at Snake River Overlook.

Nikon Z7, 24-70mm f/4, f/8, 1/800, ISO 100

Site Specifics:

Parking: The parking lot is large and can accommodate sizable vehicles.

Access: Snake River overlook is generally accessible year-round. There have been some years when the parking lot has not been plowed and is blocked off during the winter.

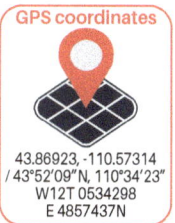

GPS coordinates
43.86923, -110.57314
/ 43°52'09"N, 110°34'23"
W12T 0534298
E 4857437N

HOTSPOT #9

Willow Flats Turnout

DESCRIPTION:

MAP 1

The Willow Flats turnout, just north of Jackson Lake Junction and just south of the Lodge, is one of the most popular stops in the park. Vistas of the Teton Range, Jackson Lake, Jackson Lake dam, and the Snake River can all be seen here.

The large meadows bring something for everyone. In the spring the meadow is a primary birthing ground for elk. The newborn calves may be visible when the mothers move them. The young elk also attract hungry grizzly bears.

Bird life is plentiful year-round as well. Even in the winter, ravens and eagles will circle high overhead in search of a meal. The best action is in spring when the young animals are born. A pair of binoculars can be helpful to identify animals before setting out to photograph them.

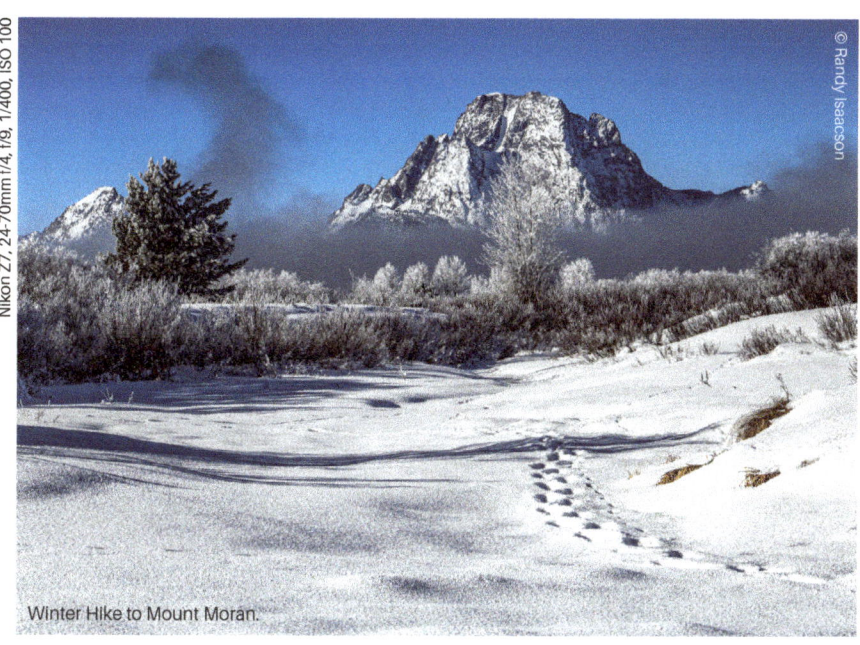

Winter Hike to Mount Moran.

Nikon Z7, 24-70mm f/4, f/9, 1/400, ISO 100

© Randy Isaacson

DIRECTIONS

Distance from Town Square

Drive north from Jackson on US 191 for 30.3 miles (48.8 km). Turn left (west) at Moran Junction. Continue for 4.2 miles (6.8 km) and turn left (west) into the Willow Flats parking lot.

HOTSPOT #9

📷 Site Specific Photography Tips

Normal to long telephoto lenses are most useful at this site. The viewpoint from the parking lot has many shrubs up close. Sometimes flowers bloom at this location, adding foreground options. For animals, bring the longest telephoto lens possible. Usually, the animal interaction can be far away and barely visible on all but the longest of lenses.

One of the best tools can be a pair of binoculars. It is far easier to first spot distant landscape and animal opportunities with both eyes. The high overlook is somewhat distant from the flatlands of Willow Flats. As a consequence, only keep eyes will first perceive still and moving animals in the distant landscape. One of the best tricks to use for the shy, beginning photographer is to look where others are pointing their spotting scopes. Chatting with others standing around is the most effective way of finding out what is going on. This helps improve the productivity of time in the field.

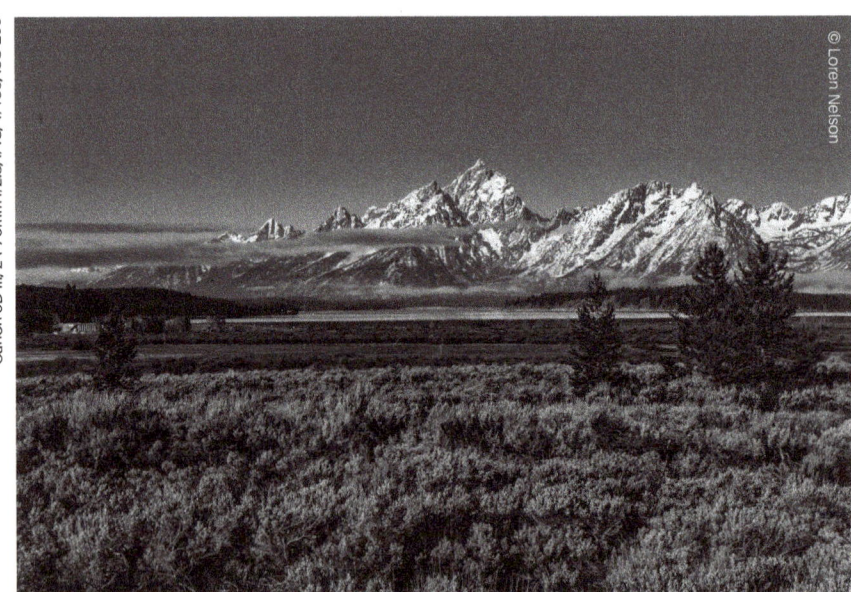

The meadow, dam, lake, mountains, and lenticular clouds created some drama under an overcast sky. The muted colors inspired a high-contrast, high-structure monochrome image.

Site Specifics:

Parking: The parking lot is large and is accessible all year unless it has not been plowed. Visitor turnover is fast, so if the lot is full, usually a car pulls out quickly.

Access: The site is drive up and walk up with easy access for disabled photographers. The high viewpoint above Willow Flats makes this an ideal location for any visitor.

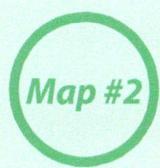

JENNY LAKE
COVERING HOTSPOTS #10-24

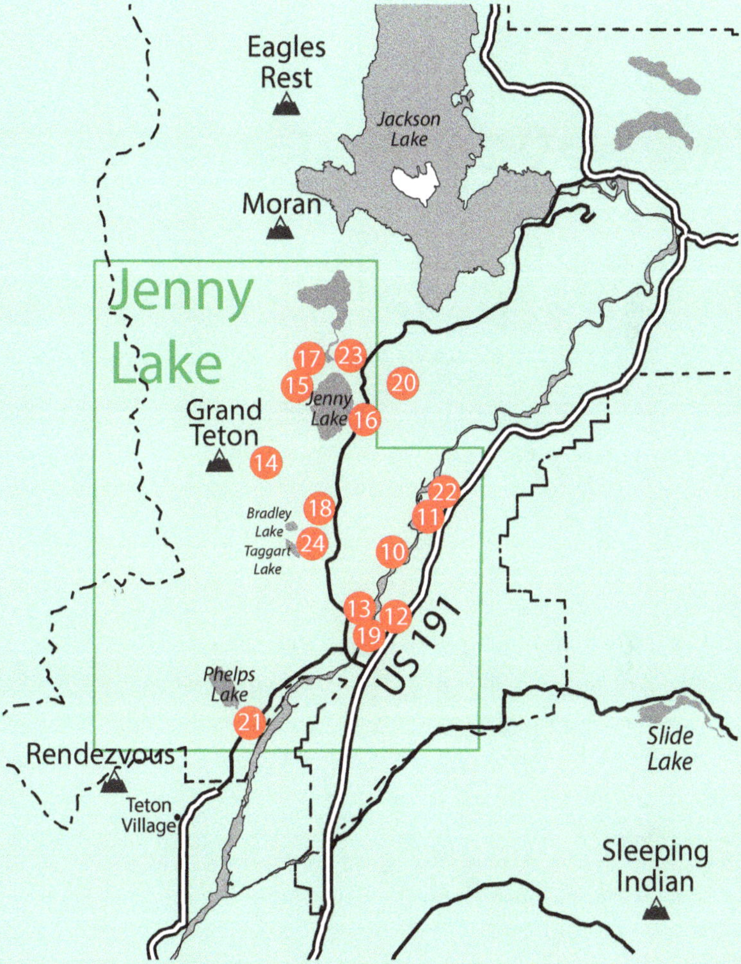

HOT SPOT #10

Bar BC Ranch

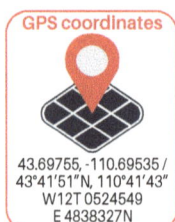

GPS coordinates

43.69755, -110.69535 /
43°41'51"N, 110°41'43"
W12T 0524549
E 4838327N

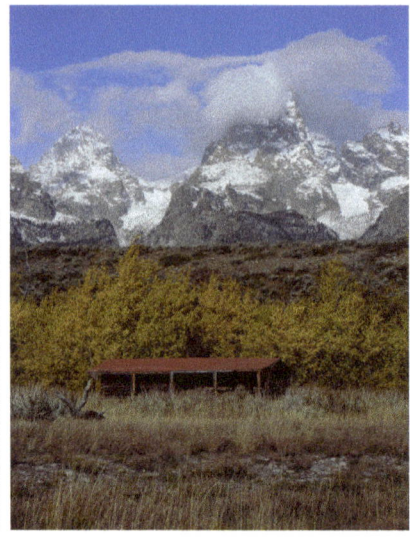

Nikon D800, 85mm f/1.4, f/13, 1/200, ISO 100

The Bar BC ranch with the Cathedral Group in the background. This ranch was one of the original dude ranches that established Jackson Hole as a tourist destination. Featured in the book *Diary of a Dude Wrangler* (available from Sastrugi Press Classics), Struthers Burt recounts his exploits of creating one of the most popular destinations in the valley for writers and actors of all kinds in the early part of the 20th century. People did not believe the photos they saw of the location and had to see it for themselves. The same can be said today of tourists who see pictures online and travel to Jackson Hole to see and experience it for themselves.

DESCRIPTION:

The Bar BC dude ranch is one of the best secrets in Grand Teton National Park. This ranch dates from 1912 and was one of the first dude ranches in Wyoming. It spans about 600 acres along the west side of the Snake River. At one time it had a dance hall, swimming pool, lodges, and cabins with hot water.

In 1990 it was declared a historic district. Unfortunately, the site's couple dozen buildings have seriously deteriorated and many collapsed. There is a current effort to re-roof and salvage some of the buildings.

Access is on the very rough south River Road and requires a high clearance vehicle and some serious patience. The road is only open from late spring to mid-autumn. Note: older maps may show River Road as a long 20-mile loop but erosion and collapse along the river closed the loop to vehicles. It is still walkable and the views worthwhile.

DIRECTIONS — Distance from Town Square

Drive north from Jackson on US 191 for 12.3 miles (19.8 km) to Moose Junction and turn left on Teton Park Road. Continue for 4 miles (6.4 km) and turn right on the unmarked rough dirt road (River Road). This turn is 1,000 feet (304 m) north of the Cottonwood Creek Picnic Area. From the steel gate, drive 1.7 miles (2.7 km) to the parking area at the wooden gate.

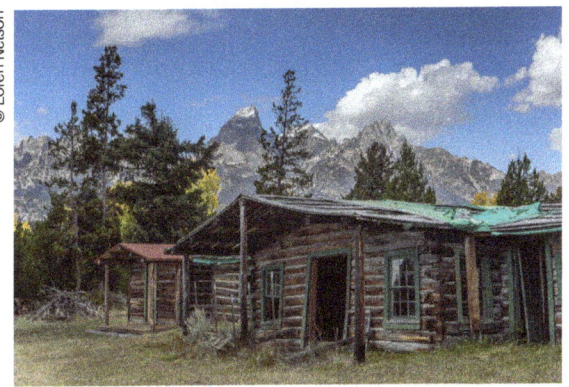

Canon 5D III, 24-70mm f/2.8, f/11, 1/160, ISO 100

One of the dilapidated buildings that is slowly being salvaged.

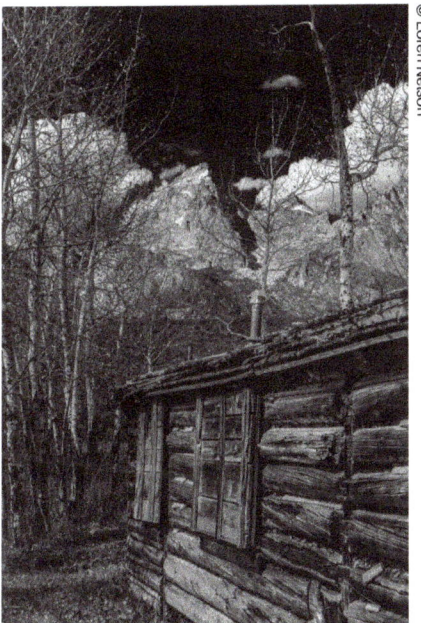

Textures in the old cabins create opportunities for great monochrome work.

History abounds at the Bar BC. Great foreground elements surround the curious photographer.

MAP 2

📷 Site Specific Photography Tips

Due to historic renovations, some of the buildings may not be accessible. This will change over time as the park rebuilds and retrofits some buildings. Plan to use a wide-angle to normal lens at this location. A lens in the 18-105mm is the perfect choice for the ranch.

The mountains peak through the aspen trees, making for unique compositions. There is a large hill (former river bench) west of the site, creating a backdrop for the buildings. The buildings are much lower than the summits, limiting the use of telephoto lenses to place the buildings directly in front of Cathedral Group.

HOTSPOT #10

Site Specifics:

Parking: The parking area above the Bar BC Ranch is small, though it is rarely full. The road to the ranch can be rough, as it is not regularly maintained.

Access: The walk to the ranch is down a moderately sloped dirt road with loose rocks. Once at the ranch level, walking around the level ranch land is easy.

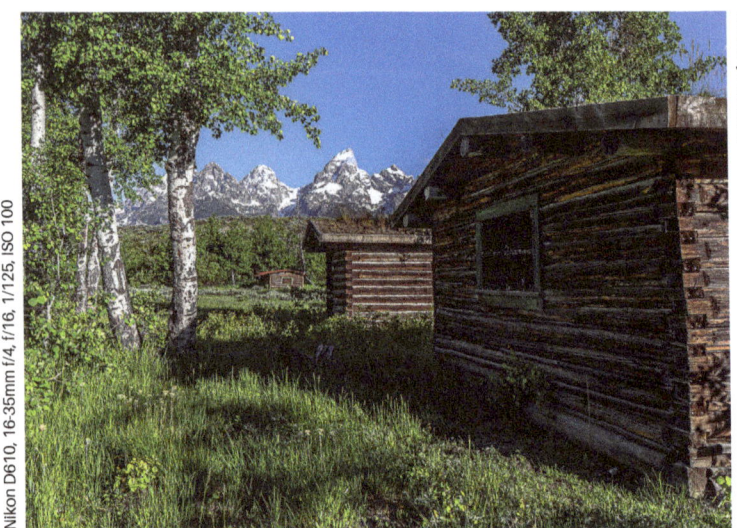

Bar BC ranch cabins.

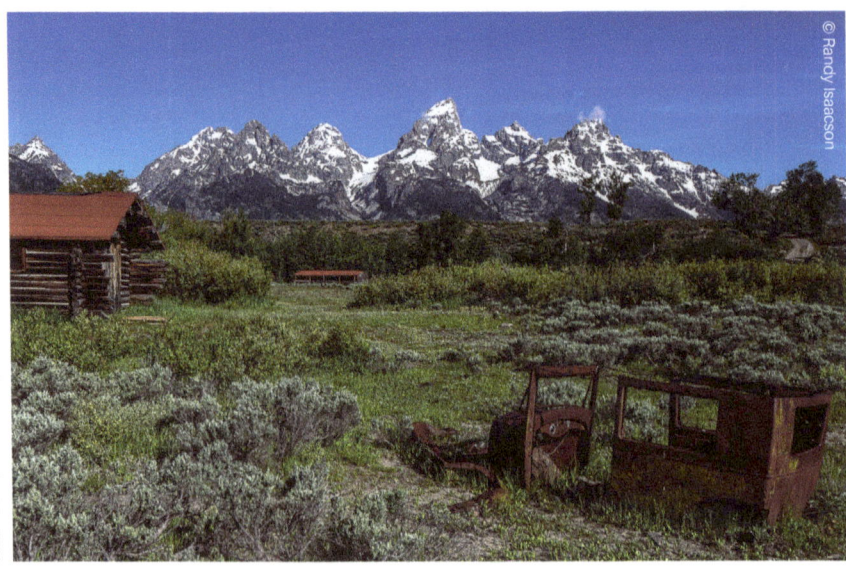

The Bar BC "Parking Lot".

HOT SPOT #11

Beaver Ponds

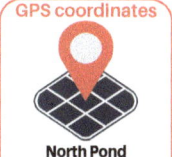

GPS coordinates

North Pond
43.71406, -110.67206
/ 43°42'51"N,
110°40'19"W
12T 0526418E
4840167N

South Ponds
43.70707, -110.67407 /
43°42'25", 110°40'27"
12T 0526259E
4839390N

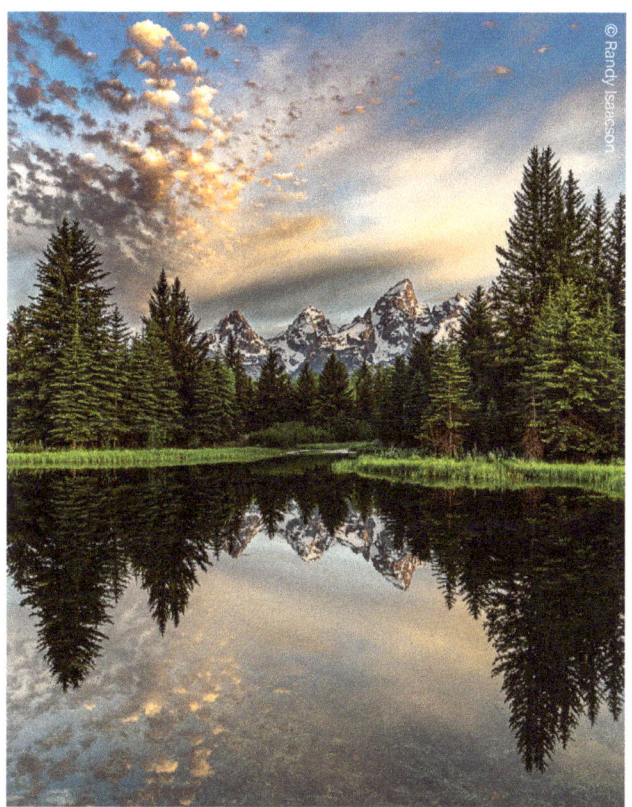

Schwabacher stunning sunrise over a beaver pond.

Nikon D610, 24-120mm f/4, f/8, 1/45, ISO 100

MAP 2

DESCRIPTION:

While Schwabacher Landing may be packed with over-lapping tripods on any summer morning, there are several beaver ponds to take classic reflection photos of. The biggest challenge is parking at this location. In the morning, there can be hoards of photographers jockeying for position at the trail's edge. However, the beaver ponds are often open.

The big beaver pond on the trail from the northernmost parking lot is the largest and most complex. There is one big dam and one large lodge in the middle of the pond. The dead trees around this particular pond may be compelling or they may be distracting.

The beaver ponds accessible at the south parking lot tend to be less busy. These particular ponds also have live conifers for a different composition option. Depending on the year, water level, and beaver activity, some of these ponds have shifted over the years.

Nikon D610, 24-120mm f/4, f/16, 1/8, ISO 100

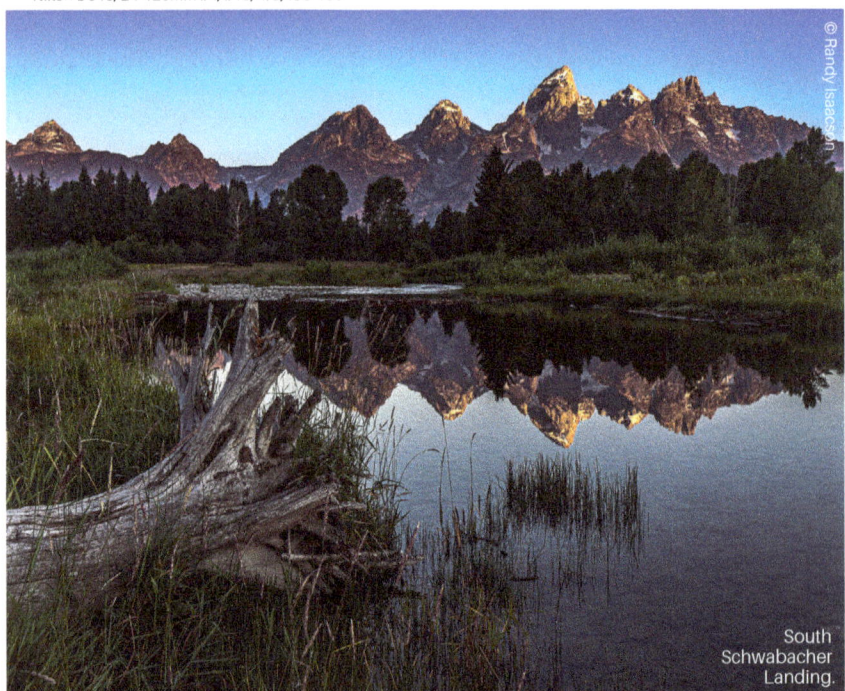

South Schwabacher Landing.

DIRECTIONS
Distance from Town Square

Drive north from Jackson on US 191 for 16.4 miles (26.3 km) and turn left at the Schwabacher Landing sign. Continue for 1 mile (1.6 km) to the large dirt lot.

Nikon D610, 24-120mm f/4, f/16, 1/8, ISO 100

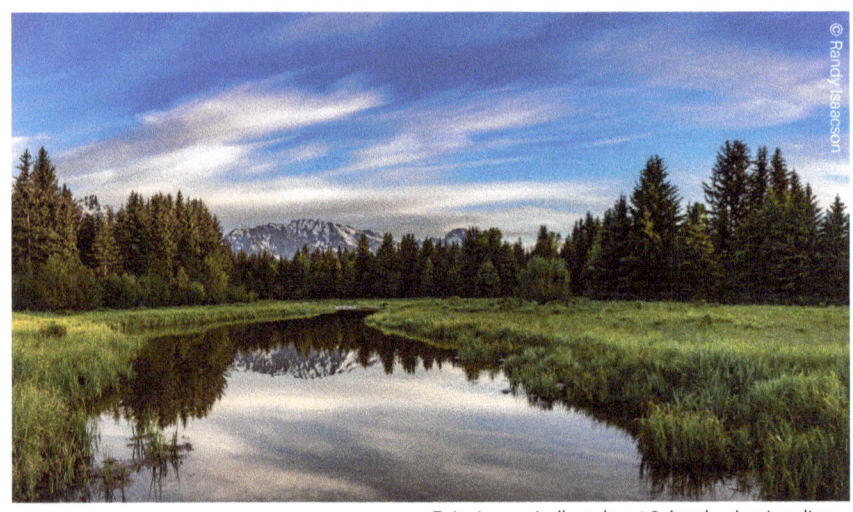

Enjoying a windless day at Schwabacher Landing.

HOTSPOT #11

Site Specific Photography Tips

The best time to photograph at the beaver ponds is in the morning. Most of the time, breezes will start by noon and persist for the rest of the day. To achieve the glassy reflection, the air must be perfectly still to create the classic photo.

Wide-angle to slightly telephoto lenses are the best choice here. A good zoom in the 18-105mm range will afford the most flexibility for composition.

When possible, consider adding a foreground element to add variety to your shots. Thistle is common most of the summer here. Flowers with petals bloom late spring through early summer.

The beaver ponds in mid-summer are calm in the early morning for good reflections. As water levels on the Snake River have changed over the years, the beaver ponds may vary considerably in their size and location. Each year is different, giving photographers the chance to take unique photographs each year.

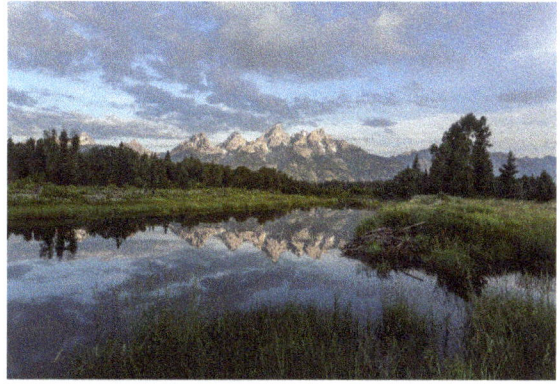
© Loren Nelson

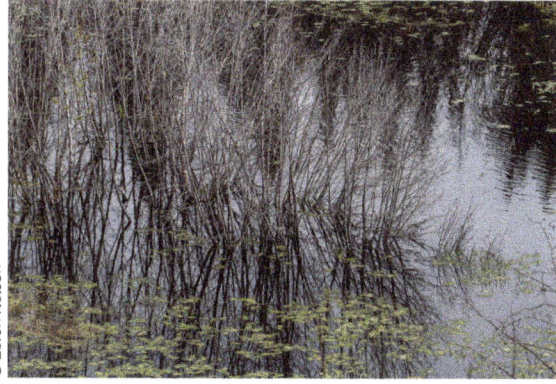
© Loren Nelson

When there are no clouds to highlight the mountains, the ponds themselves become subjects. Life around beaver ponds is dependent on the water level in the Snake River, Jackson Lake, and on the local snowpack.

Site Specifics:

Parking: Parking at the northernmost lot with the pit toilet can be a real challenge in the morning in the summer. For a less busy option, park at the southernmost dirt lot. A short stub road leads to this parking area.

Access: All of the beaver ponds at this location require hiking on a level dirt trail. The hikes are short, less than 0.2 mile (0.3 km), to reach the different beaver ponds.

HOTSPOT #12

Blacktail Ponds Overlook

GPS coordinates
43.66674, -110.69668 /
43°40'00"N, 110°41'48"
W12T 0524454E
4834904N

DESCRIPTION:

This often-bypassed overlook is on the west side of Highway 89. It is 430 feet (131 m) north of Antelope Flats Road on Highway 191. The overlook isn't visible from the highway, so fewer visitors stop at this spot. Fine views and beautiful scenery are available here and are well worth the stop.

The parking lot is a few feet from a lookout of the backwater of the Snake River. Recently, the park upgraded access, allowing visitors to hike down to the ponds. This is a new feature and is well worth taking advantage of. However, be aware that the trail is steep and demanding. During winter, drifting snow can make the hike extra challenging with the steepness in winter conditions. Be prepared.

The overlook and the surrounding ponds are gorgeous in the spring through the fall. Small streams flow through the area, leading down to a wide area of the Snake River. Bring boots because the ponds are swampy. Also, consider insect repellent and bear spray to prevent negative bear encounters.

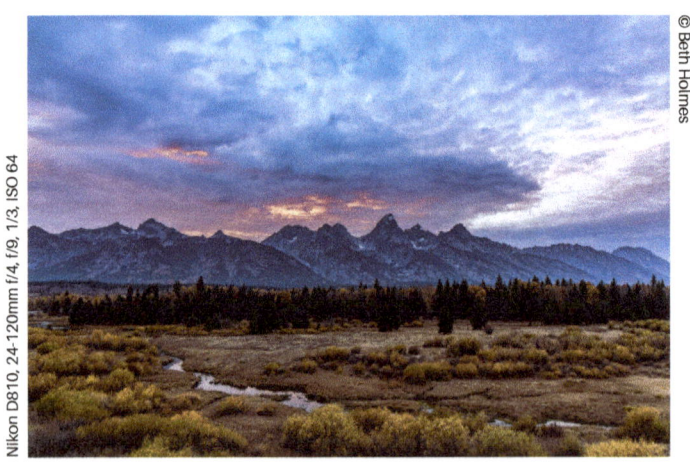

Blacktail Ponds Overlook in autumn during sunset.

DIRECTIONS

Distance from Town Square

Drive north from Jackson on US 191 for 13.8 miles (22.2 km). Turn left (west) at the Blacktail Ponds Overlook sign. Drive 0.2 mile (0.3 km) to the overlook parking area.

Site Specifics:

Parking: Parking is rarely full at the overlook. Most of the time there are few to no vehicles or visitors. The road is normally not plowed in the winter.

Access: The overlook is generally accessible from May-November unless there is an early or late snowpack.

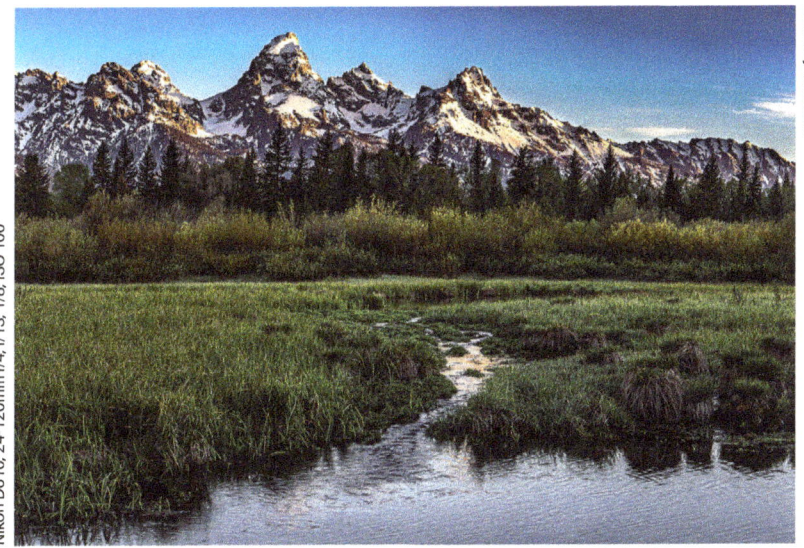

Blacktail Pond in spring.

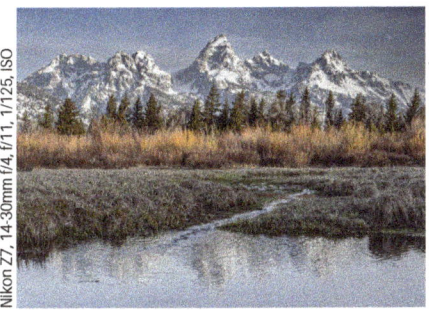

Blacktail Pond with orange willows.

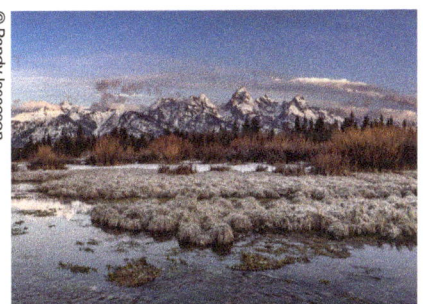

Blacktail Pond frosted and ready to bloom.

📷 Site Specific Photography Tips

Views from the overlook lend themselves to moderately wide-angle lenses to capture the ponds and mountains in the background. For images around the pond, a versatile zoom lens in the 18-70mm range is the best choice.

For the rare whitetail deer sighting, a fast, moderate zoom lens in the 300mm range is a good choice. As the deer often emerge from the tree cover near dusk, an f/4 or f/2.8 lens is a wise choice for the clearest grain-free images.

HOTSPOT #12

HOTSPOT #13

Chapel of the Transfiguration

GPS coordinates

43.66011, -110.71531
/ 43°39'36"N, 110°42'55"
W12T 0522954E
4834163N

MAP 2

Nikon D800, 50mm f/1.8, f/11, 1/400, ISO 100

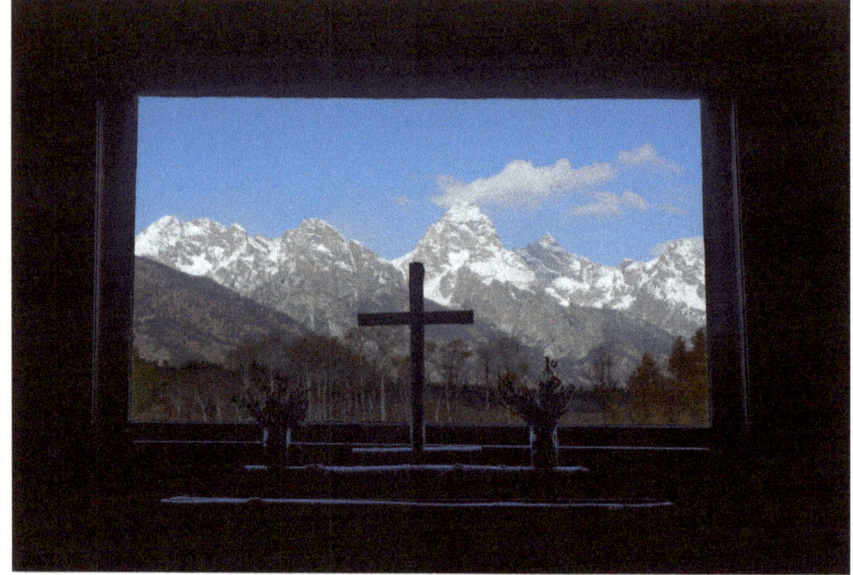

Viewing the Cathedral Group from inside the chapel.

DESCRIPTION:

This Chapel of Transfiguration is a log structure constructed in 1925. It is operated by St. John's Episcopal Church in Jackson. This historic structure is a classic fixture and is second only to the Moulton Barns for old building photography in the park.

The view from the chapel window frames the Cathedral Group. During fall, the aspens in the frame make for incredible photographic opportunities. During spring, the wildflowers including the remarkable displays of arrowleaf balsamroot dot the landscape around the chapel. It is difficult to take a poor photograph here.

The wood inside the chapel is incredibly dark. This creates difficulties with capturing the outside and inside simultaneously due to the dynamic range. Even shooting in 14-bit raw will challenge the most advanced cameras.

DIRECTIONS

Distance from Town Square

Drive north from Jackson on US 191 for 12.3 miles (19.8 km) to Moose Junction and turn left on Teton Park Road. Continue for 1.2 miles (2 km), turn right on Menors Ferry Rd, and drive 0.4 mile (0.6 km) to the Chapel of the Transfiguration parking lot.

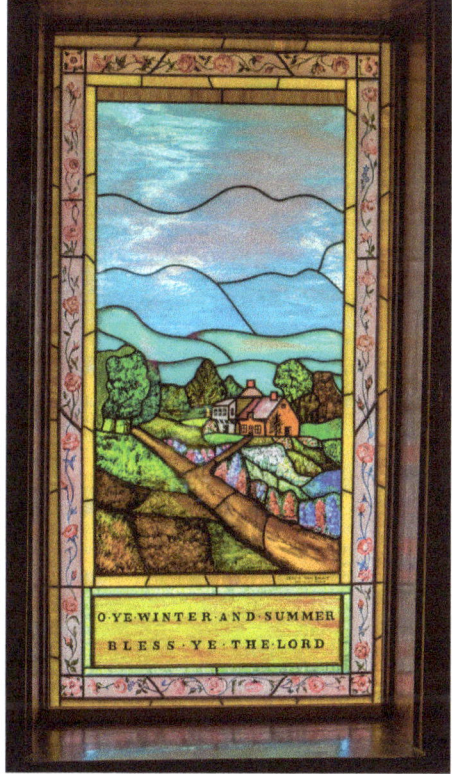

Stained glass with mountain scenes adorns the entry to the chapel.

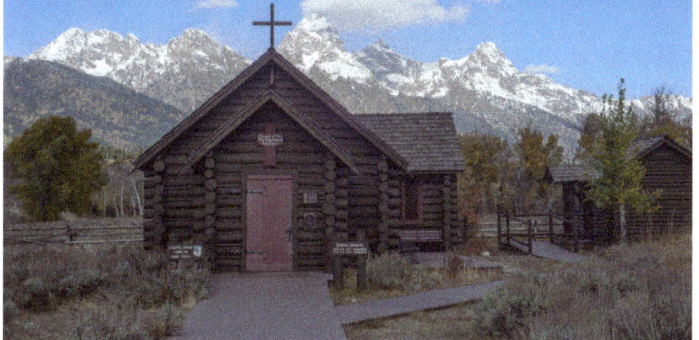

Wait for a passing cloud to reduce the contrast on the chapel's dark exterior.

HOTSPOT #13

📷 Site Specific Photography Tips

Wide and normal angle lenses are best here for photographing the building. The aspen patch northwest of the chapel makes a pleasant image with a moderate telephoto lens. Respect the posted rules of the chapel concerning tripods and flash photography.

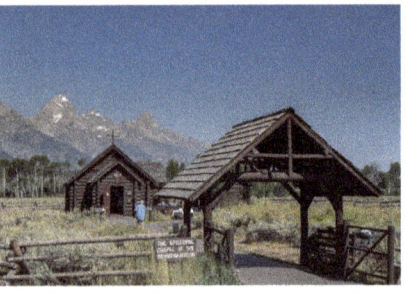

Chapel Sunday services are open to the public and the chapel is open to visitors at almost all times. Buses bring visitors in the summer and the site can get very crowded.

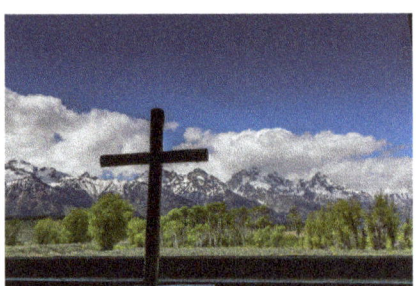

The view of the alter and window to the Teton Range.

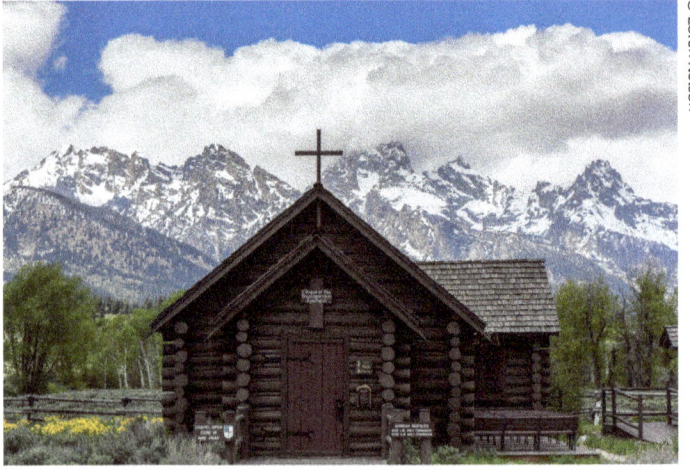

The chapel with the snow-covered Teton Range background.

Site Specifics:

Parking: Parking at the chapel is plentiful. It can accommodate tour buses and only fills up for private events (weddings, funerals).

Access: The chapel is adjacent to a large parking lot. The path to the building is paved and wheelchair accessible. It passes under a small awning with a bell that loudly clangs when the rope is pulled.

If there is an event at the chapel, access will be restricted. Please avoid walking around or into the building during services.

HOTSPOT #13

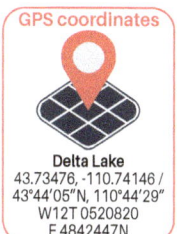

GPS coordinates
Delta Lake
43.73476, -110.74146 /
43°44'05"N, 110°44'29"
W12T 0520820
E 4842447N

HOTSPOT #14

Delta Lake

DESCRIPTION:

At one time, Delta Lake was a rarely visited off-trail lake. No longer. With the advent of social media sharing sites and apps, Delta Lake has become one of the most visited and popular backcountry lakes in Grand Teton.

The approach to Delta Lake does not reveal any of its beauty until hikers crest the final climb. Frozen until early summer, the glacial jade-green waters sit at the base of Grand Teton. When hikers catch their first glimpse of the lake, the refrain is surprise and awe. The location is simply that incredible.

Currently, the trail to the lake is unofficial. There has been some talk about the park updating this trail as an officially marked and mapped path. This has not been done as of this book's publication.

MAP 2

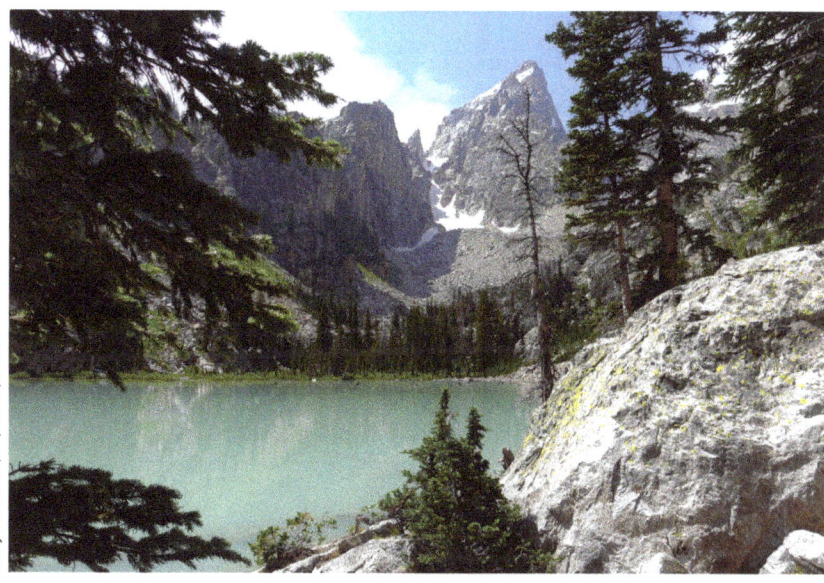

Sony RX100 VA, f/4, 1/500, ISO 80

DIRECTIONS   Distance from Town Square

Drive north from Jackson on US 191 for 12.3 miles (19.8 km) to Moose Junction and turn left on Teton Park Road. Continue for 7.2 miles (11.6 km) to the Lupine Meadows Trailhead turnoff. Turn left onto the road. Cross the wooden bridge over Cottonwood Creek, then continue on the main dirt road for 1.5 miles (2.3 km) to reach the Lupine Meadow Trailhead.

HOTSPOT #14

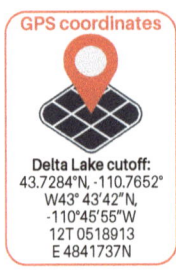

GPS coordinates

Delta Lake cutoff:
43.7284°N, -110.7652°
W43° 43'42"N,
-110°45'55"W
12T 0518913
E 4841737N

Work your way along the rough trail across several rockfalls. When crossing the rockfalls, maintain a constant elevation to reconnect with the dirt trail. Look across the rock field to identify the trail to guide yourself. Avoid climbing directly up the rocks.

The last 500 feet (169 m) is extremely steep and rocky. Avoid dislodging rocks that will fall on other hikers below you. Once you reach the flat area, Delta Lake will become visible.

📷 Site Specific Photography Tips

The location and scale of the view lend themselves to a wide-angle lens to capture both the lake and Grand Teton. One challenge at this location is balancing the composition with the lake and the mountain. Try capturing some interesting foreground objects like some of the boulders in the lake or the scraggly trees. They'll make the photo more compelling.

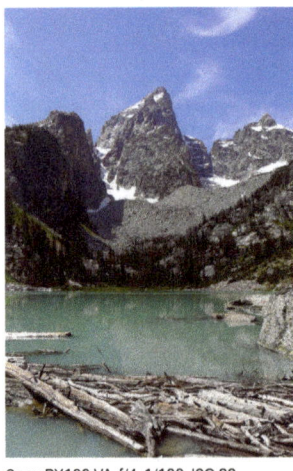

Sony RX100 VA, f/4, 1/100, ISO 80

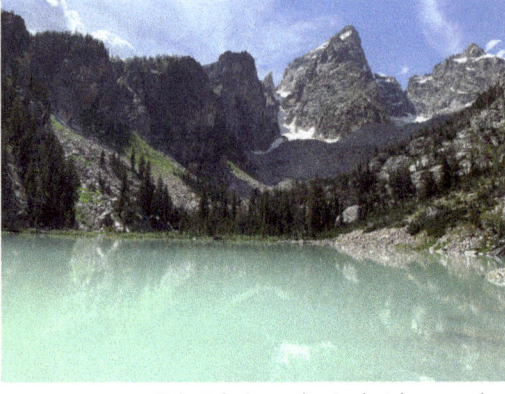

iPhone Xs, f/1.8, 1/2200, ISO 25

Delta Lake has a classic glacial green color from the glacial runoff from Grand Teton and the surrounding moraine.

HIKING DIRECTIONS

Begin at the trailhead at the end of the parking lot. The trail starts off flat, then starts uphill, curving around a hill. At 0.6 mile (1 km), cross the wooden bridge over the creek that drains Delta Lake.

The trail turns west and works its way up a ridge to the Valley Trail junction at 1.7 miles (2.7 km). The switchbacks provide expansive views of Taggart and Bradley Lakes. Continue on the trail for another 1.2 miles (1.9 km) to reach the Garnet Canyon junction.

After departing the Garnet Canyon junction, travel 1,000 feet (363 m) to the end of this switchback. Steep wooden stairs will be visible leading down a ravine on a 0.8-mile (1.4 km) trail to Delta Lake.

iPhone Xs, f/1.8, 1/2000, ISO 25

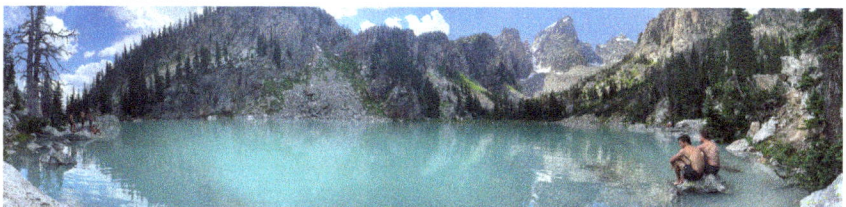

Panorama of Delta Lake with the trail that follows the shoreline.

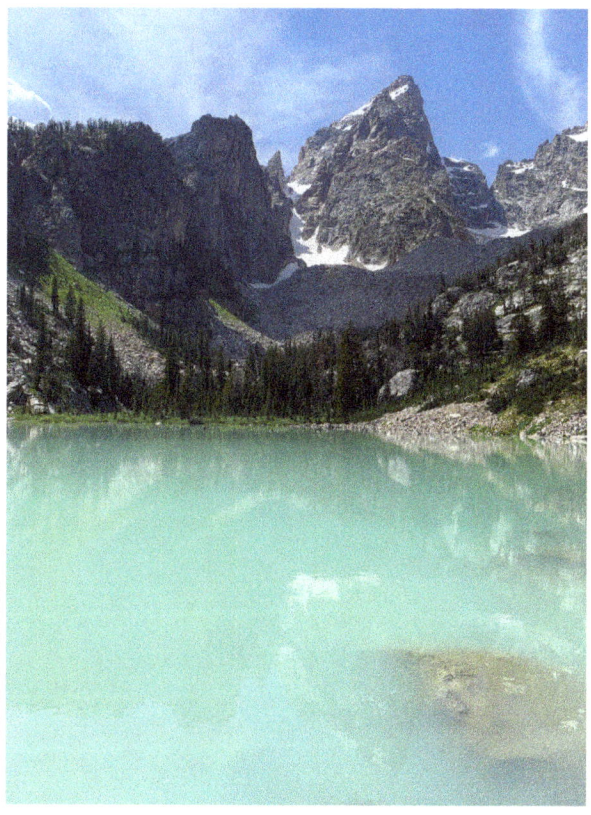

iPhone Xs, f/1.8, 1/2500, ISO 25

Site Specifics:

Parking: Park at the Lupine Meadows trailhead. Expect parking to be a serious challenge midday during the height of summer.

Access: Hiking to Delta Lake is tough. The trail cutoff from the Surprise & Amphitheater Lakes trail is unmarked. The hiker traffic makes where to go fairly obvious, though. Be mindful that it is easy to lose the path in the two boulder fields. Look well ahead and keep an eye on the extremely steep trail leading to the lake.

Dangers: Hikers may dislodge rocks higher on the trail, raining them down on hikers lower on the trail. Be attentive to whoever is above. This is a real risk, though it doesn't necessitate a climbing helmet.

HOTSPOT #14

HOTSPOT #15

Hidden Falls / Inspiration Point

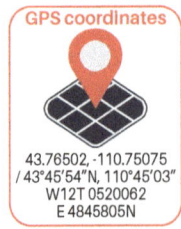

GPS coordinates
43.76502, -110.75075
/ 43°45'54"N, 110°45'03"
W12T 0520062
E 4845805N

MAP 2

© Loren Nelson

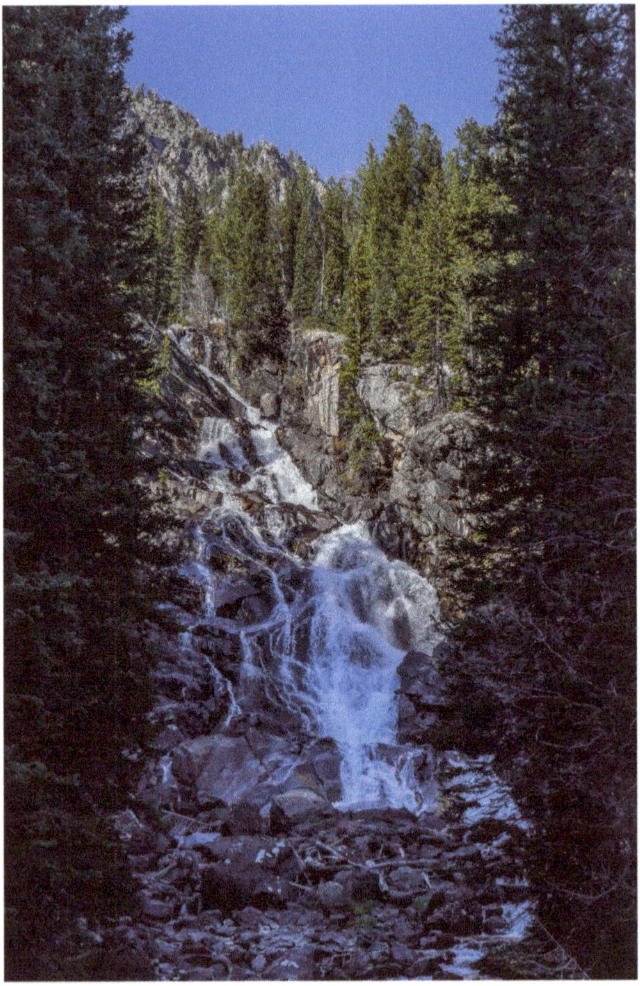

Canon 5D III, 24-70mm f/2.8, f/10, 1/320, ISO 200

Hidden Falls is a cascading falls that is difficult to capture in good light. The canyon leaves dense shadows when the light is best and the crowds preclude a tripod in the mid hours of the day.

DIRECTIONS   Distance from Town Square

Drive north from Jackson on US 191 for 12.3 miles (19.8 km) to Moose Junction and turn left on Teton Park Road. Continue past the entrance station for a total of 7.9 miles (12.7 km) to the Jenny Lake Junction, turn left, and park at the end of the lot.

DESCRIPTION:

Hidden Falls above the southwestern shore of Jenny Lake is one of the most accessible and popular waterfalls in Grand Teton National Park. It is a 200-foot cascading falls that is a short, steep hike from the Jenny Lake ferry dock. It is also accessible via a longer walk from the north or south via the Jenny Lake loop trail.

Be aware that this is one of the most crowded spots in the park in the summer months. To capture a clear, good shot arrive very early or stay until the crowd dwindles in the late afternoon. Showing up early is the best choice, as far fewer make the trek before breakfast.

Beyond the falls is a maintained but steep trail leading to Inspiration Point. This viewpoint is 0.3 mile (0.5 km) above the falls to the north. Views on the rocky precipice are well worth the climb. It is a very popular lunch spot and is crowded mid-day in the summer.

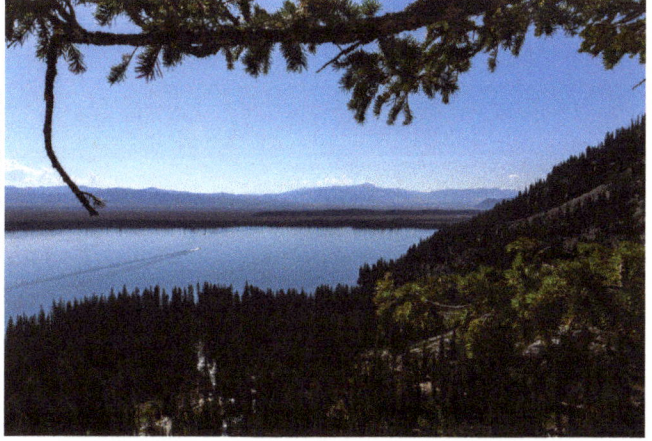

Inspiration Point is a great place to chill out and watch the boat traffic on Jenny Lake.

HIKING DIRECTIONS

Begin hiking at the trailhead toward the shuttle dock. Cross the bridge and continue on the lake trail to the Valley Trail junction at 0.7 mile (1.1 km). The trail begins gaining elevation, passes the Moose Ponds junction, then loses elevation and comes to another junction.

Note that the upper and lower trails have been under construction in past years, so mind the park signs.

Follow the trail 1 mile (1.6 km) to a signed junction toward Hidden Falls, then continue 0.25 mile (0.4 km) to another junction, turn left (W), and proceed to Hidden Falls. The falls are hidden by the trees until you reach a clearing.

To reach Inspiration Point, backtrack 200 feet (61 m) to the signed junction, then climb the steep trail 0.3 mile (0.5 km) to the overlook.

📷 Site Specific Photography Tips

Photographing the waterfall is a challenge when there is a crowd. The trees create a small window to capture the falls, so taking shots from farther away is difficult. Up close, a wide-angle lens is necessary to capture the bulk of the falls.

This particular site lends itself to photographing only a fraction of the waterfall. As the upper reaches are nearly out of sight, taking a portrait picture of the mid-section waterfall often yields good results.

Securing a tripod position by the buck rail fence requires patience. Many visitors come, take a few photos, and then leave. Give yourself time to allow people to clear out. Each shuttle boat brings a surge of visitors. Plan to stay some time to get the best shot.

To create a silky smooth waterfall, photograph using a tripod with an exposure of at least ½ second. Longer exposures create smoother water. In mid-day, a neutral density filter will be necessary to achieve long shutter times. Using a 9-stop (2.7) filter will allow for long exposures, 30 seconds or more, to smooth the water out to a wispy mist.

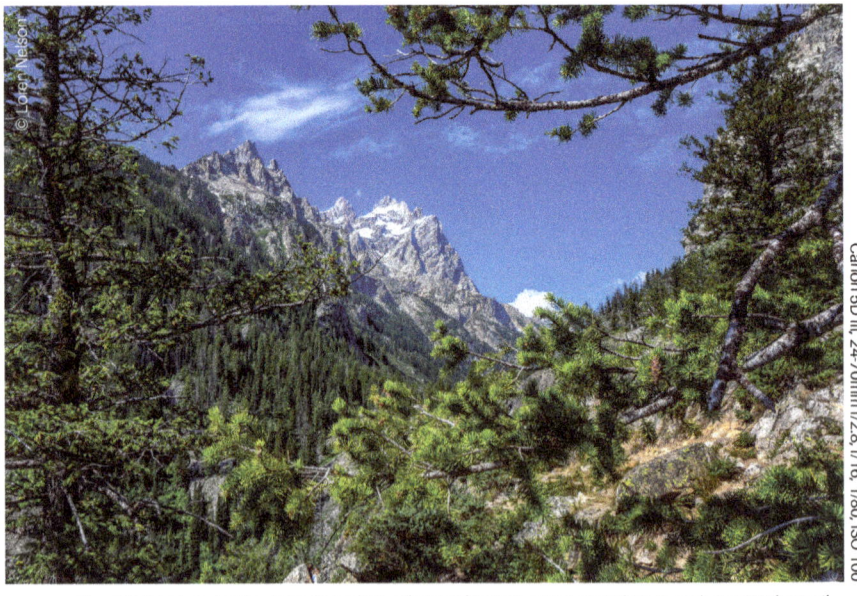

The climb to Inspiration Point is rocky and steep but the view is worth it. Past the point the trail continues to the marvelous Cascade Canyon and a great all-day hike at high altitude.

Site Specifics:

Parking: Parking is a challenge in summer in all locations.

Access: Some visitors hike around Jenny Lake to Hidden Falls and pay to ride the shuttle boat back across the lake for the complete experience. A short hike on a rocky trail is required to reach the falls from the boat ramp.

GPS coordinates
43.76789, -110.71733
/ 43°46'04"N, 110°43'0
2"W 12T 0522751E 48
46132N

HOT SPOT #16

Jenny Lake Overlook on the One Way

DESCRIPTION:

The Jenny Lake overlook is one of the few marked spots on the forested one-way paved road and bike path between String Lake and south Jenny Lake. Reflections are great in the morning before the wind comes up but the views are always spectacular. The overlook can be jammed with cars midday in the summer, but early risers and visitors in the late spring and fall will be treated to breath-taking views of the Tetons.

This road gives everyone easy access to the beauty of the lake at the foot of the Tetons. It is one lane with a bi-directional bicycle pathway on the west side and pull-offs to the hiking trail on the east side of Jenny Lake.

Vehicle access to the scenic road is limited to the early summer to mid-autumn, but you can approach as close as Taggart Lake from the south or Signal Mountain from the north. Winter access requires skis or snowshoes and a lot of stamina. The few who make it are rewarded with unmatched views.

MAP 2

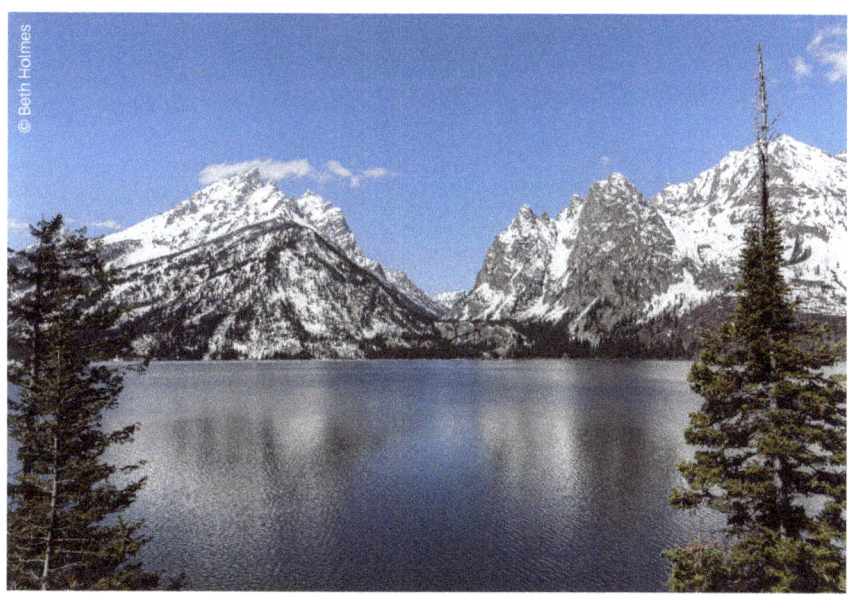

© Beth Holmes

Nikon D810, 24-120mm f/4, f/9, 1/800, ISO 200

HOTSPOT #16

63

DIRECTIONS

Distance from Town Square

Drive north from Jackson on US 191 for 12.3 miles (19.8 km) to Moose Junction and turn left on Teton Park Road. Continue past the entrance station for a total of 10.7 miles (17.2 km) to the North Jenny Lake Junction. Turn left and continue 1.5 miles (2.4 km) to String Lake Road. Continue straight where the road turns to one way for 1.5 miles (2.3 km) to the overlook parking lot.

MAP 2

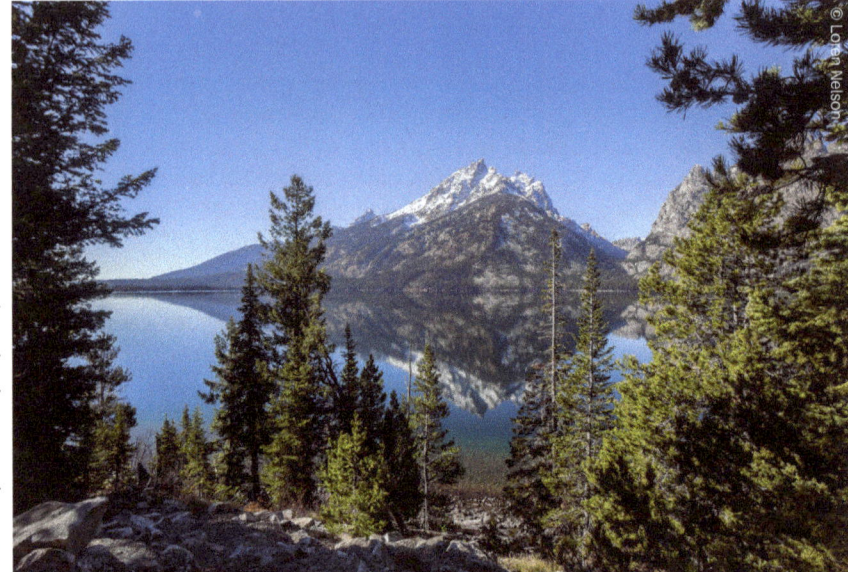

Canon 5D III, 17-40mm f/4, f/14, 1/250, ISO 400

© Loren Nelson

Walking south on the trail from the Jenny Lake overview is a classic reflection point for the Cathedral Group of the highest Teton peaks.

📷 Site Specific Photography Tips

The best time to visit is when the weather is stable and the air is windless. This viewpoint peers directly into Cascade Canyon. The site is high above the lake, making image capture as simple as it gets for any hotspot in this book.

To have the diamond sparkle off the water, photograph on a completely clear day in the afternoon. Show up early, as the sun dips behind the peaks an hour or more before sunset.

If there is atmospheric haze, the canyon and peaks will turn featureless in the afternoon. With hazy air, photographing in the morning is the best option. The haze will be minimized and the mountain features will be clearly visible.

In light smoky conditions, the afternoon light can be dramatic. The peaks sculpt the light, spraying crepuscular rays across the sky above Jenny Lake.

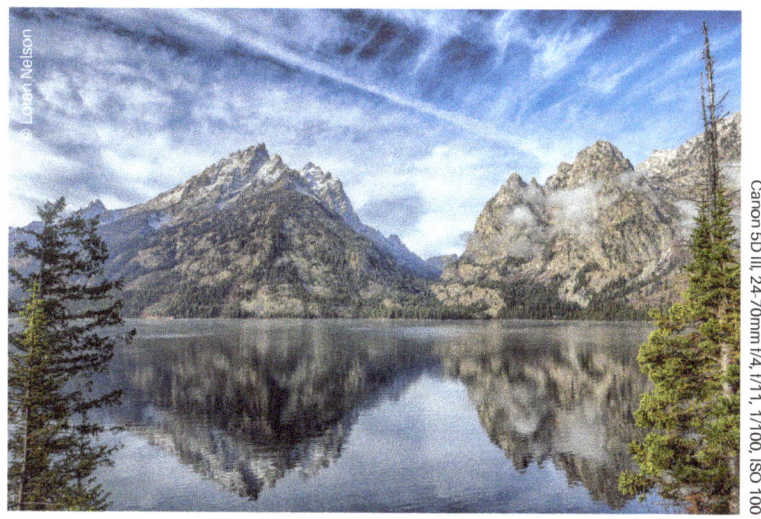

Cloudy skies add drama to the reflections at the Jenny Lake overview with Cascade Canyon and the Tetons rising from their reflections.

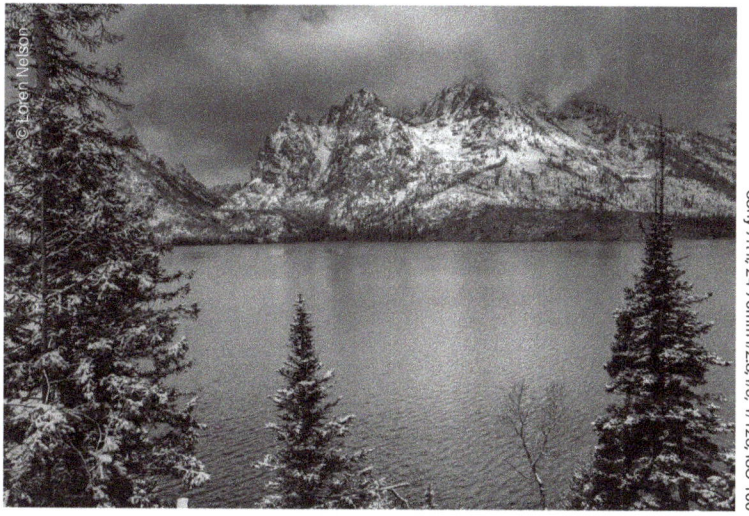

Be sure to explore monochrome images when sky and water conditions don't give perfect reflections. The road to the overlook is often open until November 1 if snow conditions allow.

Site Specifics:

Parking: The parking lot is large but summer popularity almost ensures parking difficulty from mid-day on.

Access: The site is drive-up and is disabled accessible. People who can walk down a set of stairs will be treated to a lower angle view. Both are equally good. The inner park road is not accessible by car from November 1 to April 30. You can still ski or snowshoe into this location. Plan for a several-hour trip to this site in the winter.

HOT SPOT #17

Jenny Lake Trail

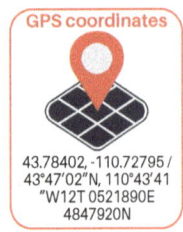

GPS coordinates

43.78402, -110.72795 /
43°47'02"N, 110°43'41"W
12T 0521890E
4847920N

DESCRIPTION:

The Jenny Lake trail leading from the String Lake parking lot is a flat trail that leads along the northwest side of Jenny Lake. There are views all along the path for nature scenery. Waterfalls, creeks, rough paths, overlooks, and steep greenery slopes are all available along this popular pathway.

The best part of this walk is the mild gain in elevation. There are few trails in Grand Teton that are like this. As a result, more energy can be spent on photographing lake views combined with the mountain than elsewhere.

There are multiple starting points for the Jenny Lake Trail, including String Lake, South Jenny Lake, and the Overlook. This path is 7.5 miles (12 km) long and travels all the way around Jenny Lake with nearly endless photographic opportunities.

Jenny Lake is undoubtedly the most popular and crowded area in all of Grand Teton National Park. In the summer months, it is common for all parking to be filled by mid-morning. Visitors park on both sides of the highway, up to a half-mile (0.8 km) away, along the Jenny Lake Loop Road.

The reasons for the popularity are clear: beautiful views, hiking and biking paths, the visitor area, camping, and access to the ferry across Jenny Lake to the popular Hidden Falls and Inspiration Point. Jenny Lake has it all.

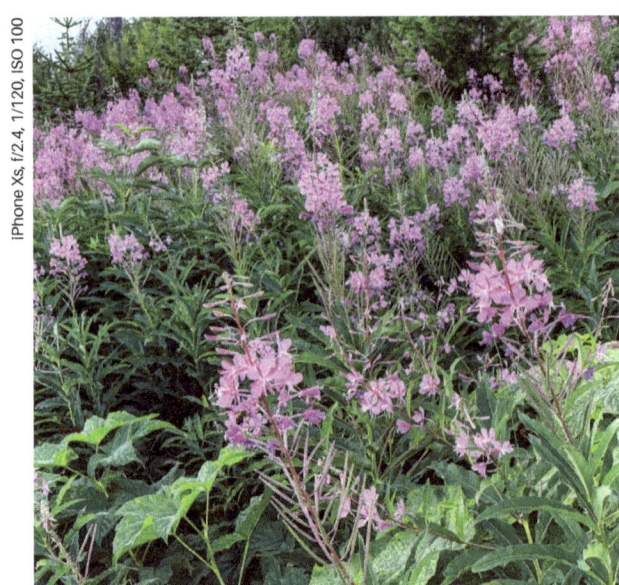

iPhone Xs, f/2.4, 1/120, ISO 100

Fireweed between String Lake and Hidden Falls.

DIRECTIONS

Distance from Town Square

Drive north from Jackson on US 191 for 12.3 miles (19.8 km) to Moose Junction and turn left on Teton Park Road. Continue past the entrance station for a total of 10.7 miles (17.2 km) to the North Jenny Lake Junction. Turn left and continue 1.5 miles (2.4 km), then turn right and park in the first (south) String Lake parking lot.

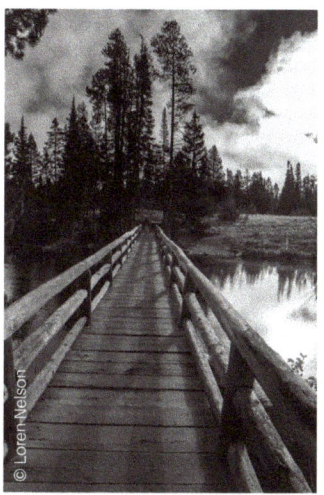

The bridge crossing the String Lake outflow is the start of the Jenny Lake trail.

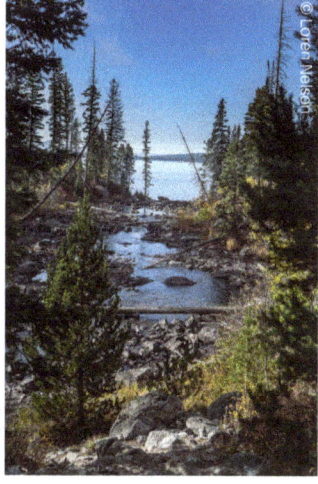

The outflow from String and Leigh Lakes into Jenny Lake is a great spot for varied terrain, flowing water, wildlife, and hiking.

HIKING DIRECTIONS

Begin the hike at the String Lake Trailhead at the first parking lot at String Lake. Cross the large wooden bridge over the String Lake outlet. Hike 0.3 mile (0.5 km) to the first trail junction and follow the sign toward Hidden Falls and Jenny Lake Outlet.

Hike along the nearly level trail along the northwest section of Jenny Lake across a series of short wooden bridges and one large bridge crossing a large creek for a total of 1.2 miles (1.9 km). There is a signed trail junction for Cascade Canyon and Lake Solitude.

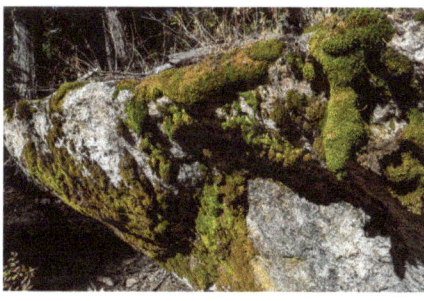

The trail around Jenny Lake not only is a great way to see the lake at the base of the Grand Teton but also is a route to the spectacular Cascade and Paintbrush Canyons. This is a shot of rock covered with lichens and moss that can enhance wider scenic shots.

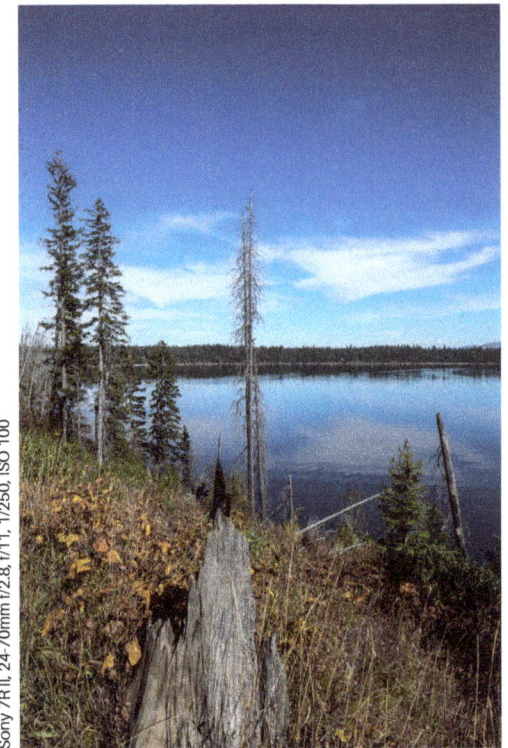

Sony 7R II, 24-70mm f/2.8, f/11, 1/250, ISO 100

The quiet side of Jenny Lake.

Expect and be prepared to see a variety of wildlife along the trail to Cascade Canyon and the back (west) side of Jenny Lake. Here is a bull moose that lead hikers up the trail for nearly a mile one day. Bears are often seen more than half of the days – be prepared.

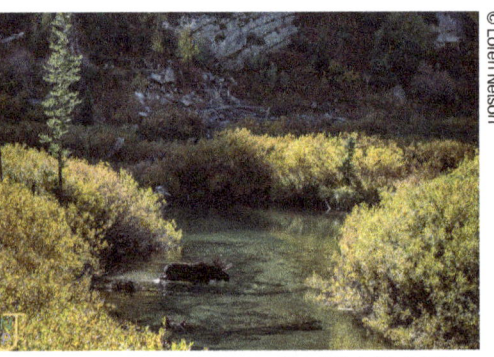

Sony 7R II, 24-70mm f/2.8, f/3.5, 1/400, ISO 100

📷 Site Specific Photography Tips

Wide-angle, normal, and macro lenses are the best choice along this trail. The views up and down the trail are unmatched in the park, as there are unobstructed views of the lake on nearly the entire hiking trail.

For anyone bringing a telephoto, be aware Jenny Lake is large. The opposite shore from the Jenny Lake Overlook is 1 mile (1.6 km) to the southeast. Elk and deer can be found along this trail but often they are so close, a normal to moderate telephoto lens will be more than adequate.

HOTSPOT #17

Site Specifics:

Parking: Parking will be challenging during the summer months. The site is incredibly popular. It can often fill up by early morning. Parking along the roadway has been actively discouraged by the park, so be prepared to come early and stay for an extended amount of time.

Access: The hiking trail from String Lake toward Jenny Lake is easy and relatively flat. It only gains 66 feet (20 meters) from the parking lot to the shuttle boat dock.

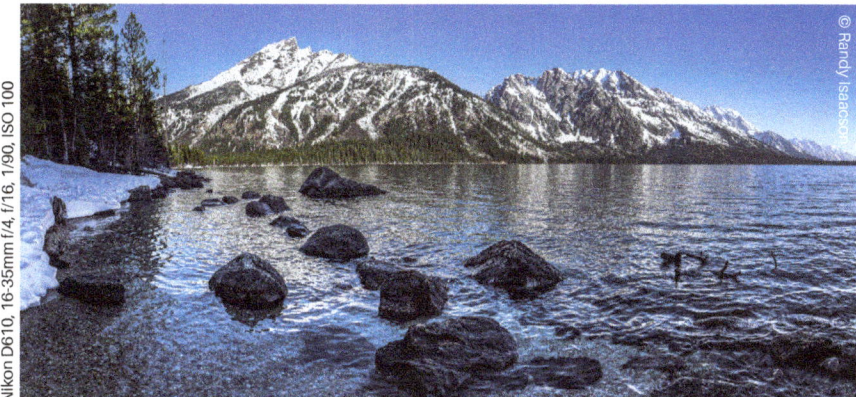

Jenny Lake boat launch.

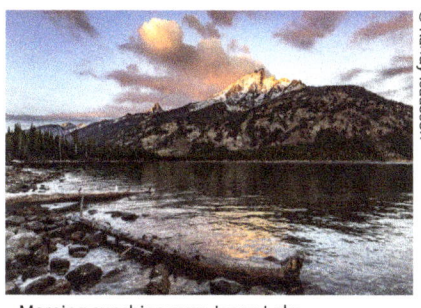

Morning sunshine over Jenny Lake.

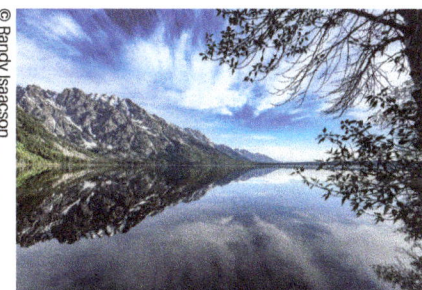

View north from Jenny Lake boat launch.

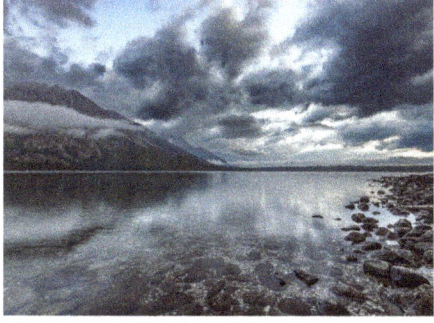

Storm approaching Jenny Lake.

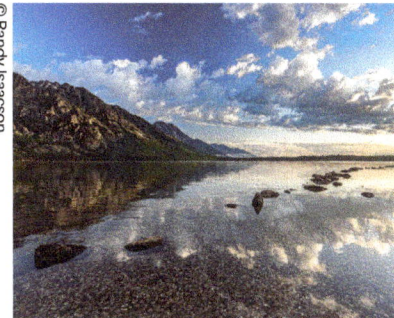

Sunrise along Jenny Lake.

HOTSPOT #18

Lucas-Fabian Homestead

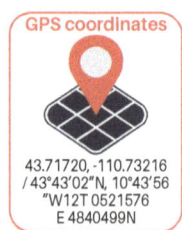

GPS coordinates
43.71720, -110.73216
/ 43°43'02"N, 10°43'56"W
12T 0521576 E 4840499N

MAP 2

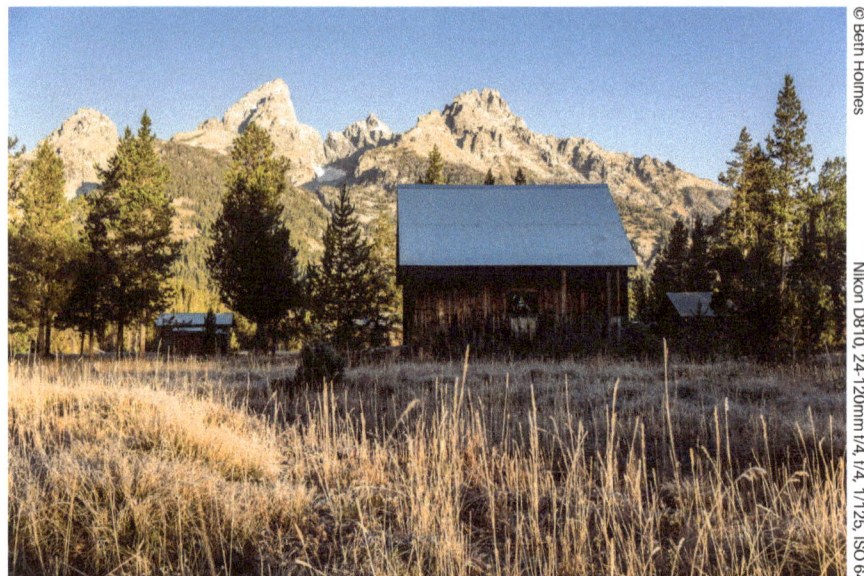

Lucas-Fabian homestead in late summer.

DESCRIPTION:

The Geraldine Lucas and later Harold Fabian homestead contains eleven historic buildings donated to GTNP in the mid-1900s. They are a hidden treasure along Cottonwood Creek. This collection of buildings is in an arrested state of decay. Although the buildings are old, the Park Service maintains the roofs to prevent the buildings from disintegrating.

The views from the base of the Tetons are spectacular from any of the buildings. The best view is from the last cabin with the wrap-around porch. Sandhill cranes can be regularly seen and heard in the open area. All of the cabins are locked so it's not possible to access the interiors.

In the winter, the homestead is accessible by skis or snowshoes from the Taggart Lake parking area. There are only a few feet (meters) of elevation gain from the parking area to the cabins. This makes the trek mild even in cold winter conditions.

DIRECTIONS

Distance from Town Square

Drive north from Jackson on US 191 for 12.3 miles (19.8 km) to Moose Junction and turn left on Teton Park Road. Continue past the entrance station for a total of 5.3 miles (8.6 km) to a small, unmarked dirt lot on the west side of the road. A wooden gate and sign reading "Service Road Only" marks the lot. It is easy to miss, as the turnoff is on a slope not easily visible from the road when driving north.

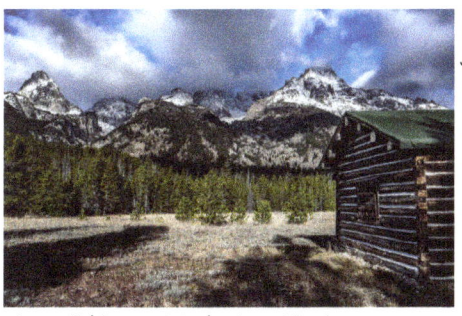

Lucas-Fabian as winter begins setting in.

Arrowleaf Balsamroot at Lucas-Fabian cabins.

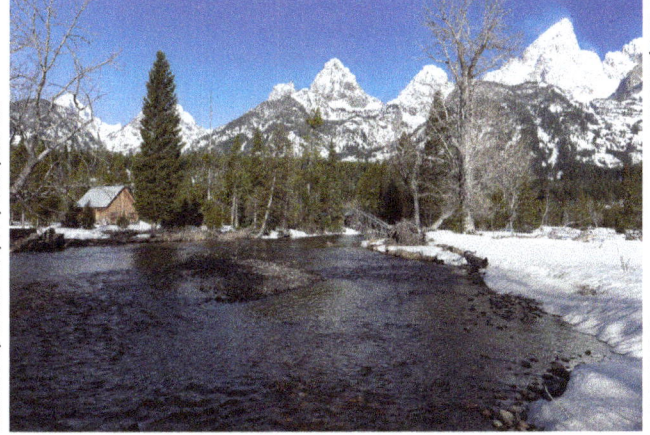

Cottonwood Creek winding through the Lucas-Fabian cabin area.

📷 Site Specific Photography Tips

Using the buildings for compositions lends itself to using wide-angle and normal lenses. The open field to the south allows telephoto images of the site. The two main cabins have porches that provide options for taking framed images of the mountains and surrounding environment.

The trail that leads to the south connects with a junction that splits off to Burned Wagon Gulch. Along with this trail is a large rock with a plaque commemorating Geraldine Lucas's pioneering spirit. She was the second woman in modern history to reach the summit of Grand Teton. This path is featured on the cover of Aaron Linsdau's book, *Jackson Hole Hiking Guide, 1st ed.*

HOTSPOT #18

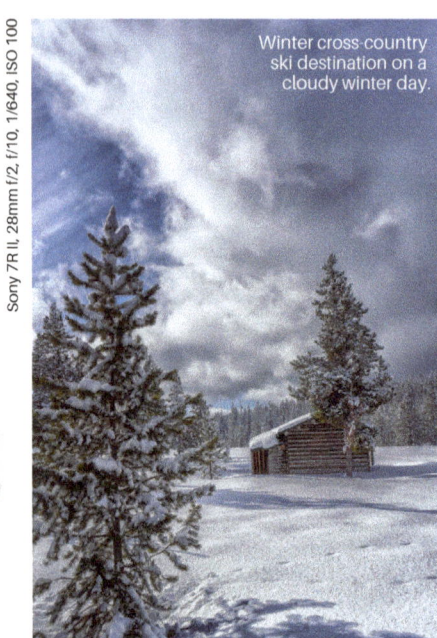

Winter cross-country ski destination on a cloudy winter day.

© Loren Nelson

Sony 7R II, 28mm f/2, f/10, 1/640, ISO 100

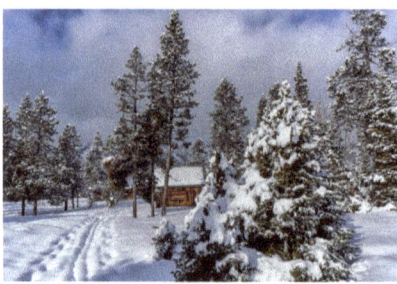

Winter cabin with a ski trail.

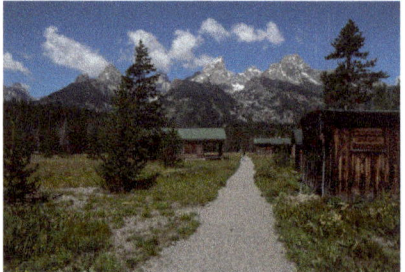

Summer approach to the cabins.

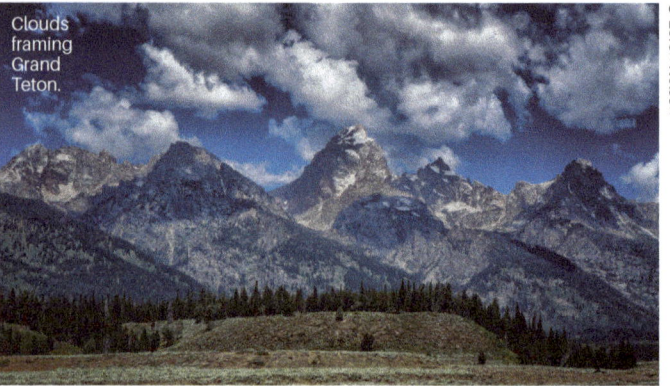

Clouds framing Grand Teton.

© Loren Nelson

Sony 7R II, 24-70mm f/2.8, f/8, 1/500, ISO 100

Site Specifics:

Access: Located a quarter-mile off the highway between the Glacier View turnout and Lupine Meadows Road, the turn-off is unmarked and difficult to see while driving northbound. There is a wooden gate blocking the dirt road leading from the parking lot toward Cottonwood Creek. This is the path to walk along to reach the cabins.

A large wooden bridge spans Cottonwood Creek, making access easy.

Parking: The small dirt parking lot has room for a few vehicles. Note that the dirt slope leading to the parking lot is steep. Low-riding vehicles may scrape their undercarriage when returning to the road.

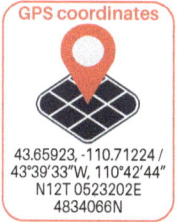

GPS coordinates
43.65923, -110.71224 /
43°39'33"W, 110°42'44"
N12T 0523202E
4834066N

HOT SPOT #19

Menors Ferry

DESCRIPTION:

From the late 1800s to the late 1920s, the cable ferry of William Menor was used to shuttle people and commerce across the Snake River at Moose. The original ferry is gone but a replica was built near the general store building. The ferry was operational only a few years before the writing of this book.

The location provides perfect views of the river and is near the drop-off point for many of the scenic raft trips. It is a hotspot for wildlife, as they access the river for water and crossings. Multiple historic information signs are sprinkled through the area. They are helpful to provide context and photographic inspiration.

MAP 2

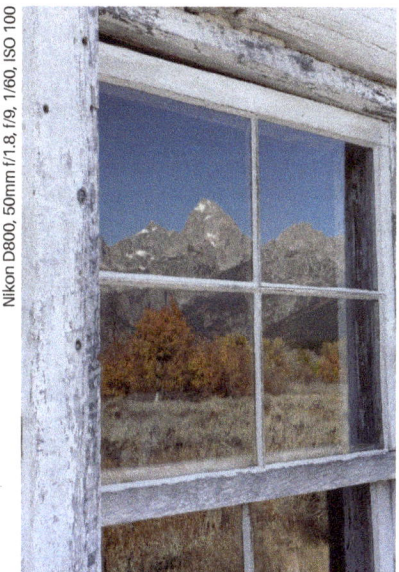

Nikon D800, 50mm f/1.8, f/9, 1/60, ISO 100

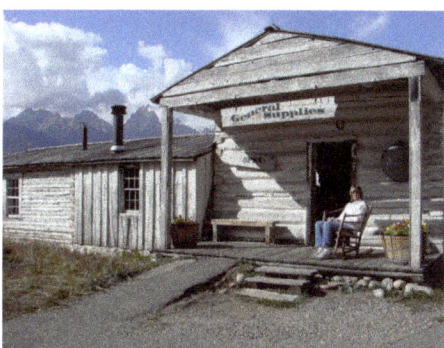

© Loren Nelson

The Menor historical area store is open in the summer and a good spot to talk with the volunteer staff who know the park's history well.

DIRECTIONS

Distance from Town Square

Drive north from Jackson on US 191 for 12.3 miles (19.8 km) to Moose Junction and turn left on Teton Park Road. Continue for 1.2 miles (2 km), turn right on Menors Ferry Rd, and drive 0.4 mile (0.6 km) to the Chapel of the Transfiguration parking lot.

Follow the trail signs across the parking lot from the Chapel of Transfiguration toward Menors Ferry. The hike to the ferry and general store is 0.2 mile (0.3 km) on a nearly flat trail.

HOTSPOT #19

📷 Site Specific Photography Tips

The ferry is visible near the general store and historic vehicle barn. Multiple angles of the white-washed buildings with the Cathedral Group in the background. Taking medium-telephoto images to compress the buildings on the mountains is challenging but possible.

One of the most unique image opportunities is on the backside of the general store. The old frame window captures a reflection of Grand Teton when shot with a normal to slight telephoto lens. A close-up wide-angle image is a possibility as well.

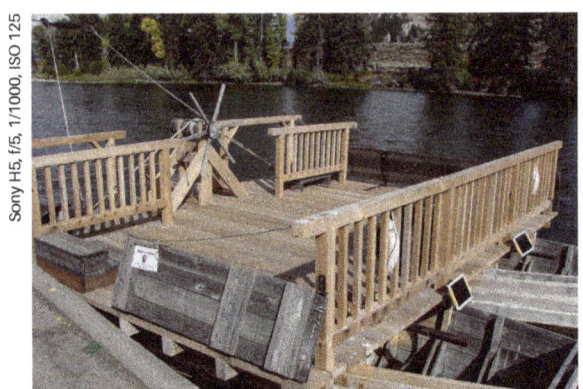

The replica of the original ferry is on display.

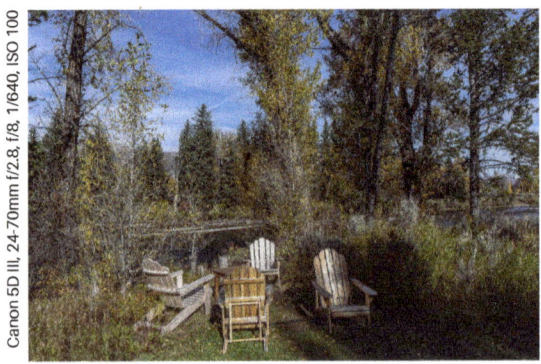

View of the ferry from Dornan's across the river and a perfect autumn day.

Site Specifics:

Parking: Parking at Menors Ferry is plentiful and accommodates large vehicles. Only when there is an event or multiple buses show up at once does the parking lot fill up.

Access: Start at the western edge of the parking lot at the park information kiosks. Follow the broad, flat trail east toward the river. In 400 feet (126 m), the ferry will come into view. The general store is situated 200 feet (68 m) to the northeast of the ferry.

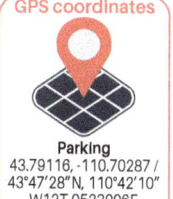

GPS coordinates

Parking
43.79116, -110.70287 /
43°47'28"N, 110°42'10"
W12T 0523906E
4848721N

Patriarch Tree
43.78329, -110.69800 /
43°47'00"N, 110°41'53"
W12T 0524300E
4847848N

HOTSPOT #20

Patriarch Tree

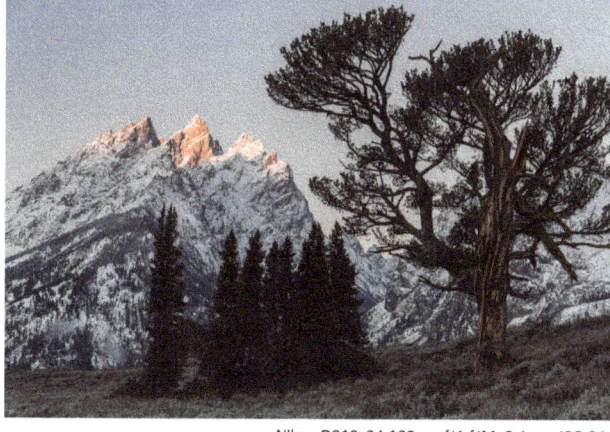

The Patriarch Tree at first light.

Nikon D810, 24-120mm f/4, f/11, 0.4 sec, ISO 64

DESCRIPTION:

Known as the Patriarch Tree, this old gnarled limber pine lies in the middle of a sagebrush field. Originally along the inner park road, the pine now requires an off-trail walk to visit it. The road was realigned in 1990, relegating this majestic tree to relative obscurity.

Limber pines are excellent photographic subjects due to their rough-looking bark. The tree looks like it has been around a thousand years. This look gives context to the landscape, adding character to the otherwise sagebrush-strewn landscape.

It is well worth the walk from late spring to late fall. During winter, visiting this famous photography spot requires a long ski trip.

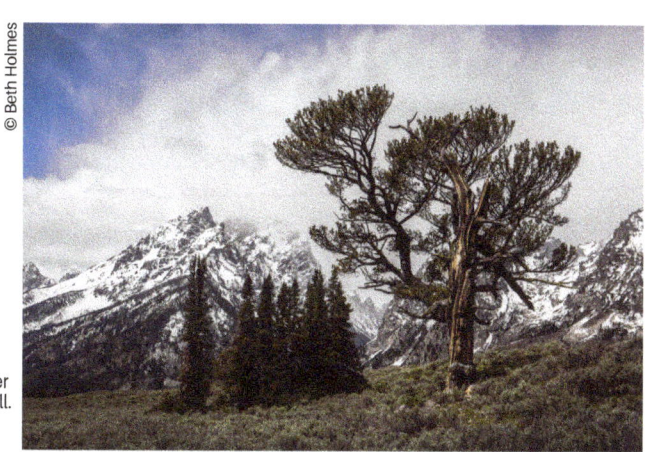

© Beth Holmes

The Patriarch Tree after a snow squall.

Nikon D810, 24-120mm f/4, f/11, 1/160, ISO 64

HOTSPOT #20

DIRECTIONS

Distance from Town Square

Drive north from Jackson on US 191 for 12.3 miles (19.8 km) to Moose Junction and turn left on Teton Park Road. Continue past the entrance station for a total of 10.7 miles (17.2 km) to the North Jenny Lake Junction. Turn left and park in the turnout on North Jenny Lake Road.

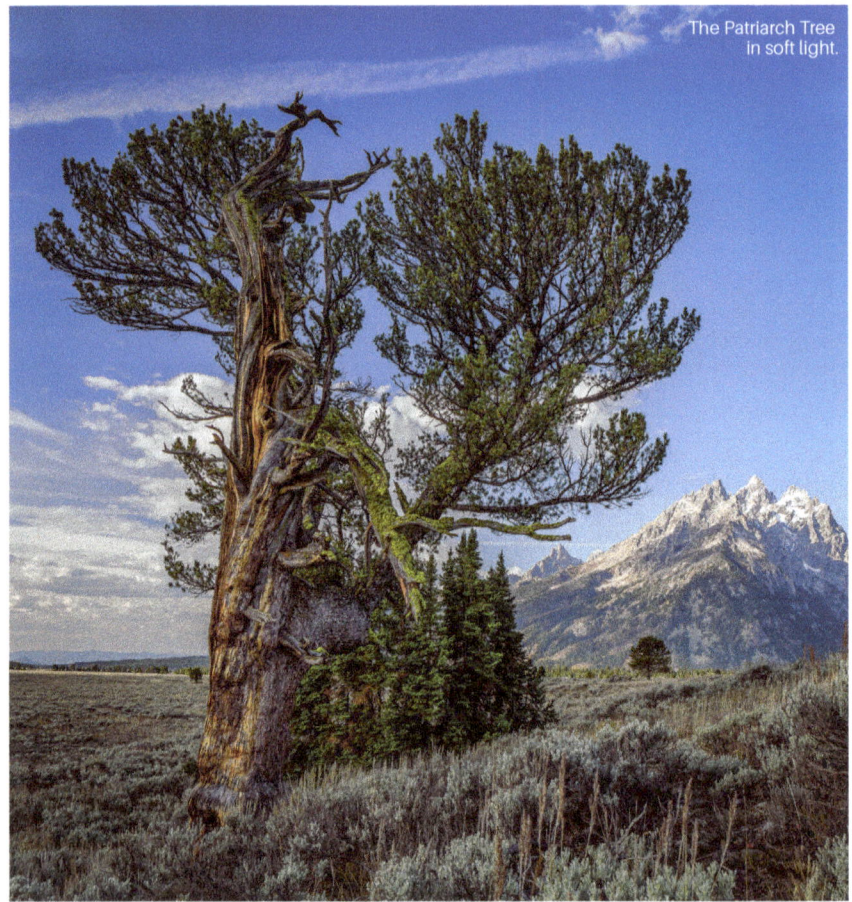

The Patriarch Tree in soft light.

© Loren Nelson

Sony H5, f/5, 1/1000, ISO 125

MAP 2

📷 Site Specific Photography Tips

The classic composition is to use a wide lens at this site. Place the Patriarch Tree in the right of the frame with the Cathedral Group over the small cluster of younger conifers. As the young conifers grow, this image will become more difficult to create. Eventually, they will block the summit views, changing this image forever.

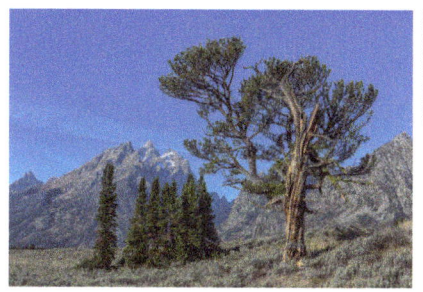
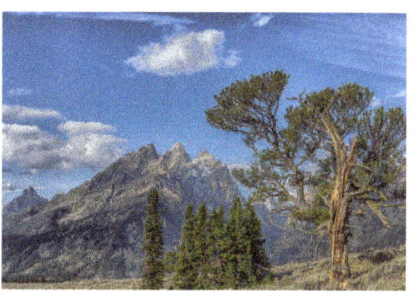
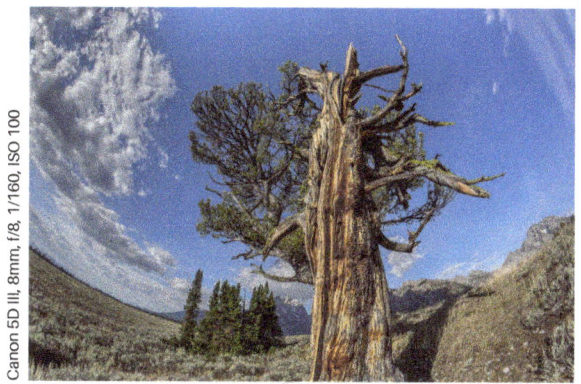
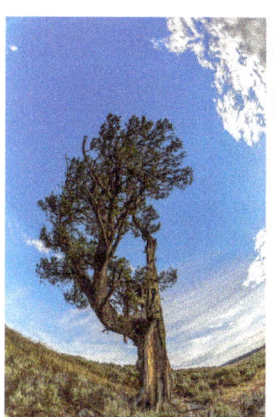
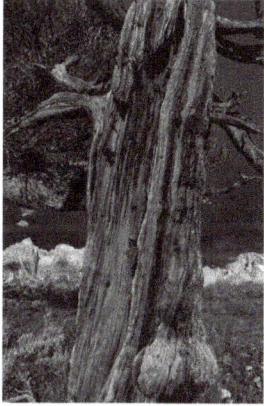
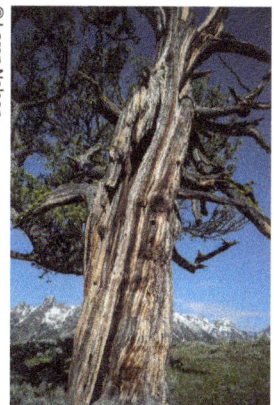

Site Specifics:

Parking: The safest parking area is on Jenny Lake Road at the turnout 400 feet (126 m) northwest of the North Jenny Lake Junction. Park off the main road.

Access: The Patriarch Tree is reached by a 0.5 mile (0.8 km) bushwhack through a sagebrush meadow on a bearing of 156° southeast. From North Jenny Lake Junction, walk in a straight line toward the Gros Ventre slide. The tree is not visible until after descending the first two steps of the moraine.

HOTSPOT #21
Phelps Lake

DESCRIPTION:

GPS coordinates

43.63466, -110.79080 /
43°38'05"N, 110°47'27"
W12T 0516875E
4831318N

Phelps Lake and the surrounding trail network is a lesser-visited location in Grand Teton. This spectacular lake is only accessible by an easy hike. The effort and sweat are well worth it. The waterfalls, meadows, and beaches all make this walk worthwhile.

Hiking the full distance around Phelps Lake will take some time. The trail is generally flat with only one elevated section in the southwest corner of the lake. Views up Death Canyon are continuous around the lake. The views change slowly but the light in the canyon changes rapidly. Rocks and beaches circle the lake, providing ample photographic opportunities.

The lake is accessed from Moose-Wilson Road. This dusty, narrow road has significant traffic during the summer months. Bear activity along the north section of the road can cause closures. The road opens in May and closes in November or earlier depending upon snow conditions. It is open for cross-country skiing or snowshoeing in the winter. Wildlife is plentiful in the area with waterfowl. Deer, elk, moose, and both black and grizzly bears are common.

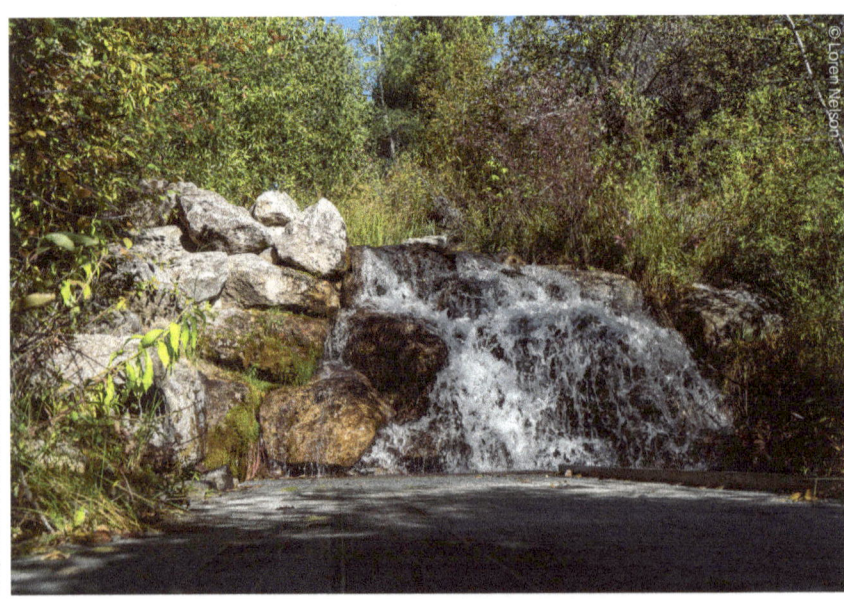

Lake Creek Falls is located on Moose-Wilson Road and limited parking is available near the bridge. A high bank on both sides of the creek makes the approach steep. The approach from LSR is nearly flat.

DIRECTIONS

Distance from Town Square

Drive north from Jackson on US 191 for 12.3 miles (19.8 km) to Moose Junction and turn left on Teton Park Road. Continue for 0.7 mile (1.1 km) and turn left on Moose-Wilson Road. Drive south for 3.7 miles (5.9 km) and turn left at the Laurance S. Rockefeller Center turnoff. Drive south 0.3 mile (0.5 km) to the parking area.

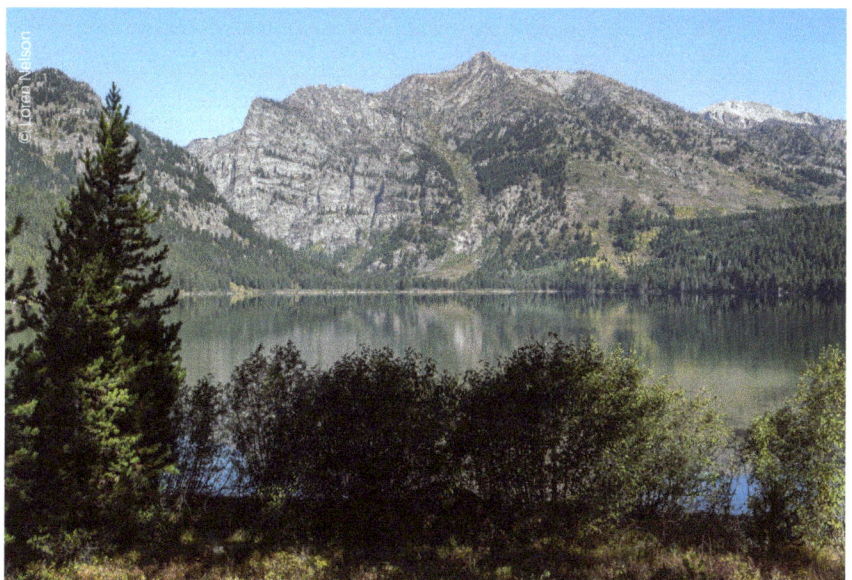

Phelps Lake can be reached using the network of trails near the Rockefeller Preserve. Early morning and late afternoon are great times to visit but watch for bear activity.

HIKING DIRECTIONS

Begin the hike at the Laurance S. Rockefeller building. Walk west from the parking lot toward the LSR Center building. At the west end of the building, continue on the trail for 0.1 mile (0.2 km) to the junction near the waterfall. Continue along the Woodland Trail, staying to the right (E) of Lake Creek.

At 0.6 mile (1 km) farther, the trail intersects the Woodland and Aspen Ridge Cutoff Trail as well as the Boulder Ridge Trail junction. Continue on the Woodland Trail north.

Hike for 0.7 mile (1.1 km) to Phelps Lake, then turn right (NE) and begin circling clockwise around the lake.

HOTSPOT #21

Site Specific Photography Tips

For the wide variety of photo opportunities, the suggested lens is a zoom covering wide-angle to moderate telephoto focal lengths. A 24-70mm or 18-105mm will serve well at this site. Along the lakeshore, there are multiple beaches. Most beaches are easy to find, though a few are only accessible with some off-trail travel.

If you feel brave, bring swimming attire. There is a popular rock to jump off into Phelps Lake midway along the northern shore. During summer, there is a regular crowd at this spot, as social media has made it more widely known.

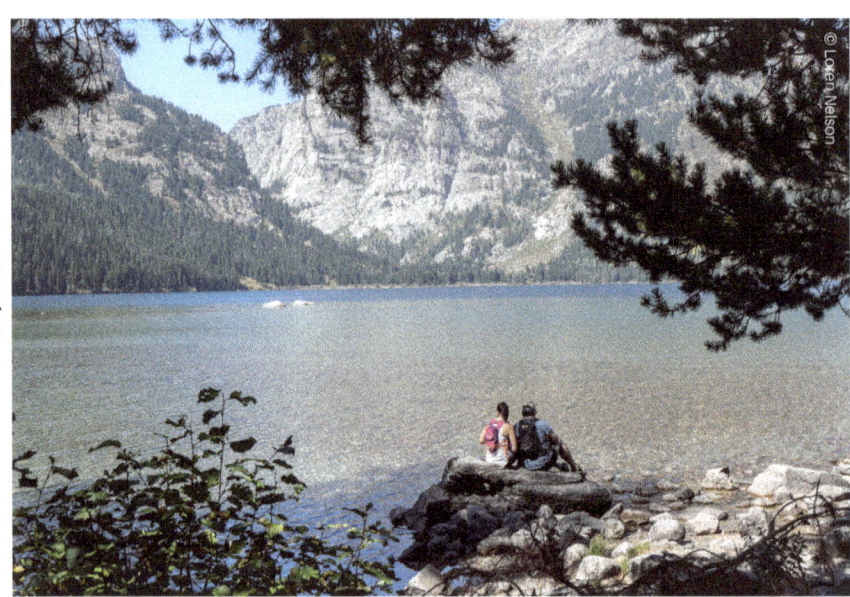

Phelps Lake is a popular place to chill out in the summer and the trails can be quite crowded.

Site Specifics:

Parking: Parking can be a substantial challenge at the Laurance Rockefeller Preserve on Moose-Wilson Road. There are a limited number of parking spaces compared to the number of vehicles that regularly visit the area. There is often a line of cars waiting to park in the middle of the summer.

Access: The hikes to Phelps Lake from the main parking lot are flat and easy. Hiking to the lake from the Death Canyon trailhead requires walking up a hill before descending again to the lake.

GPS coordinates
43.71152, -110.67030 /
43°42'41"N, 110°40'13"
W12T 0526561E
4839885N

HOT*SPOT* #22
Schwabacher Landing

DESCRIPTION:

Schwabacher Landing is one of the premier photography sites in Jackson Hole. The location almost appears especially created for photographers to take the iconic photographs of the Cathedral Group in Grand Teton National Park.

As the river meandered over the years, Schwabacher Landing became a small branch off the main river channel. It used to be accessible to bigger boats but over time, the water has subsided. Now, there is sometimes enough water for kayaks and canoes to ply these popular waters.

Beavers and other larger mammals are common here. Although the high amount of foot traffic can disturb animals, others seem habituated to humans. Always be mindful that all animals are wild and potentially dangerous. Give them the appropriate space required by the park.

MAP 2

Nikon D800, 24mm f/2.8, f/4, 15 sec, ISO 1600

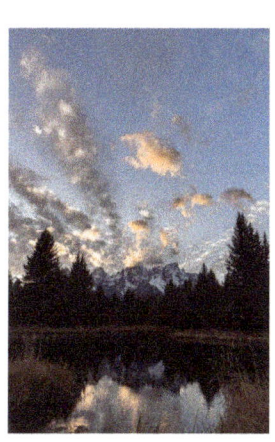

© Beth Holmes

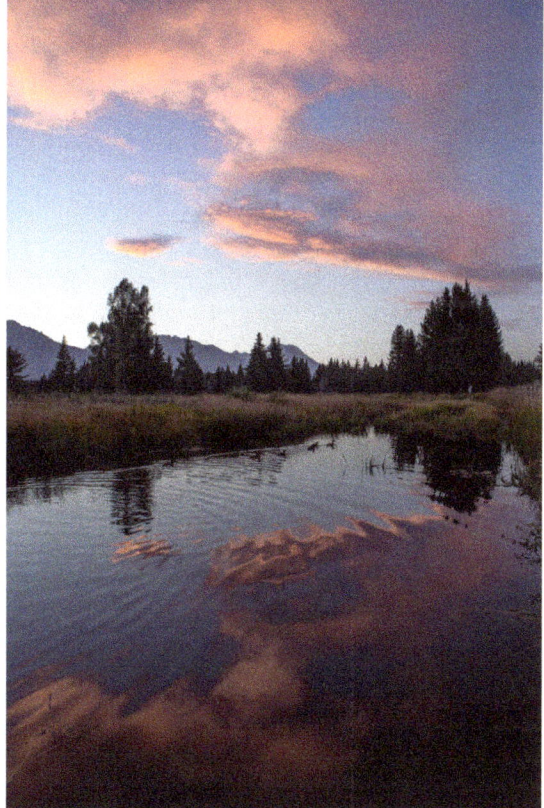

Nikon D800, 20mm f/2.8, f/8, 1/15, ISO 200

HOTSPOT #22

📷 Site Specific Photography Tips

Check the weather before venturing out to Schwabacher Landing. The most iconic images at the landing are best made when there is no wind. If the forecast calls for strong winds, the water's mirror effect will be wiped out. If a storm is anticipated the next day or a storm has departed the area the day before, expect windy conditions. This spot is a great spot regardless of the weather but for the premium image, perfectly still water is the most desirable.

An 18-70mm lens is the most effective for this location. Crouching at the water's edge with a wider lens will make the range look impressive in a still reflection. Standing above the water on the trail is a more classic view. Due to the positioning of the creek and trail, longer lenses usually are not as effective for image compression at this location.

Schwabacher is one of the most popular sunrise photography locations in the park. Expect a large crowd on a summer morning. It is best to arrive well before sunrise (at least an hour) to establish a photography spot. If possible, scout a location the day before to be prepared for the next morning. Have a backup location prepared. Rushing about trying to compose an image while other photographers are doing the same is a sure recipe for frustration and suboptimal images.

Consider that Schwabacher is also a good sunset location. Not nearly as many people will be here compared to the morning. Plan to show up at least two hours before sunset, as the sun disappears behind the mountains well before the official sunset time. If it happens, the sky will not shift in color until half an hour before to half an hour after the official sunset time. Do not expect the sun visible for a classic sunset shot. The best chance for a dramatic image is during unsettled weather for sunsets. Clear blue skies result in bland color. With storms or clouds, the water may not be smooth but the sky will be more interesting.

Beavers are common at this location. They can be seen swimming around in the day. At night, they wander onshore. They ripple the water but can make a unique image. The Schwabacher beaver pond is described in more detail in Hotspot #11 in this book.

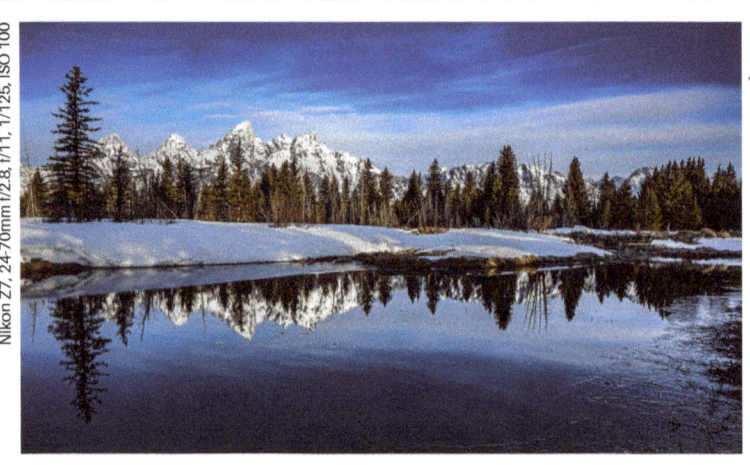

Nikon Z7, 24-70mm f/2.8, f/11, 1/125, ISO 100 © Randy Isaacson

HOTSPOT #22

DIRECTIONS

Distance from Town Square

Drive north from Jackson on US 191 for 16.4 miles (26.3 km) and turn left at the Schwabacher Landing sign. Continue for 1 mile (1.6 km) to the large dirt lot.

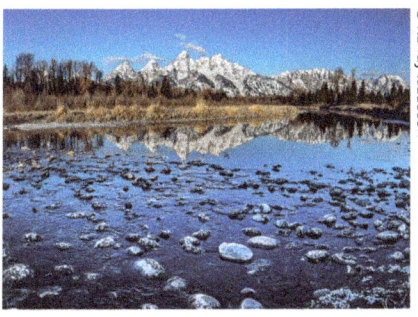
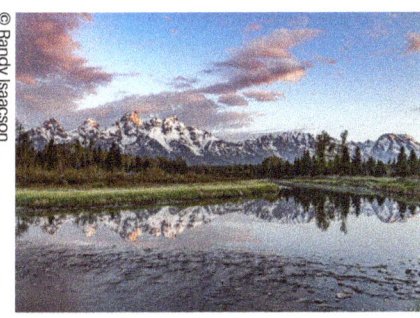

Schwabacher Landing offers photographers a large variety of options depending on seasonal and daily weather conditions.

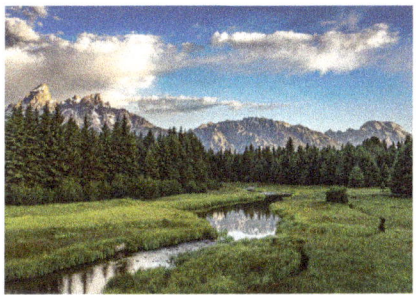
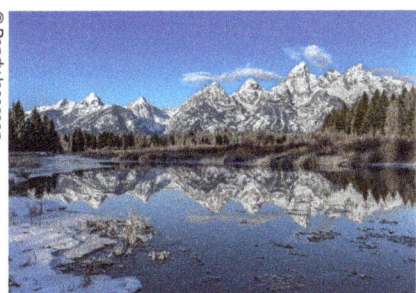

The three areas of Schwabacher Landing vary greatly in visitation and parking availability. The south parking lot is often open while the north lot is packed.

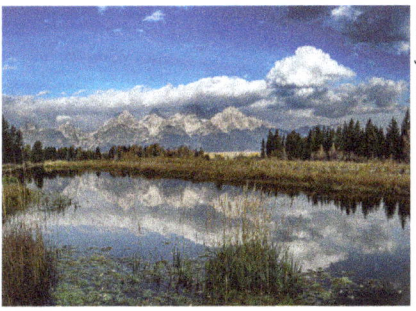
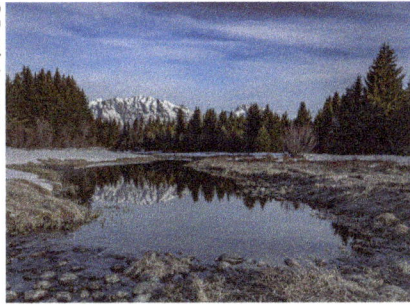

Early snowfall or heavy winter snows can make for excellent options for compositions. Waterways in the area rise and fall depending on the snowpack.

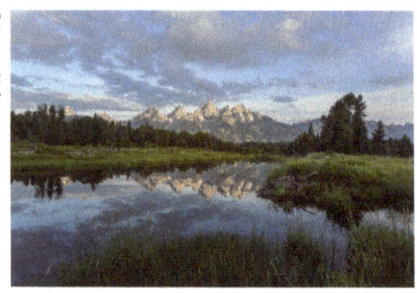

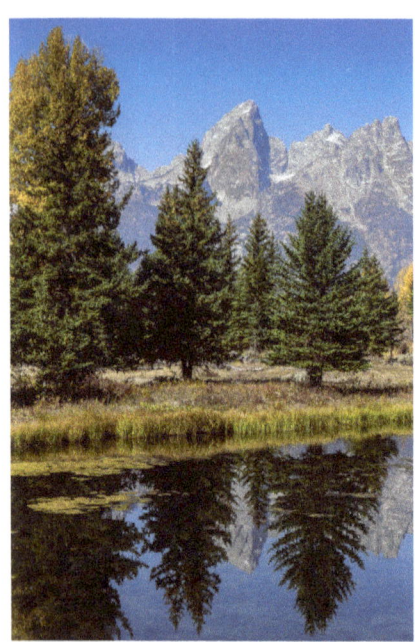

Afternoon clouds will add variety to the views. However, the deep shadows of midday light can create challenges in managing contrast. Mildly cloudy days are some of the best options for photography. Clouds before or after storms are often dramatic, though windy conditions before or after storms can eliminate the mirror reflection of flat water.

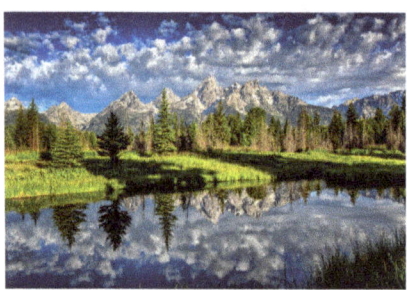
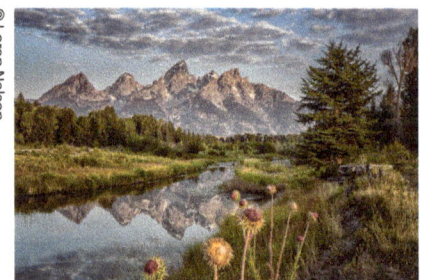

Site Specifics:

Parking: During the summer, the north parking lot regularly fills to capacity during the day. For sunrise, be prepared to park at one of the roadside turnouts. Show up well before sunrise to secure a spot. Plan to leave Jackson at least 30 minutes prior to your desired time.

If the main parking area is full, park farther south in the obvious turnouts. There is also a smaller parking lot 0.6 mile (0.9 km) south of the main lot on a spur road.

Access: The road to Schwabacher Landing is normally closed from late fall to early spring. It's possible to hike down to the landing until the seasonal closure, usually around December 1. Check with the Park Service for current access dates at 307-739-3399 or 307-739-3300.

During the summer, the steel gate is open and it is possible to drive to the landing.

HOTSPOT #23

String Lake

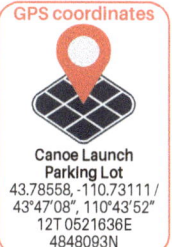

GPS coordinates

Canoe Launch
Parking Lot
43.78558, -110.73111 /
43°47'08", 110°43'52"
12T 0521636E
4848093N

MAP 2

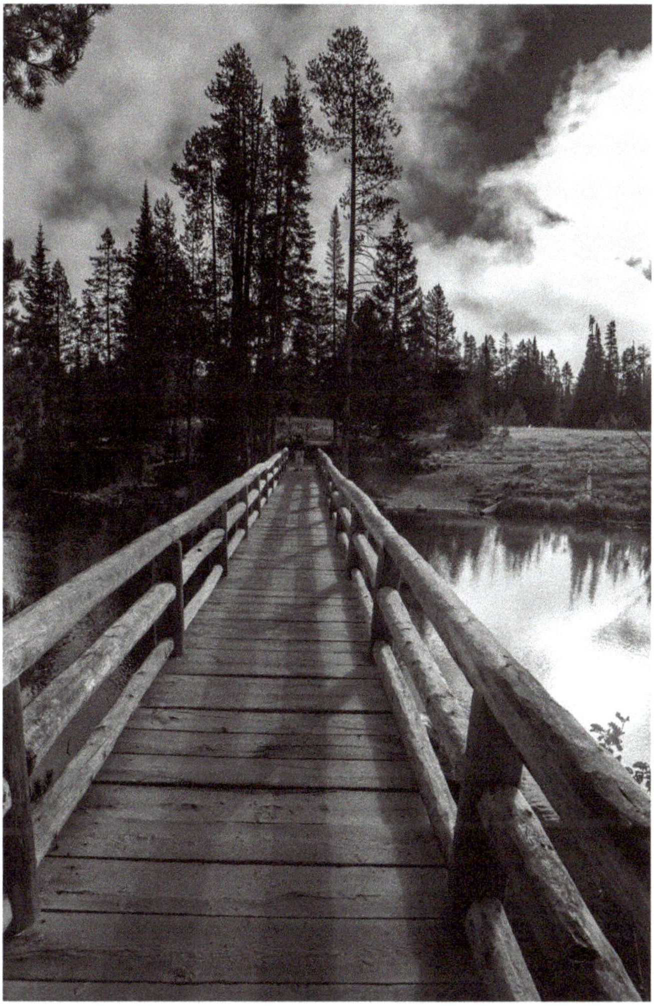

© Loren Nelson

Sony 7R II, 24-70mm f/2.8, f/10, 1/125, ISO 100

Monochrome of foot bridge over String Lake outflow into Jenny Lake.

DIRECTIONS   Distance from Town Square

Drive north from Jackson on US 191 for 12.3 miles (19.8 km) to Moose Junction and turn left on Teton Park Road. Continue past the entrance station for a total of 10.7 miles (17.2 km) to the North Jenny Lake Junction. Turn left and continue 1.5 miles (2.4 km), then turn right and park in the first String Lake parking lot.

DESCRIPTION:

String and Leigh Lakes are north of Jenny Lake on North Jenny Lake Road. These are favorite spots for summer paddleboarders and kayakers, filling the parking lots early. String Lake is drive-up accessible until the park road closes for winter.

Arrive early for calm water to achieve the mirror reflection of Teewinot on String Lake. From here, Teewinot is in front of Grand Teton. First-time visitors confuse the two due to the perspective. During the first few weeks of spring access, ice rings the lake. The canoe launch on String Lake is the best starting point for photography with mountains in the background.

The trail starting from the southern String Lake parking lot leads to Jenny Lake. This access point allows hikers to circumnavigate Jenny Lake. It is also a good starting point to reach the west side of Jenny Lake, Hidden Falls, Observation Point, and the spectacular Cascade and Paintbrush Canyons.

MAP 2

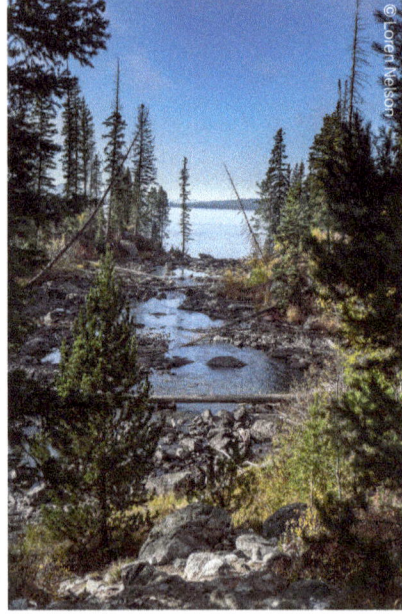

Sony 7R II, 24-70mm f/2.8, f/4.5, 1/320, ISO 100

The outlet from String Lake into Jenny Lake has a photogenic bridge and cascades.

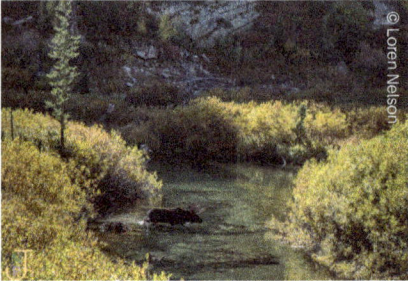

Bull moose in the outlet from String Lake in the autumn.

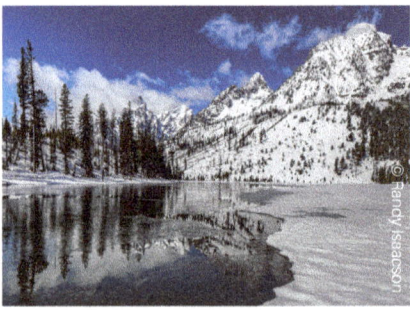

String Lake in late spring.

📷 Site Specific Photography Tips

When accessible by car, the location is highly busy during the mid-summer months. During the winter, the only way to access String Lake is by ski or snowshoe.

HOTSPOT #23

Site Specifics:

Parking: The three parking lots at String Lake are large. However, the traffic can be intense during the peak summer season. Park personnel sometimes mark the areas as "Parking Full." Arrive early in the day or late in the afternoon for the best chance at a parking space.

Access: The walk to String Lake is easy. A trail circles all the way around the lake. The trail on the east side of the lake is nearly flat. The west side trail gains some elevation but is not too intense.

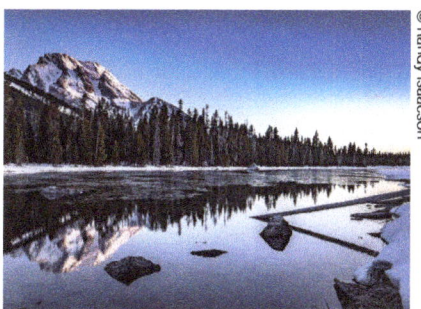

String Lake sunrise.

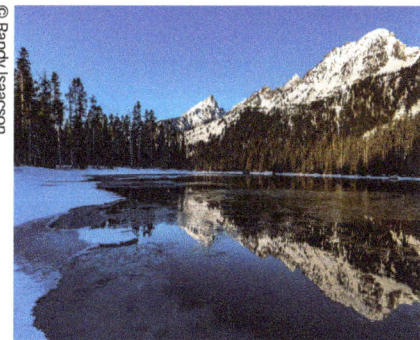

String Lake to Grand Teton.

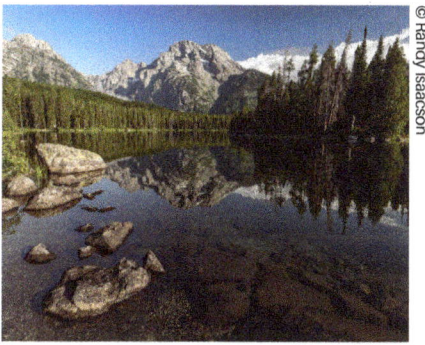

Hiking around String Lake provides plenty of photographic opportunities.

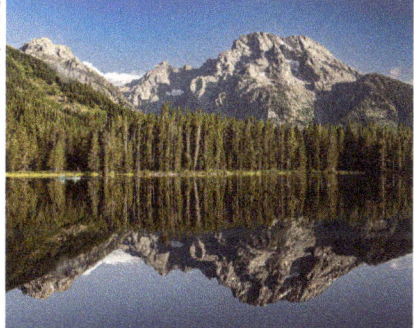

String Lake in mid-summer.

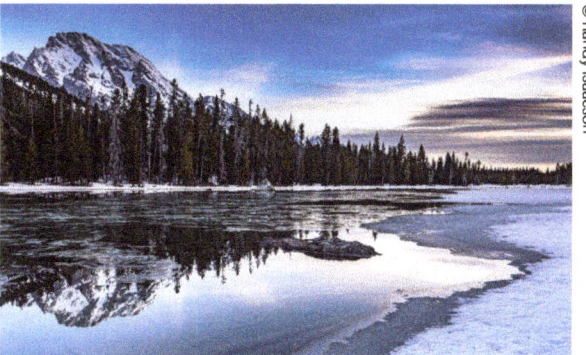

Ice floes can stay on String Lake well into early May.

HOTSPOT #23

HOTSPOT #24

Taggart Lake

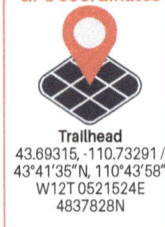

GPS coordinates

Trailhead
43.69315, -110.73291 /
43°41'35"N, 110°43'58"
W12T 0521524E
4837828N

Lake
43.70085, -110.75161 /
43°42'03"N, 110°45'06"
W12T 0520014E
4838677N

MAP 2

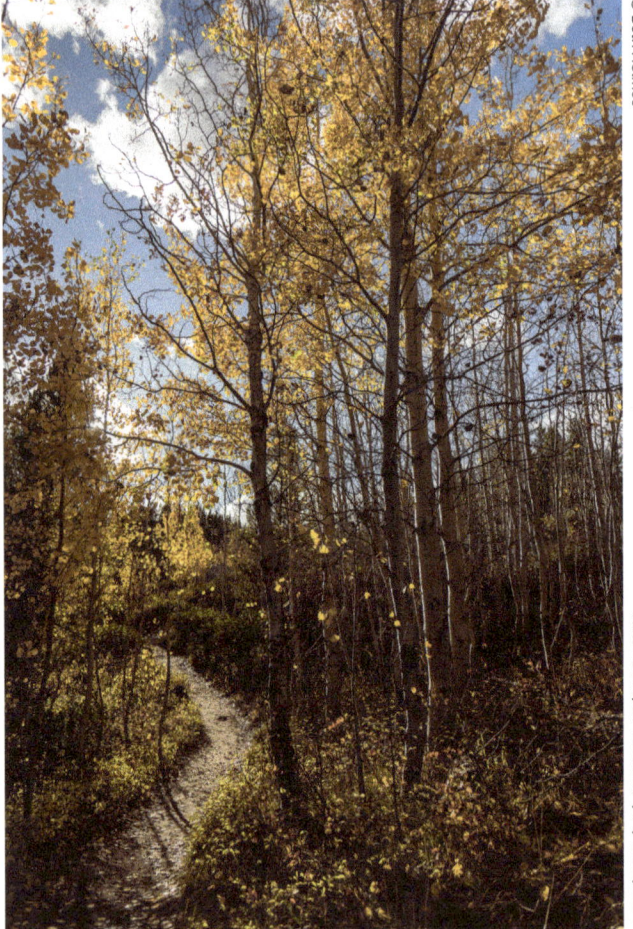

© Beth Holmes

Nikon D810, 24-120mm f/4, 1/320, ISO 64

DESCRIPTION:

There are many hiking trails up into the Teton Mountain Range. Many of these trails are very steep and require many miles to arrive at your location. Taggart Lake (and Bradley Lake) are only 1.6 miles (2.6 kilometers) from the trailhead parking lot. The trail only gains 511 feet (156 m) of elevation. All along the trail to the lake, there are many different compositions with Grand Teton as a backdrop.

One advantage to Taggart Lake compared to other lakes in Grand Teton is that this lake is accessible year-round. The ski or snowshoe trek to the lake is manageable for the novice. It is not nearly as intimidating as accessing other backcountry lakes in Grand Teton. The north loop trail from the parking lot is broad and easy to follow.

DIRECTIONS Distance from Town Square

Drive north from Jackson on US 191 for 12.3 miles (19.8 km) to Moose Junction and turn left on Teton Park Road. Continue past the entrance station for a total of 3.6 miles (5.7 km) to the Taggart Lake Trailhead parking lot.

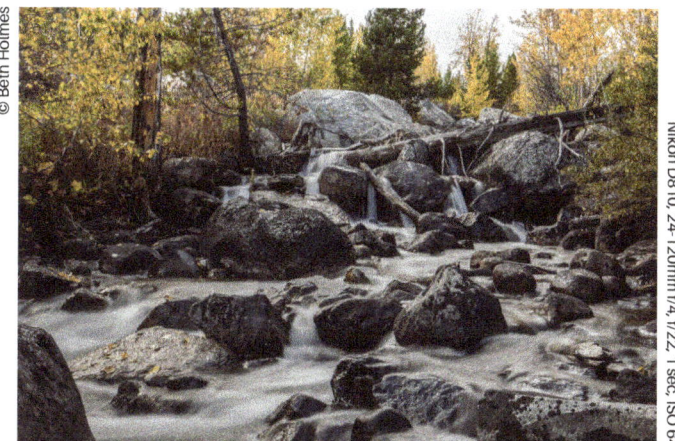
© Beth Holmes
Nikon D810, 24-120mm f/4, f/22, 1 sec, ISO 64

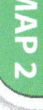
MAP 2

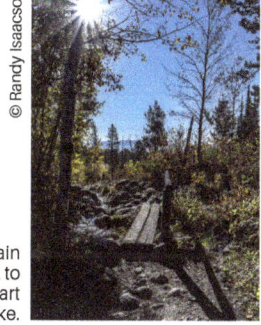
© Randy Isaacson
The main trail to Taggart Lake.

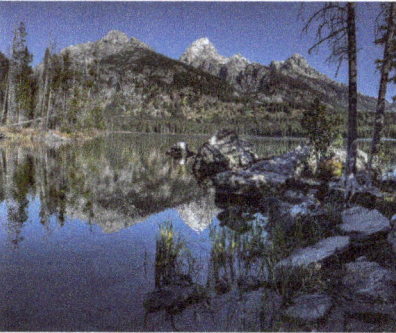
© Randy Isaacson
Taggart Lake in the fall.

HIKING DIRECTIONS

Start the hike near the concrete restroom building at the information and map kiosk. The wide trail leads through an open field toward the mountains and a tree-covered hill.

Take the first right (N) trail fork toward Bradley and Taggart lakes in 0.1 mile (0.2 km) from the trailhead. In 0.2 mile (0.3 km), the trail merges with the Beaver Creek Trail and curves northeast toward the horse corrals. It then curves left (NW) and gains elevation through a stand of trees.

The Bradley Lake cutoff trail is 0.7 mile (1.1 km) from the horse corrals. Take the left fork and continue another 0.5 mile (0.8 km) to Taggart Lake.

HOTSPOT #24

📷 Site Specific Photography Tips

Most of the views at Taggart Lake are up close. A wide to normal lens will be the most useful here, with a mid-range zoom being a good versatile choice. The long wooden bridges that span the south and northeast sections of the lake allow for overwater shots. They, too, can be incorporated into your composition. The length of the bridges is such that a wide-angle lens can make them seem incredibly long.

There is wildlife in the area, especially moose at Taggart Creek and in the marshy areas southeast of the lake. Be mindful when hiking this section of the lake trail, as sightlines are obscured by the meandering trail. Make plenty of noise to warn animals of your presence.

MAP 2

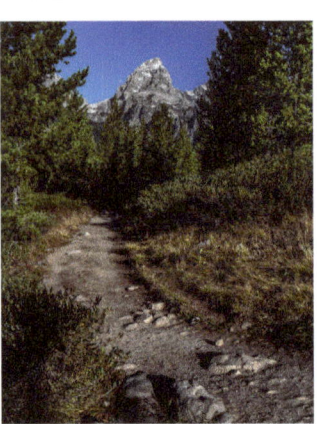

The main trail to Taggart Lake offers perfect alignment with Grand Teton.

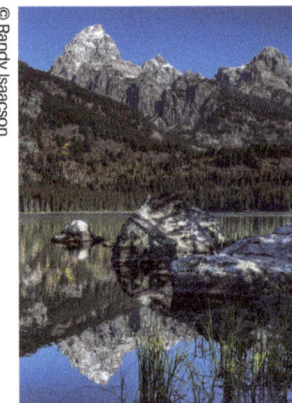

Up close to the shoreline of Taggart Lake.

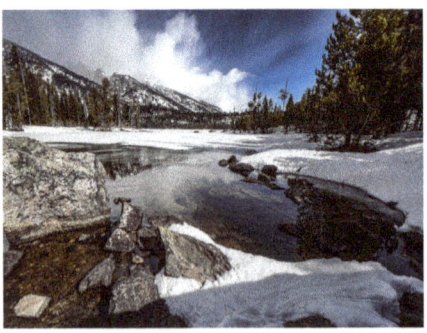

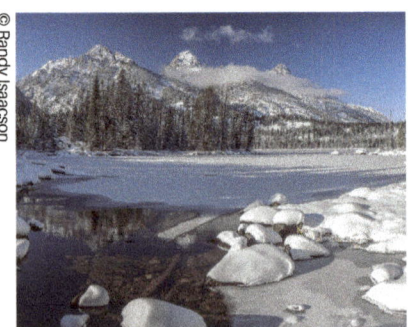

Taggart Lake early April can have significant snow.

Mid-November at Taggart Lake.

Site Specifics:

Parking: Parking is extremely busy during the summer. The Taggart Trailhead parking lot will overflow during the summer. Parking is generally available on the roadside.

Access: Taggart Lake is a hike-accessible destination. The hike is easy to moderate and gains little elevation. Do bring bear spray for the chance bear encounter.

HOTSPOT #24

CENTRAL JACKSON
COVERING HOTSPOTS #25-29

Map #3

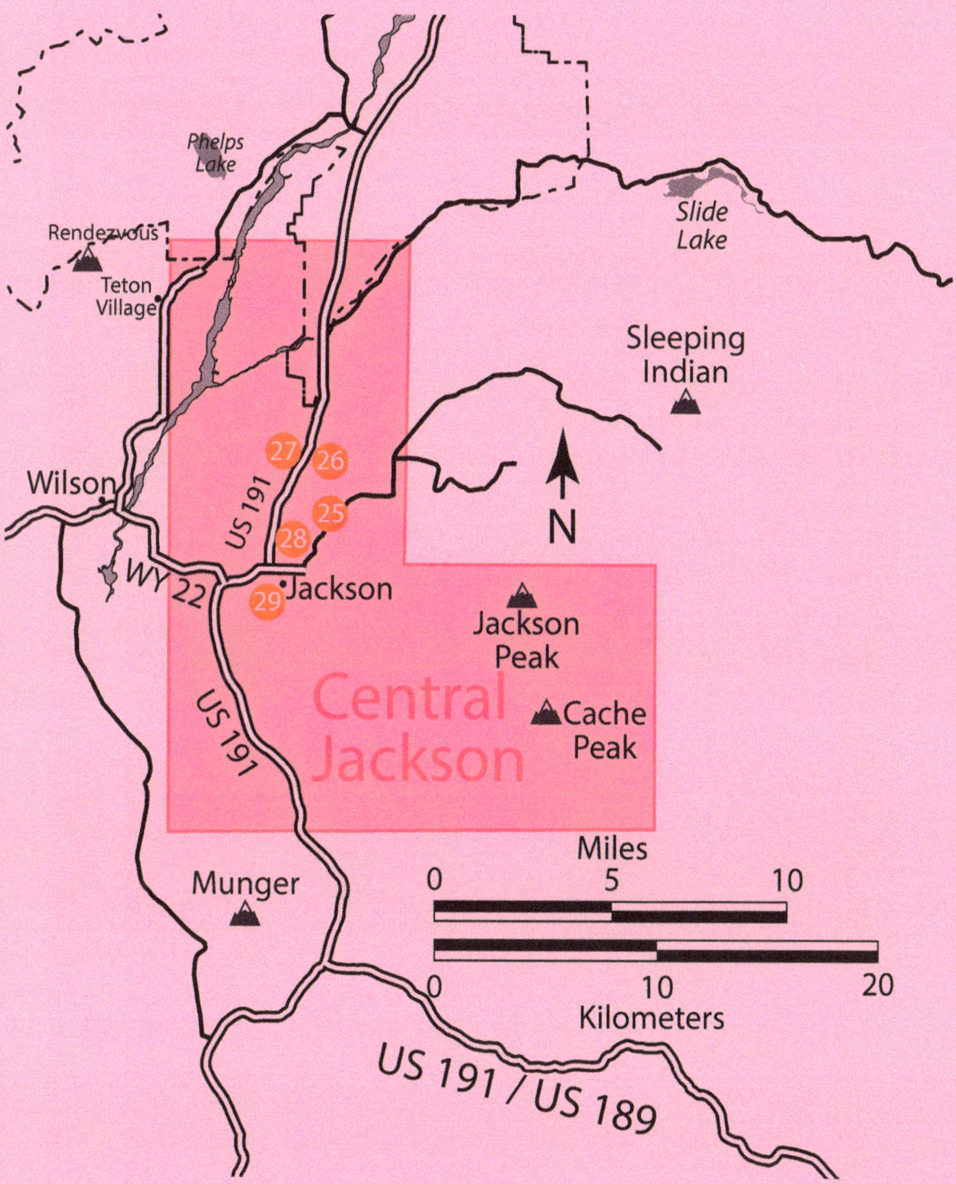

*HOT*SPOT *#25*

Miller House

DESCRIPTION:

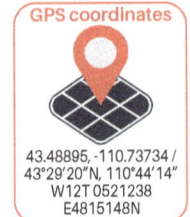

GPS coordinates
43.48895, -110.73734 /
43°29'20"N, 110°44'14"
W12T 0521238
E4815148N

Located in the National Elk Refuge along the Refuge Road, this historical building is one of the best-preserved in the area. When it is open during the summer season, docents meet visitors at the park bench or porch outside the building. They can provide a broad historical overview of the building and its former occupants before entering.

The interior of the Miller House is well-preserved and beautifully decorated. The irreplaceable historic artifacts inside provide ample opportunities for creating interesting images. The upstairs is inaccessible, as it is used by the staff. A convenient gift shop occupies one of the rooms of the house. Funds from this shop help cover the cost of maintaining and operating the building for guests to visit and enjoy.

MAP 3

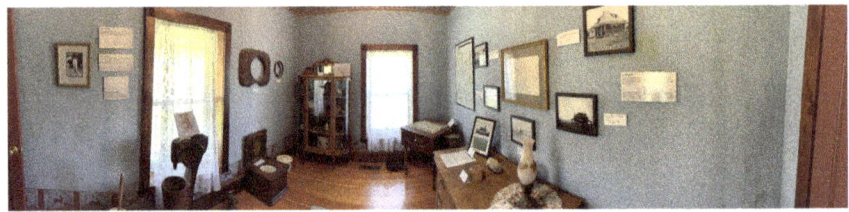

Panoramas of the interior of Miller House provide a sense of the era and feeling of the building's interior. Spending time to understand the people who lived here will provide the industrious photographer with a useful historical perspective.

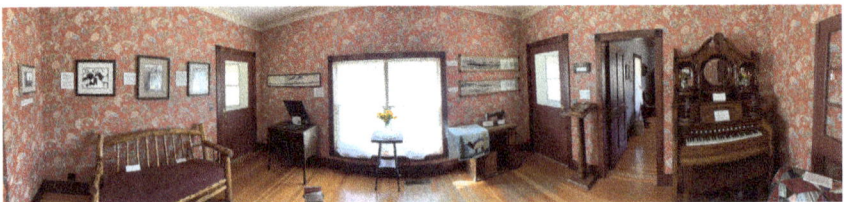

The Miller House with old-style wall paper.

DIRECTIONS

Distance from Town Square

Drive 1 mile (1.6 km) east from the Town Square to the end of the road. Turn left (N) onto the dirt refuge road. Continue 0.7 mile (1.2 km) to the Miller House turnoff.

Canon 7D, 100-400mm, f/5, 1/500, ISO 100

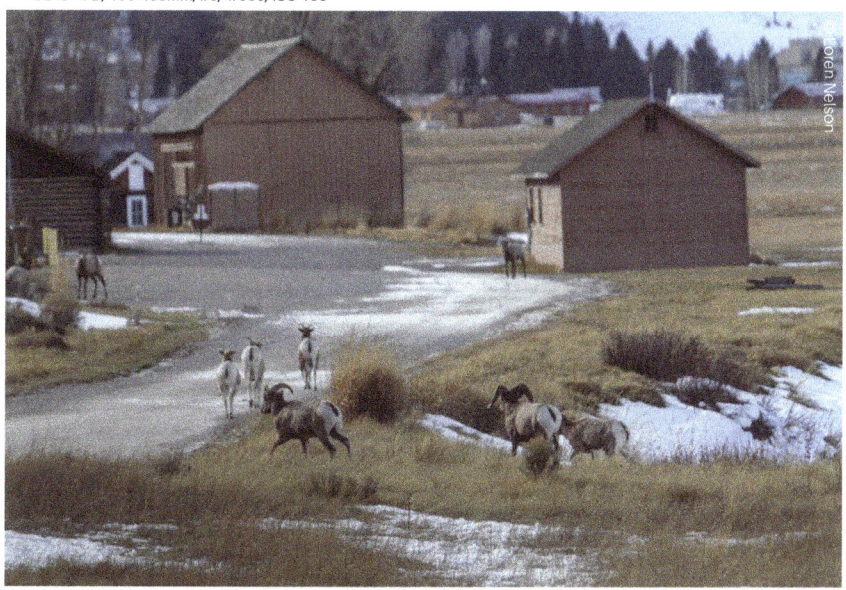

Bighorn sheep parade across the Miller House property with minimal fear of humans and vehicles. This condition makes for one of the easiest photographic opportunities of large mammals in Jackson Hole.

Early fall dustings of snow add visual interest to an otherwise tan and brown landscape. Caught at the right angle, snow can sparkle, adding twinkle to the buildings and the landscape.

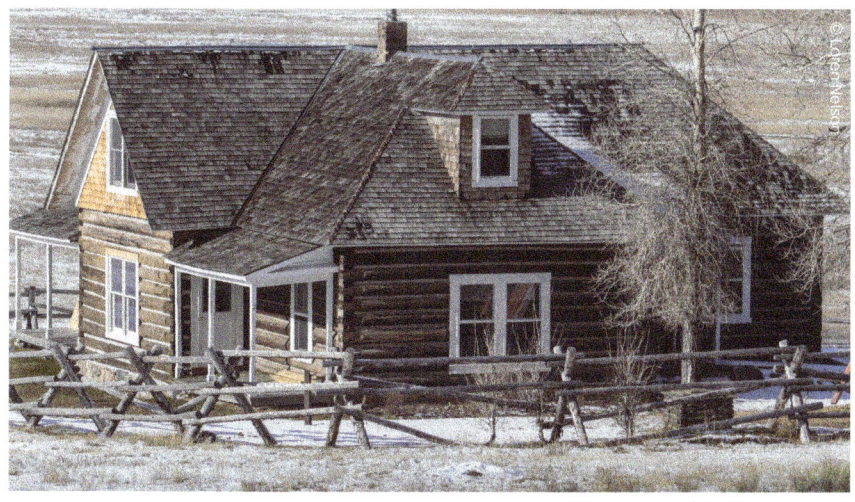

Canon 7D, 100-400mm, f/7.1, 1/500, ISO 100

HOTSPOT #25

Site Specific Photography Tips

One of the prettiest photos of the Miller House is taken a moderate distance south of the building on the Refuge Road. Frame the house in an ideal composition point and use a telephoto to compress the building against the butte farther away.

Note that parking and stopping along the roadside have been restricted over the years. If this restriction is in place, park at the Refuge Road entrance dirt pullout at the east end of East Broadway Avenue. Walk along the roadway or the trail to the west side of the road until you find the ideal composition point with the house, butte, and surrounding mountains.

It is possible to wander around to create interesting compositions using the house, fencing, and historical artifacts. Foggy mornings make the house appear as though it hovers inside of a watercolor painting. This is especially true in the winter in cold conditions.

Nikon D810, 70-300mm, f/4.5, 1/1000, ISO 110

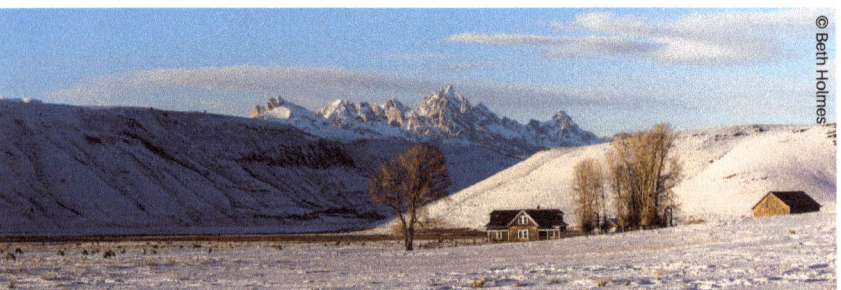

Pink late-afternoon light gracing the Miller House in early December.

Site Specifics:

Parking: There is a large dirt parking lot at the house. It is easily accessed and found along the Refuge Road.

Access: The Miller House is normally open during the summer with normal business hours. It is closed to access otherwise with a locked gate preventing access.

Check with the National Elk Refuge for current operating hours.

Phone: 307-733-9212

Also, stop by and check at the Greater Yellowstone Visitor Center for Miller House access information.

532 N. Cache Street, Jackson, WY 83001

Volunteers staff and maintain the site. If the volunteers are unavailable, the site cannot be accessed.

HOTSPOT #26

National Elk Refuge

GPS coordinates
43.47971, -110.74328 /
43°28'47"N, 110°44'36"
W12T 0520761E
4814120N

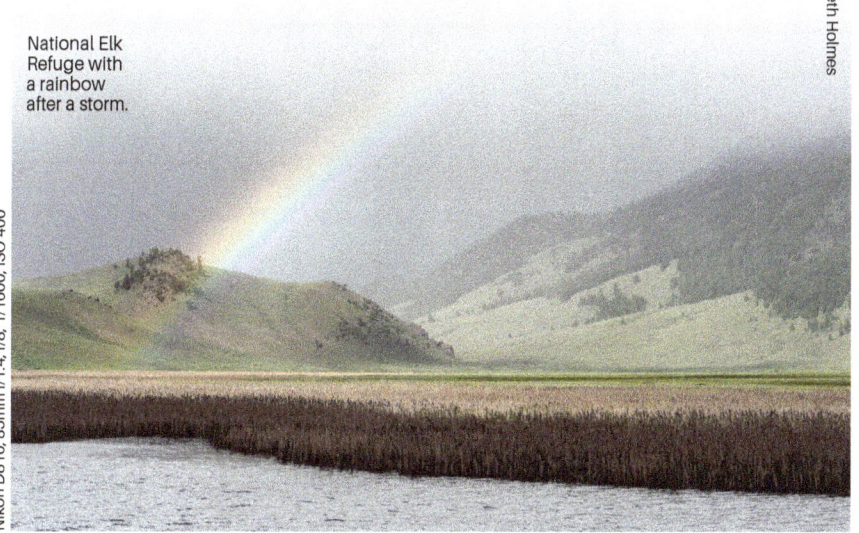

National Elk Refuge with a rainbow after a storm.

© Beth Holmes

Nikon D810, 85mm f/1.4, f/8, 1/1600, ISO 400

DESCRIPTION:

In the early 1900s, people had started feeding elk in the meadows north of Jackson and south of what would later become Grand Teton National Park. Feeding originally protected elk from starvation in especially harsh winters. In 1913, a reserve was created and managed by various state and federal agencies. In July 1940, it was declared a refuge and feeding continued.

When the town of Jackson grew in the 1960s, it blocked the traditional migration path for thousands of elk heading south from Yellowstone. Without the elk feeding, they would have great difficulty in finding enough food for the winter.

It has become a huge area of grassland and wetlands and the source of Flat Creek. In the summer, it is home to many species including pronghorn, mule deer, bald eagles, trumpeter swans, coyotes, wolves and others. In November, the winter snows drive elk into the valley by the thousands. During a typical winter, upwards of 9,000 animals are a common sight.

The winter also brings bighorn sheep down to the Miller Butte area on the east side of the refuge, north of Jackson. The roads are maintained on each side of the refuge and accessible throughout the winter. Be aware that the refuge has contributed to an abundance of elk so hunting is allowed and appropriate care must be taken.

DIRECTIONS

Distance from Town Square

Drive directly north of town to see the Elk Refuge from the highway. To access the Elk Refuge Road, drive east from the town square along Broadway for 1 mile (1.6 km) to the end of the road. Turn left onto the dirt road marked "National Elk Refuge."

"It is almost impossible to capture an image that does justice to the thousands of elk that span miles of the refuge. I have tried panoramas, wide-angle shots, close-ups with telephoto shots and have concluded it is best just to enjoy the experience and take what shots you can get. You can shoot from the National Museum of Wildlife Art on the west to get above the herd or from the Miller Butte Road extending from east Broadway in the town of Jackson. A great shot is the spring and fall crossing of the Gros Ventre River only a short walk in the snow from the Kelly Road."
—Loren Nelson

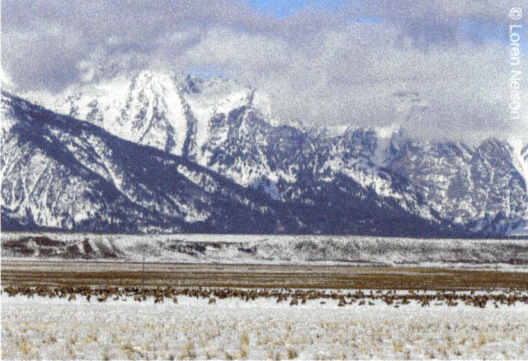

Canon 7D, 100-400mm, f/8, 1/800, ISO 100

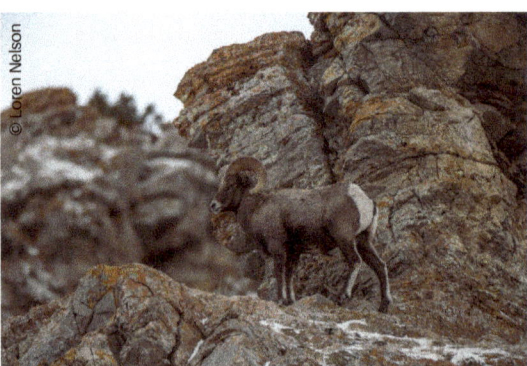

Canon 5D III, 600mm f/4 + 1.4x, f/5.6, 1/320, ISO 200

The rocky Miller Butte on the east side of the refuge is a local favorite for bighorn sheep. The sheep come down to the paved refuge road in mid-morning every day and return to the Butte in late afternoon. This is one of the few places you don't want to get up early for the wildlife—they will be high in the hills. The bighorns come down to the road and will approach cars to lick mineral deposits. This is potentially harmful and should not be allowed. If the sheep approach, take your photo and move your vehicle away.

Site Specifics:

Parking: Park in designated turnouts along Highway 89 adjacent to the Refuge and along the Refuge Road. During fishing season on the Refuge, the northern parking lots may be completely full.

Access: Purchase sleigh ride tickets at the Jackson Hole & Greater Yellowstone Visitor Center at 532 N. Cache St. in Jackson from 9:00 am – 4:00 pm.

The Refuge Road from the east end of Broadway into the Refuge is open year-round. During the winter, the road is closed at Twin Creek Ranch.

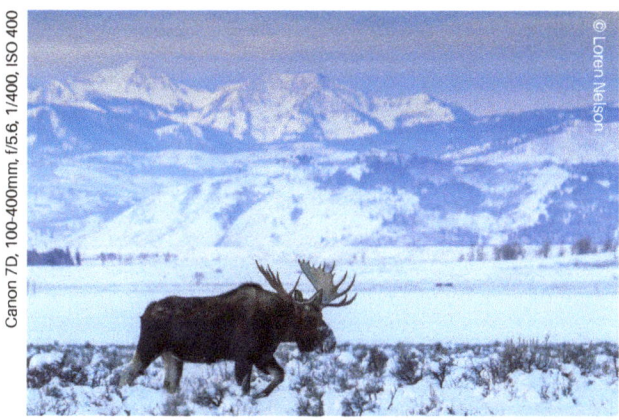

The Elk Refuge is not just about elk. Moose are very common on the north of the refuge along the Kelly Road from September to November and then scatter throughout the southern and eastern parts of Grand Teton National Park for the rest of the winter. The big bulls start losing their racks in late December and vanish into the hills again by April.

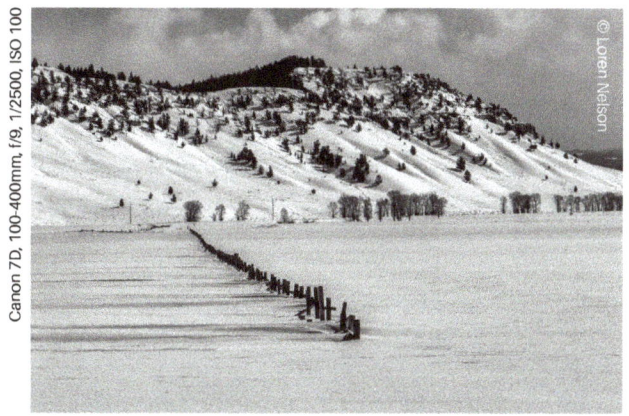

A snow buried fence becomes a long abstract line.

📷 Site Specific Photography Tips

The elk are often far away during the winter. Sometimes they stand up near the fence. However, stopping along the roadside may be dangerous or not permitted. The best option to view the elk up close is to take the sleigh or cart ride from the Refuge gate. On this ride, the sleigh will be quite close to the elk. Only a moderate telephoto will be necessary. A broad range zoom will be a good versatile choice.

Along the Refuge Road, bighorn sheep may be right along the roadside. The best choice is to bring a normal to moderate telephoto lens for sheep along the road and a longer telephoto for sheep on Miller Butte.

The Refuge Road is the access point to Curtis Canyon which penetrates many miles (kilometers) into the Gros Ventre range. Views from high on the hills along the eastern side of the Refuge offer excellent landscape photography options.

HOTSPOT *#27*

National Wildlife Museum

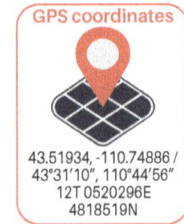

GPS coordinates
43.51934, -110.74886 /
43°31'10", 110°44'56"
12T 0520296E
4818519N

DESCRIPTION:

One of Jackson Hole's treasures is the National Museum of Wildlife Art on Highway 89. It is 2.9 miles (4.7 km) north of Jackson. Both the permanent collection and visiting shows keep the museum fresh and always interesting for visiting photographers.

There are few better views of the National Elk Refuge than from the museum. The outside statuaries are perfect foreground elements or primary subjects themselves. Natural rock walls help the building blend into the background. This gives photographers the chance to create fun architectural compositions with nature as a background.

During the winter, the views of thousands of wintering elk are impressive. On occasion, wolves can be seen prowling the refuge, hunting for their next meal. Capturing the moonrise or sunrise above Sleeping Indian from the outside of the museum is a great option, too.

MAP 3

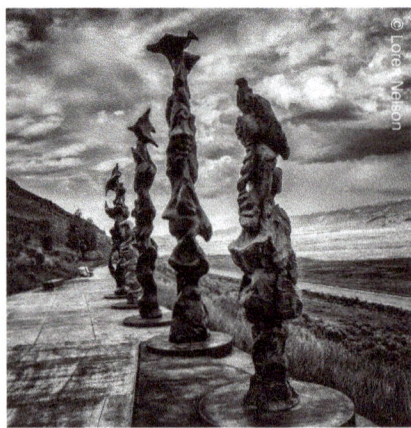

Sony 7R II, 24-70mm f/2.8, f/9, 1/250, ISO 320

© Loren Nelson

The Spirit Totems are magnificent pieces up to about 14 feet tall. This image earned the photographer a personal call from Herb Alpert himself.

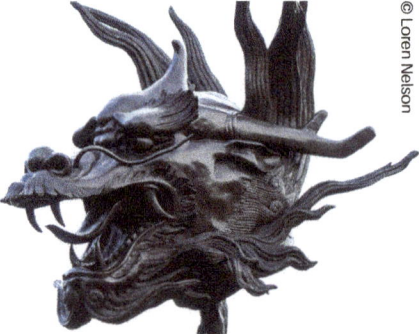

© Loren Nelson

Visiting exhibits to the museum come from around the world. This is a Circle of the Zodiac piece by artist Ai Weiwei.

DIRECTIONS

Distance from Town Square

Drive 2.9 miles (4.7 km) north from Jackson Town Square. Turn left (W) into the driveway leading up to the museum.

Site Specifics:

Parking: Parking is plentiful and nearly always available. The only time the lot is full is if the museum is hosting an event.

Access: The site is drive-up and there are disabled access ramps.

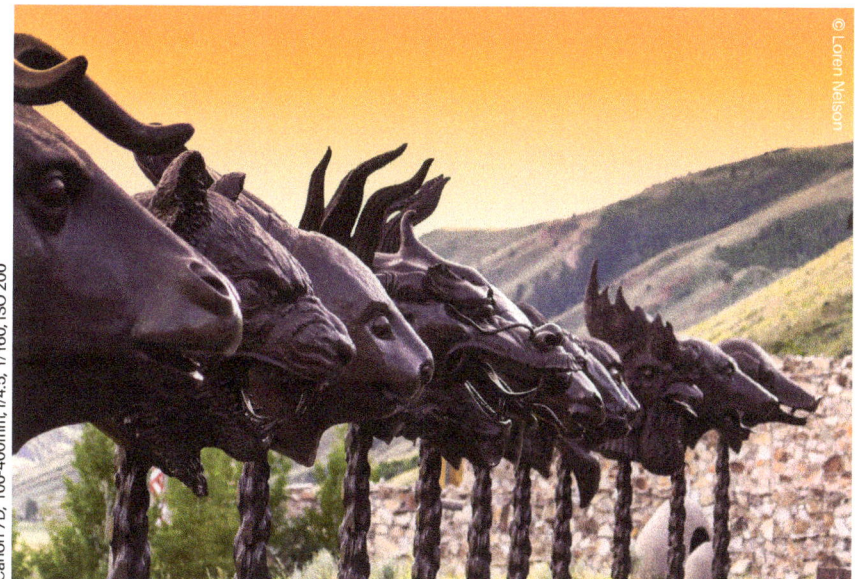

The complete Zodiac Circle on display in 2015.

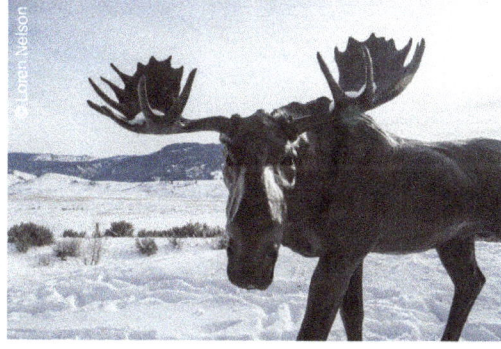

The museum's outdoor collection is open year-round and creates many photogenic opportunities.

📷 Site Specific Photography Tips

The site lends itself to a wide variety of photographic techniques. Nearly any lens will be useful in creating excellent compositions. The sculptures at the museum lend themselves to placing art in a northwest Wyoming landscape.

For the rare chance to photograph wolf interactions with the elk herd in the refuge, bring the longest telephoto possible. The view of the refuge is expansive but it is also far away.

Note that photography is not allowed in the museum.

HOTSPOT #28

Park Sign North of the Fish Hatchery

GPS coordinates
43.54663, -110.73288 /
43°32'48"N, 110°43'58"
W12T 0521578E
4821555N

DESCRIPTION:

One of the most photographed signs in all of Jackson Hole is the Grand Teton park sign north of the fish hatchery. Located on the top of the rise when leaving the lower area of the National Elk Refuge, the pullout is the edge of the park.

This location is a must-stop for people who love to take proof of presence images. One of the biggest challenges is the distance of the peaks. From the sign, the Cathedral Group is 13.8 miles (22.3 km) away on a bearing of 345° northwest. When photographing with a wide-angle lens common on smartphones and pad devices, the peaks will appear diminutive and far away.

Interestingly, the location of this park sign is on the current southern edge of Grand Teton National Park. As Highway 191 travels through the park, there is no checkpoint entrance for this section of the park. This roadway is the main artery between Jackson, Dubois, Yellowstone, and points beyond.

MAP 3

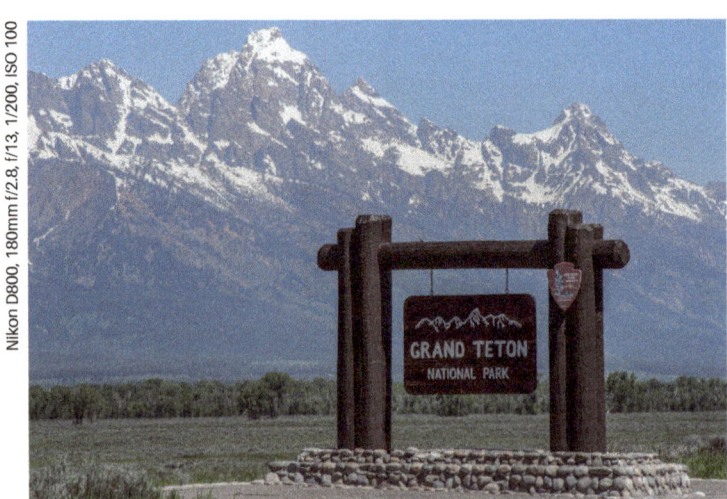

Nikon D800, 180mm f/2.8, f/13, 1/200, ISO 100

DIRECTIONS

Distance from Town Square

Drive north from Jackson on US 191 for 5 miles (8 km) to Grand Teton park sign turnout.

Site Specific Photography Tips

The classic photo is taken from the sidewalk in front of the sign. There is a large stone pedestal holding up the posts of the sign. It is easy to take this photo.

However, there are two better possibilities. First, have whoever you're taking photographs of step about 15 feet (4.5 m) from the sign. Photograph them in a portrait landscape format with their waist at the bottom of the frame and the top of their head near the top of the frame. Place the sign to the right of the subject with the summits in the background. This composition creates a beautiful portrait worthy of hanging on the wall.

The most striking photo is taken with a moderate to long telephoto as far away from the sign as possible. The best position is halfway to the fence. Using about a 180mm lens will create a striking photo. People will ask where this sign is and insist that the southern park sign isn't this photo. An image taken this way compresses the Tetons, making them dominate the sign with a commanding perspective.

Nikon D800, 80-400mm, f/8, 1/800, ISO 200

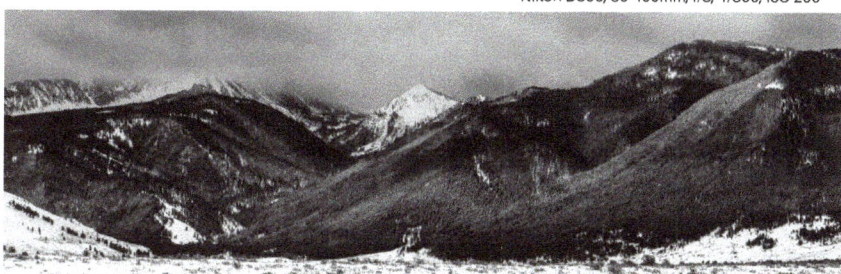

Looking toward Nelson and Jackson Peaks from the park sign turnout in Grand Teton. Stormy conditions make for dramatic pictures. Convert images to B&W with dull color to bring the image to life.

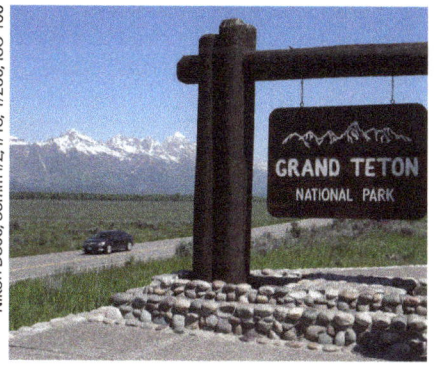

Nikon D800, 35mm f/2, f/13, 1/250, ISO 100

The classic tourist shot taken from the southern boundary sign at the turnout makes the Teton Range look diminutive. Use the techniques of perspective shifting to change the scale of foreground and background objects to make a more impressive statement. This shot, taken from a short distance from the sign, guarantees small mountains. Stepping back as far as possible will create a more compelling image.

Site Specifics:

Parking: There is plenty of parking at this site. It can be busy but vehicles don't stay long as the sign is the only attraction.

Access: The site is paved and disabled accessible.

HOTSPOT #29

Snow King Overlook (of Jackson)

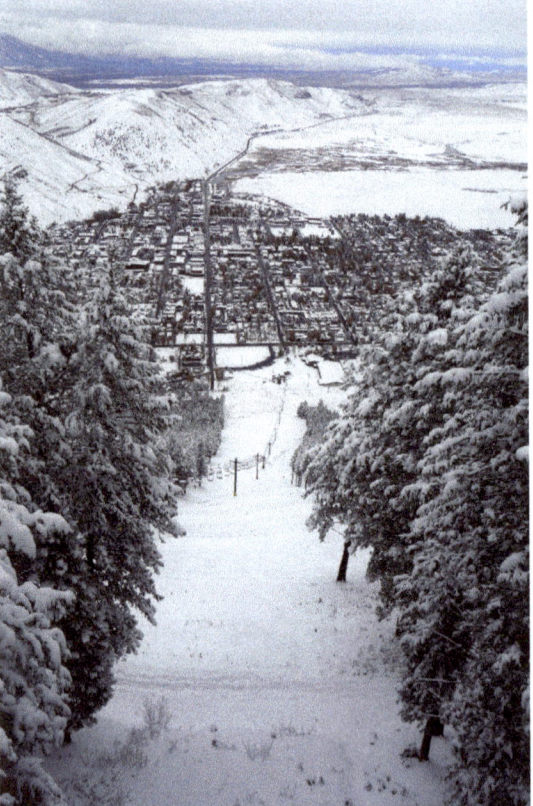

Sony RX100, f/5.6, 1/800, ISO 125

GPS coordinates

Trailhead
43.47191, -110.76038 /
43°28'19"N, 110°45'37"
W12T 0519381E
4813250N

Overlook
43.46325, -110.76297 /
43°27'48"N, 110°45'47"
W12T 0519174E
4812288N

MAP 3

Hiking up the boot pack on Snow King can be a grueling experience. The few who make the trek up the mountain in the cold depths of winter will be rewarded with a enjoyable perspective of this famous town and the valley. Make sure to follow current uphill travel regulations for the ski resort to maintain your safety and that of downhill travelers.

Site Specific Photography Tips

The high point of the overlook is a large wooden deck that soars over the Exhibition Ski run. Any number of lenses will work, from wide-angle to long telephoto. The metal plaque at the corner of the ski hut provides orientation for the different summits and features of the area.

The view directly down from the deck is a tree tunnel. This provides a leading line and guiding options for composition.

Mid-morning and mid- to late-afternoon are the best times to photograph. The mountains to the east in Cache Creek shade the town well into the morning past the official local sunrise time. Mid-day can be hazy, creating blue-tinted images. A polarizer can help darken the sky and reduce the appearance of blue haze visible on a mid-summer day.

DIRECTIONS

Distance from Town Square

Drive south on South Cache from the Town Square for 0.4 mile (0.6 km) and turn left (E) on E. Snow King Avenue. Park in the parking lot at Phil Baux Park.

DESCRIPTION:

At the top of Snow King near the gondola summit and ski patrol hut is the best overlook of Jackson and the surrounding mountains. Rising over 1,571 feet (479 m) above the town, there is no more accessible location for a broad view of central Jackson Hole, Flat Creek, the Elk Refuge, Grand Teton, and the surrounding areas.

There is a small cabin hidden in the aspens south of the summit. Nearby is the Wyoming Stargazing observatory as well. A trail leads west along the ridgeline toward Josie's Ridge. To the south of the summit are Wilson and Adams Canyons.

The main trail ("Slow Trail") is the most popular way to reach the summit. Access is free, even if the hike isn't easy. The former chairlift and now gondola provide paid access to the summit for those not interested in a strenuous hike.

The overlook looks down Exhibition, a 55° double black diamond ski slope. There is also the Boot Pack Trail which directly ascends Exhibition and is an extremely strenuous hike that provides immediate overlooks of Jackson and the Snow King complex.

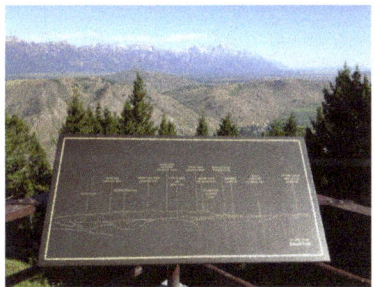

The metal sign at the corner of the summit hut is illustrated with identifiable mountains and important Jackson Hole locations of note. From this location, most of the major summits of Grand Teton National Park are visible. One large summit that is obscured by the closer mountains is Mount Moran which is only visible farther north.

Site Specifics:

Parking: The parking lots at Phil Baux Park and the Snow King Event Center provide ample parking to access the summit area. The park is located at 100 E Snow King Ave, Jackson, WY 83001.

Access: Either hike up Snow King on several of the trails or purchase a lift ticket during operating hours. Note that the trail is steep and strenuous with an unrelenting slope. Bring plenty of water (at least one liter) during the heat of the day.

Visit the Snow King website for updated hours at: www.snowking.com or call at 307-733-5200.

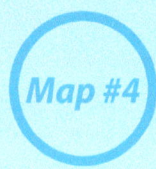

GROS VENTRE NORTH
COVERING HOTSPOTS #30-36

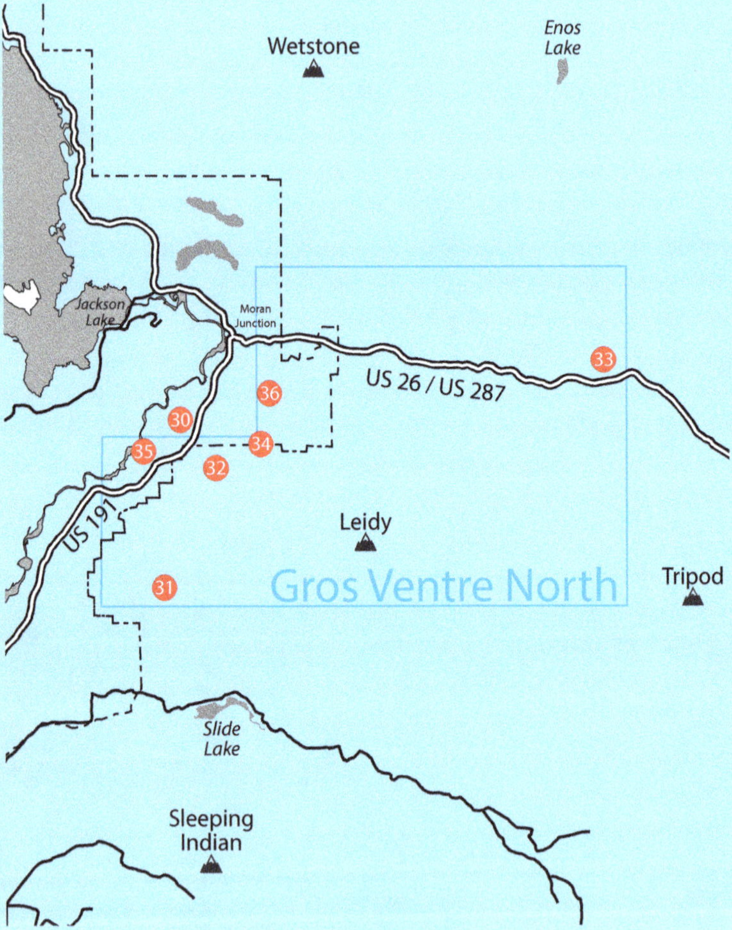

HOTSPOT #30

Cunningham Cabin

DESCRIPTION:

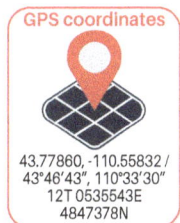

GPS coordinates
43.77860, -110.55832 /
43°46'43", 110°33'30"
12T 0535543E
4847378N

Best-known for the shootout that happened in 1893, the Cunningham Cabin is an accessible historical structure for photography. The location is noted by a road sign along the highway, though the cabin is not visible from the highway. A mystery persists to this day about the characters at the cabin and the causes of the deadly shootout.

The building is short so taller visitors will need to mind their heads. The two rooms of the cabin are attached by an open wall roof, providing sun protection in the middle of summer. As the cabin has a dirt floor, there is no danger of falling through a rotten floor.

There are several meadows beyond the cabin. Sometimes they have horses from a nearby dude ranch depending on the season. Also, there is a good chance that roaming wildlife will happen to pass through.

A small kiosk at the parking lot may have a flier for historical cabin information. Over the years, the roof beams have been repaired or replaced. The roof is maintained to prevent the building from disintegrating in the harsh Jackson Hole winters.

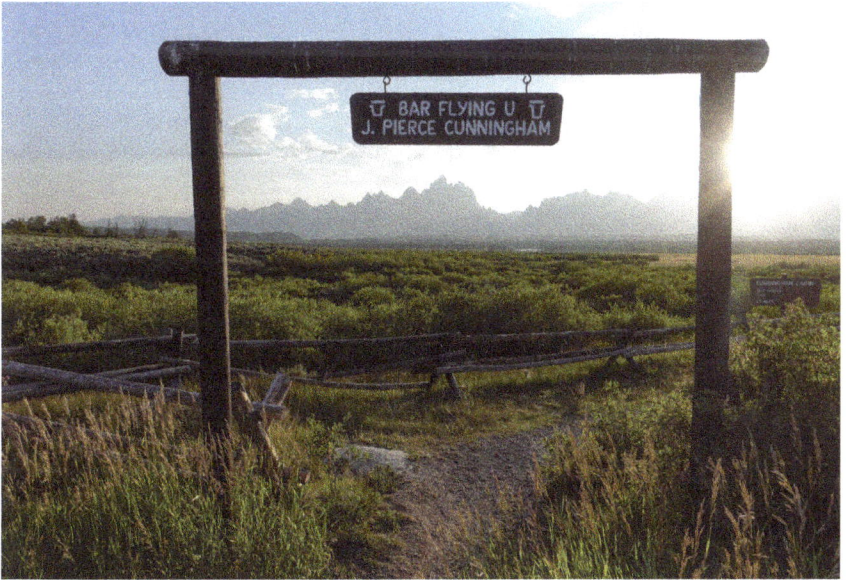

Sony RX100 VA f/4, 1/500, ISO 125

DIRECTIONS

Distance from Town Square

Drive north from Jackson on US 191 for 27.1 miles (43.6 km). Turn left at the Cunningham Cabin sign and continue 0.36 mile (0.58 km) to the parking area.

Nikon 810, 24-120 f/4, f/9, 1/6, ISO 64

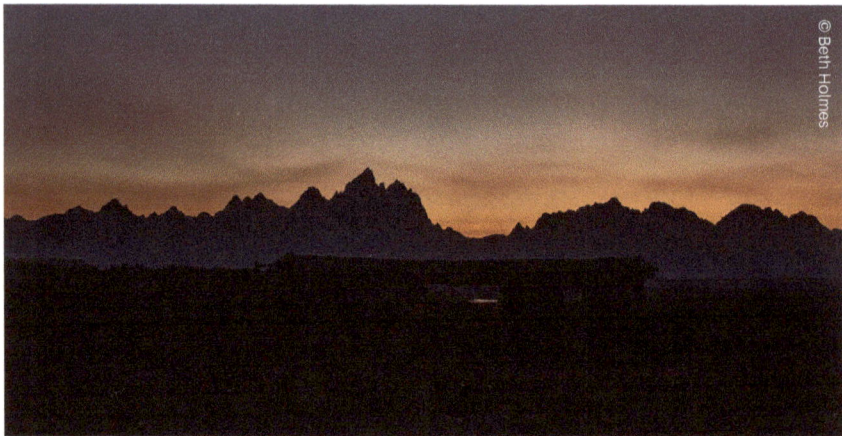
© Beth Holmes

Cunningham Cabin is unique in Jackson Hole for having a historical building with clear views of the Cathedral Group, Cascade Canyon, and the northern portions of the Teton Range. This site is good for both sunset and sunrise images, which makes it more flexible than many locations in the valley.

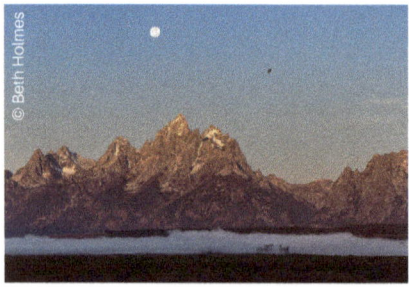
© Beth Holmes

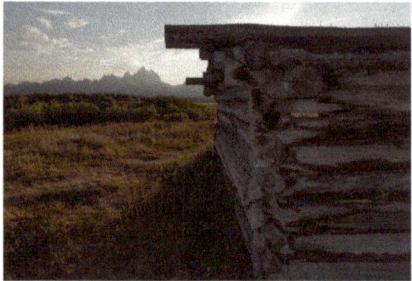

📷 Site Specific Photography Tips

It is possible to photograph the Cathedral Group through the awning between the two rooms of the cabin. The position requires placing the camera near or on the ground to achieve this composition. The roof is low-slung, so achieving a telephoto image with the mountains through the cabin is a challenge.

The ground around the cabin is flat. There is a buck rail fence as well as an intermittent creek to the north of the cabin. They may be useful as compositional elements. There are no obstacles around the cabin preventing a clear view of the Cathedral Group.

MAP 4

HOTSPOT #30

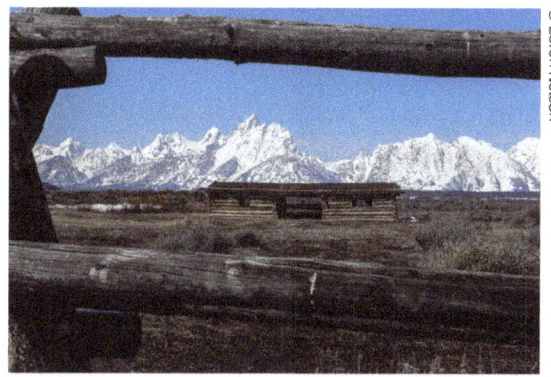

Using buck rail fences to create images with framed mountains.

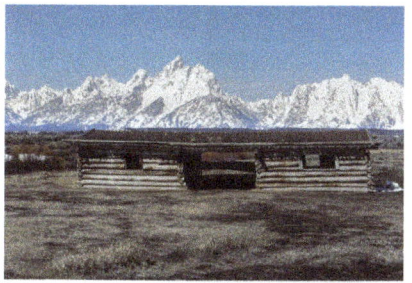

The historic cabin is a perfect foreground element to offset the mountains.

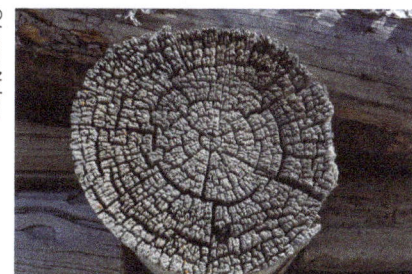

Macro textures are also options at this site.

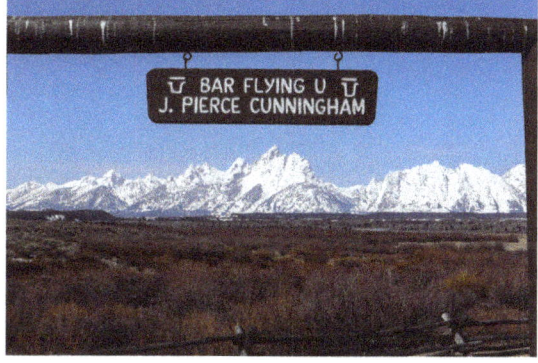

Entrance sign to the trail leading to Cunningham Cabin.

Site Specifics:

Parking: The paved parking area is large and accommodates many vehicles. Turning around a large van or an RV may be a challenge but it is possible.

Access: Start walking at the large wooden post and lentil western-style gate toward the cabin. The path wanders a short distance before opening up at the cabin. There is a small creek flowing through the area. A 0.3-mile (0.5-km) trail looks around the historic property.

Dangers: There are numerous badger holes hidden in the grasses around the cabin. Many a wary visitor and photographer has fallen up to their hip in some of these holes. Be mindful to prevent injuries from an unexpected fall.

HOTSPOT #31

Shadow Mountain

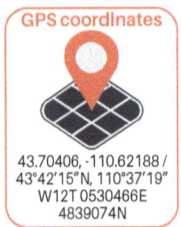

GPS coordinates

43.70406, -110.62188 /
43°42'15"N, 110°37'19"
W12T 0530466E
4839074N

DESCRIPTION:

Shadow Mountain is located in the Bridger-Teton National Forest just east of the park and the area is accessible via a rough dirt road north of the town of Kelly. The road opens in May and is usually drivable until early November.

Views from Shadow Mountain of northern Jackson Hole are excellent and open. The tree cover is not as dense as other areas. This makes selecting photography spots much easier than in other areas in Jackson Hole. Wildflowers are prevalent in the early to mid-summer.

The road can be extremely rough. A high-clearance vehicle and ideally a four-wheel drive is recommended for this road. There are multiple off-road vehicle trails and campsites to explore.

MAP 4

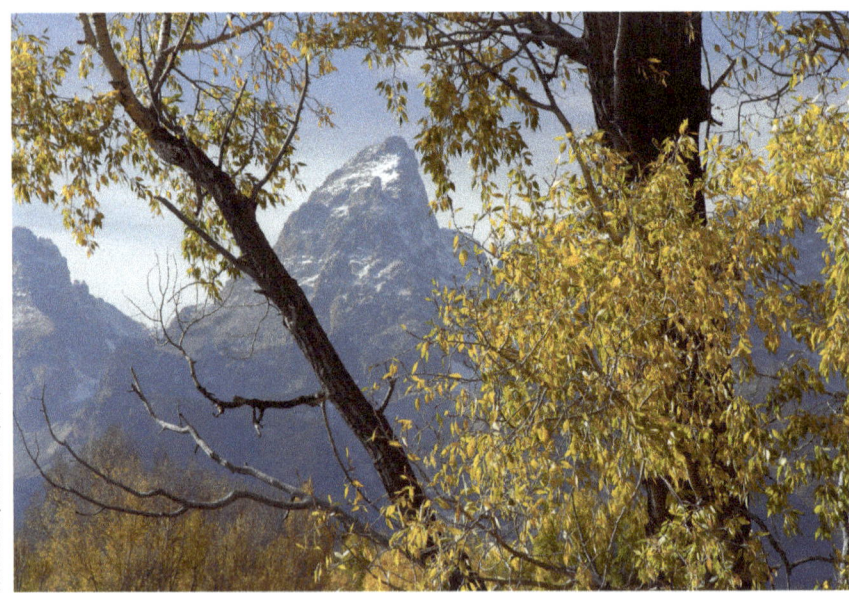

Nikon D200, 85mm f/1.4, f/13, 1/30, ISO 200

DIRECTIONS

Distance from Town Square

Drive north from Jackson on Cache Street to US 191 for 13.6 miles (21.8 km) past Moose and turn right on Antelope Flats Road. Drive 3.3 miles (5.3 km), then turn left on Shadow Mountain Road and continue 1.6 miles (2.5 km) to the dirt road. Drive 0.8 mile (1.2 km) to the parking and camping area.

📷 Site Specific Photography Tips

The variety of photographic opportunities on Shadow Mountain are truly endless. Macro, wide, normal, and telephoto lenses are all options on this large mountain. For wildflowers with the Tetons in the background, a normal to moderate telephoto is a good choice.

Shadow Mountain's altitude allows for balanced images of the Tetons compared to photographs taken from the lower valley. Groves of aspen and some cottonwoods make for excellent fall foreground objects. These trees work well any time of the year when the mountain is accessible.

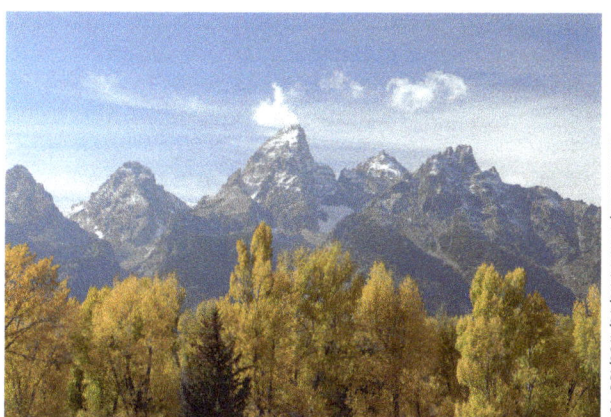

Nikon D200, 50mm f/1.8, f/8, 1/50, ISO 100

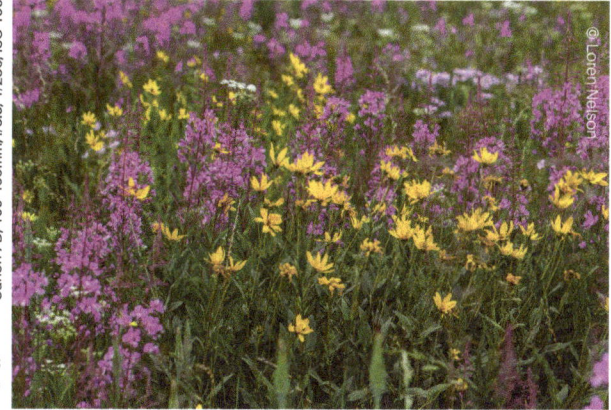

© Loren Nelson

Canon 7D, 100-400mm, f/5.6, 1/250, ISO 100

Endless seas of wildflowers dot Shadow Mountain in late June until late July.

Site Specifics:

Parking: Park off the roadway in turnouts or designated campgrounds. The road is narrow and rough.

Access: Most photography points are easily accessible on Shadow Mountain with a high-clearance vehicle. Areas like Forest Service Road 30340B, a stub off the main road, require mild hiking to find the best wildflower points.

HOTSPOT #31

HOTSPOT #32

The Observatory

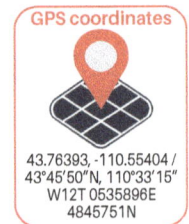

GPS coordinates

43.76393, -110.55404 /
43°45'50"N, 110°33'15"
W12T 0535896E
4845751N

DESCRIPTION:

The Observatory (as named by locals) is one of the few elevated views on the eastern side of the valley that is easy to access. The elevated view located north of the Cathedral Group is unmatched in the whole valley.

Locals named this The Observatory for the commanding views of the Tetons in the morning and the clear sky views at night. On a moonless night, the number of visible stars can overwhelm the senses. During the correct time of year, the Milky Way galaxy stripe is easily visible from this location.

One of the challenges in recent years is the popularity of the site on free camping location mobile apps. The entire platform can be occupied by campers and RVs.

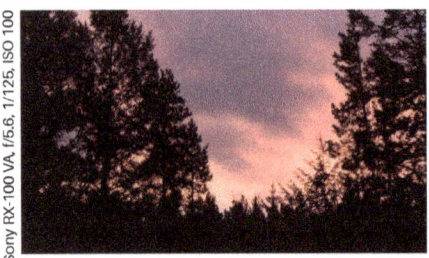
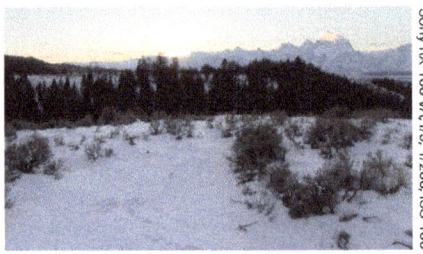
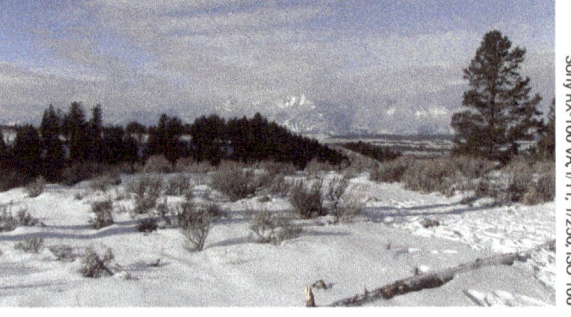

DIRECTIONS

Distance from Town Square

Drive north from Jackson on US 191 for 27.1 miles (43.6 km). Turn right (E) on Toppings Lake Road (FS 30310) across the highway from the Cunningham Cabin. Drive on the dirt road for 0.8 mile (1.3 km) to a junction. Continue on FS 30310 around a hairpin turn for 0.4 mile (0.7 km) to the first junction after the road levels out. Turn left (NW) to enter the open, flat area.

Site Specifics:

Parking: Parking can be a challenge in the summer in the day and night. Often campers will occupy much of the space in the wide expanse. Most of the time people are friendly and will allow you to skirt their campground so you can take photos at the edge. Strike up a conversation. Many will be willing to take a photo of you with the iconic Tetons in the background.

Access: The site is drive-up and easy for anyone to access.

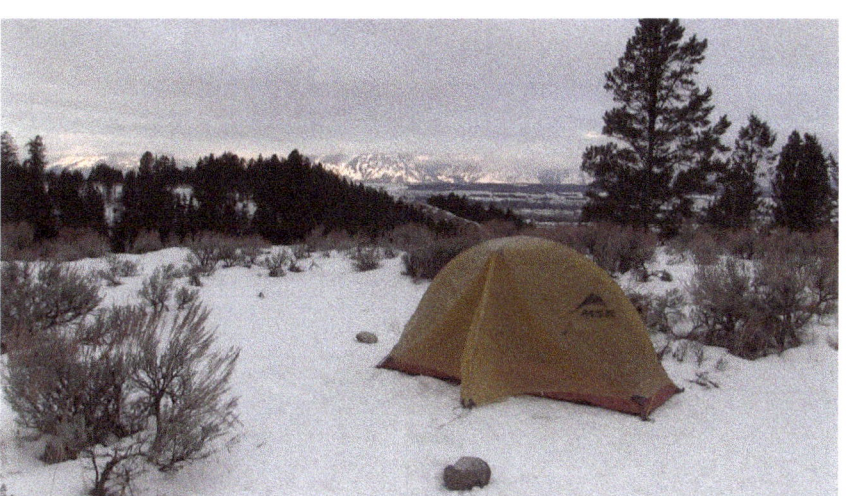

Canon G20, f/5.6, 1/60, ISO 200

To make capturing morning images easier, camping is a good way to go. During the winter, this location can be quite cold. Temperatures register below -20º F (-29ºC) regularly. Be prepared for personal safety and also to make sure camera batteries still have enough power to take pictures.

Site Specific Photography Tips

All types of lenses are useful at this site. Spring and early summer flowers are best photographed with a wide-angle, using the mountains in the background. Normal lenses are best for capturing general views of the valley floor and the Tetons together. On clear days, telephotos can be used to capture a different angle of the Cathedral Group.

This is one of the better spots in the valley to create panoramic images. The elevated viewpoint helps reduce boring or overwhelming foreground objects.

Astrophotographers may find this site to be enjoyable or difficult to photograph from. The people and vehicle traffic can cast light across a lens which will wash out long exposures. However, shot from farther back, an enterprising night photographer can use a campfire to add fun compositional elements to an otherwise two-dimensional image.

HOTSPOT #32

HOTSPOT #33

Togwotee Overlook

GPS coordinates
43.82144, -110.19401 /
43°49'17"N, 110°11'38"
W12T 0564813E
4852356N

DESCRIPTION:

The road to Togwotee Pass is an absolute must for landscape photographers. The road gives broad overlooks of northern Jackson Hole and the Tetons. The four-season scenery is unmatched along this roadway which parallels the Buffalo River.

Proximity to Togwotee Lodge makes this a good stopping point between Jackson and Dubois. The most prominent mountain is Mount Moran which dominates the northern Jackson Hole skyline. The Cathedral Group is farther away from this viewpoint and is still quite spectacular due to the jagged nature of the peaks.

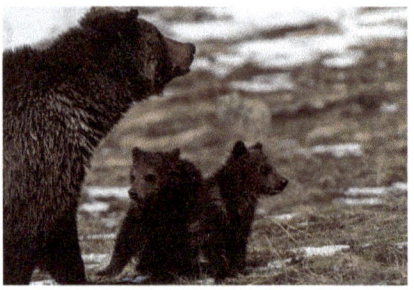

Grizzly bears and other wildlife frequent the road to Togwotee Pass.

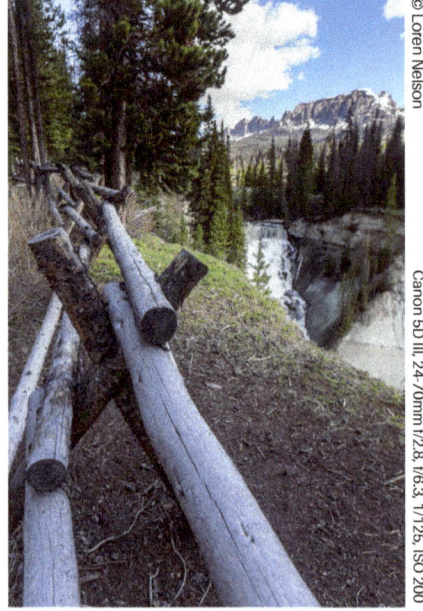

Lakes, rivers, streams, canyons, forests, and craggy mountain peaks await the landscape photographer driving up Togwotee Pass. The Falls campground near Brooks Lake has history, a waterfall, and spectacular views of the Pinnacles.

DIRECTIONS

Distance from Town Square

Drive north from Jackson on US 191 for 30.3 miles (48.8 km) to Moran Junction. Continue past the junction, staying on US 26 / US 287, driving an additional 16.9 miles (27.2 km) to the sign marked Togwotee Overlook and turn on FS 30033. This road is 0.5 mile (0.8 km) east of Togwotee Lodge. Drive 0.25 mile (0.4 km) to the overlook dirt parking area.

📷 Site Specific Photography Tips

All four seasons at this spot provide normal and telephoto opportunities. The arrowleaf balsamroot flowers are prevalent in the area. The yellow petals provide a pleasant contrast against the purple and blue mountains in the distance. The overlook is the most northwesterly location to view and photograph the Tetons from the Togwotee direction. There are a few roadside positions farther east but none provide broad and safe parking along the highway.

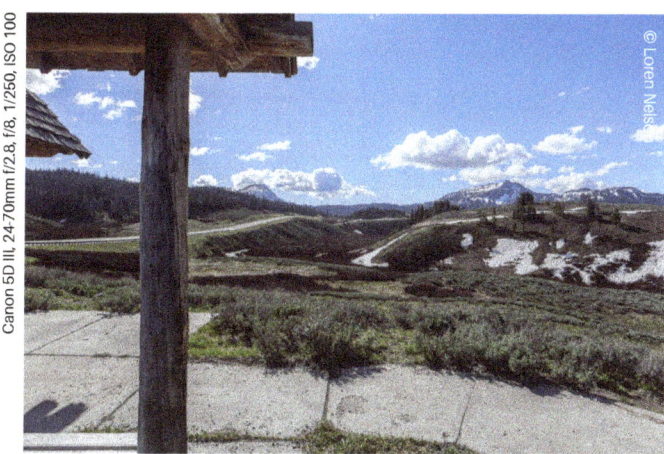

One of several overlooks along the highway to Togwotee Pass.

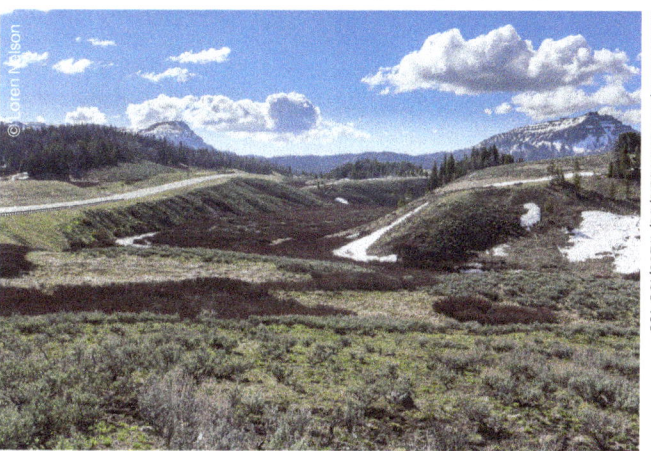

There is four-season access to the pass with dramatic changes from lush summers to hundreds of inches of snow in late winter.

Site Specifics:

Parking: There is plenty of parking at the site. Generally, there are only a few vehicles at any time at this location.

Access: This viewpoint is a drive-up location. The edge of the viewpoint is fully accessible by walking and, in dry conditions, is disabled-friendly.

HOTSPOT #33

HOTSPOT #34

Toppings Lake Ridge

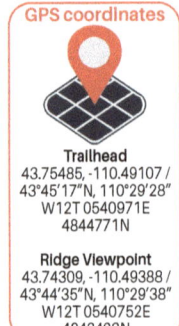

GPS coordinates

Trailhead
43.75485, -110.49107 /
43°45'17"N, 110°29'28"
W12T 0540971E
4844771N

Ridge Viewpoint
43.74309, -110.49388 /
43°44'35"N, 110°29'38"
W12T 0540752E
4843463N

DESCRIPTION:

This little-known ridge is one of the best valley landscape photography locations in the entire Jackson Hole region. The trail is easy to follow but lightly used, meaning photographers will likely not be competing for tripod positions.

One of the major advantages to this location over others is the ability to compose a three-dimensional landscape image. So often photographs of the Teton range are bland two-dimensional affairs. Toppings Lake Ridge affords the intrepid photographer a chance to stand out from the crowd.

The top of the ridge is not blocked by stands of trees, making it easy to choose a camera position. Be aware that if there are other people on the ridge, excluding them from the photo will be a challenge. Arriving early to secure a good spot will pay off.

The ridge is aligned along a bearing nearly pointing to the Cathedral Group 14.6 miles (23.4 km) away at 267° west. The Teton Range isn't visible until the top of the ridge which may instill doubt of the photographic value of the location. As soon as you crest the ridge, the image potential will be excitingly obvious. Few photographers venture here, making the payoff with a unique image of the valley worthwhile. The chance of encountering other hikers or photographers is low, even in the height of the hiking and tourist season. That said, arrive early to ensure a prime location should the rare hiker have the same idea.

MAP 4

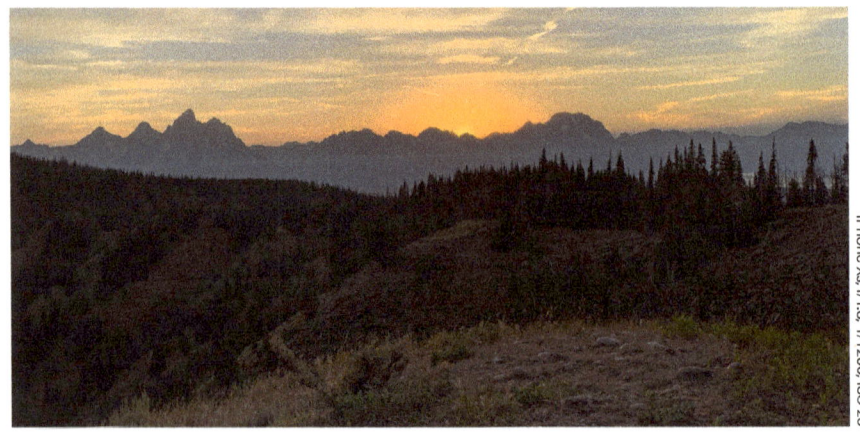

iPhone Xs, f/1.8, 1/1200, ISO 25

DIRECTIONS

Distance from Town Square

Drive north from Jackson on US 191 for 27.1 miles (43.6 km). Turn right on Toppings Lake Road (FS 30310) across the highway from the Cunningham Cabin. Stay on FS 30310 for 5 miles (8 km), bypassing the spur service roads. Park by the green steel gate. The road may require a high-clearance vehicle. Give yourself time to find the trail junction off the dirt road past the gate.

iPhone Xs, f/1.8, 1/2000, ISO 25

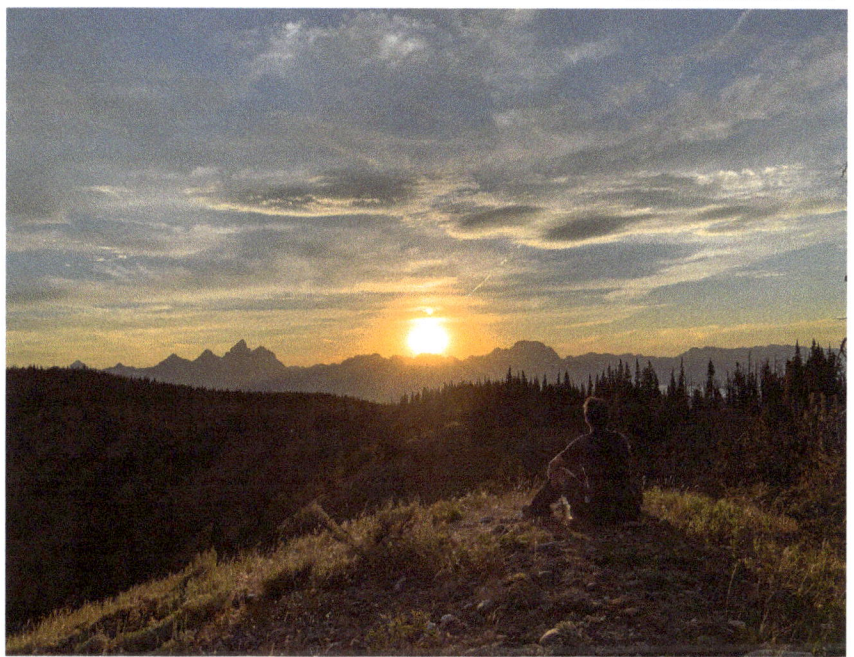

Looking west, enjoying the sunset overlooking Jackson Hole.

HIKING DIRECTIONS

Start by walking past the steel gate and continuing on the old dirt road. Hike for 0.18 mile (0.29 km) to a trail junction on the right (S) side of the road. It may be marked with a rock cairn and orange poles. It is easy to miss the junction. Once you see it, the trail is well-traveled and apparent.

The trail is easy to follow through the forest. Hike for 0.8 mile (1.3 km) along a heavily forested path to a junction and turn right. The trail proceeds up a series of steep switchbacks to the ridge, gaining 570 feet (174 m). The trail disappears at the west end of the ridge which is a perfect sunset or picnic spot.

📷 Site Specific Photography Tips

This hike is strenuous. It may take some time to reach the top of the ridge. Plan for an hour hike to reach the ridge. The last vertical distance of 570 feet (152 m) to the ridge of the trail is steep. Keeping a free hand is a good idea.

Plan to arrive on the ridge at least an hour before sunset to choose an ideal composition. Although the ridge is at 9,000 feet (2,743 m), the sun is hidden by the Teton Range at the actual horizon sunset. During the summer, the sun is north of the Cathedral Group.

One of the challenges of this location is the likelihood of having the sun in the frame. Test your camera and lens to make sure both handle direct sun and flares well. Should your camera suffer from minor flares, they can be digitally touched up. Significant lens and aperture flares need to be planned for.

Digitally removing flares or imperfections is a subject of debate. Consider what level of retouching is acceptable to your style.

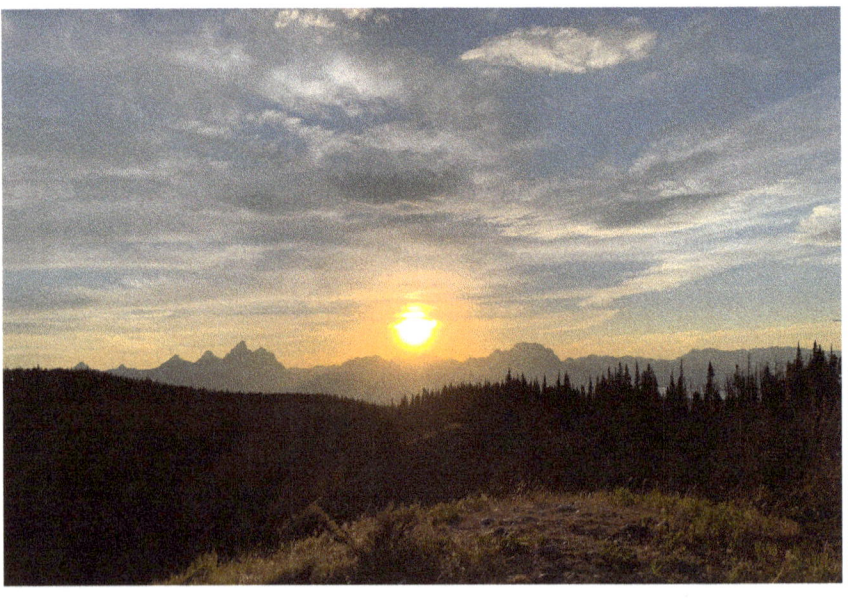

iPhone Xs, f/1.8, 1/3400, ISO 25

Site Specifics:

Parking: There is ample parking at the end of Toppings Lake Road. As this location is lightly visited, parking is not an issue. There is one campsite next to the parking area and steel gate.

Access: During the late spring to early fall, access along the dirt road is easy. Once the area snows in, driving can be treacherous and is not recommended. The trail is strenuous and rough.

GPS coordinates
43.77005, -110.57019 /
43°46'12", 110°34'13"
W12T 0534592E
4846424N

HOT*SPOT* #35

Triangle X Ranch Meadow

DESCRIPTION:

Triangle X is a dude ranch located 24.4 miles (39.2 km) north of Jackson on an in-holding in Grand Teton National Park that dates back to the 1920s. In the early 1930s, the working cattle ranch and hunting outfitter transformed into a dude ranch. It has now morphed into a western-style luxury lodge with 20 cabins.

More than 300 acres in the heart of the park gives guests opportunities for horseback riding, rafting, hunting, hiking, and pack trips in a setting with abundant wildlife and magnificent Teton views. During the summer, the ranch regularly rides visitors from the lodge to the Snake River.

Horses and, less frequently, bison, coyotes, and even wolves are seen in the ranch meadow west of the highway. These animals create a pastoral scene with the Tetons in the background.

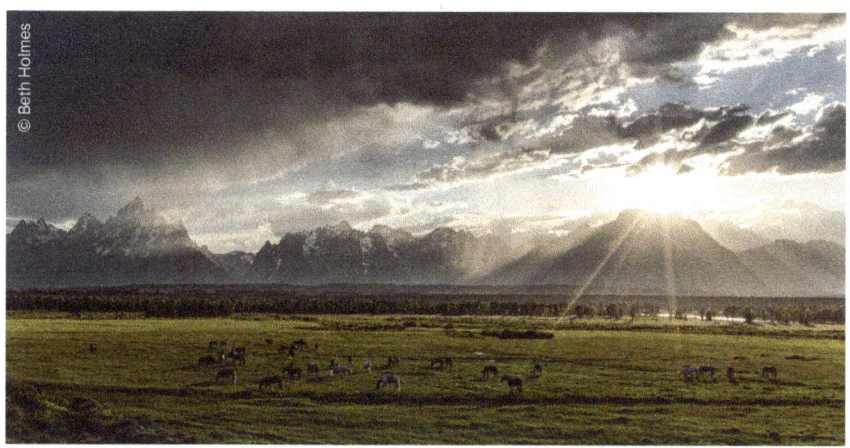

© Beth Holmes

Nikon D810, 24-120mm f/4, f/18, 1/250, ISO 400

DIRECTIONS

Distance from Town Square

Drive north from Jackson on US 191 for 24.4 miles (39.2 km) to reach Triangle X Ranch Road.

📷 Site Specific Photography Tips

A variety of lenses will work well at this site. Wide angles work well to capture the old fence, flowers, and any animals that might be present. Normal lenses work well to bring animals closer while still keeping a perspective of the surrounding areas. Telephoto lenses are the best choice when the animals are far away or you want to make them appear much closer to the mountains than they are.

Nikon D810, 85mm f/1.4, f/8, 1/1250, ISO 200

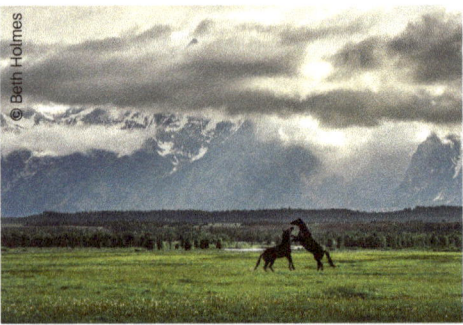

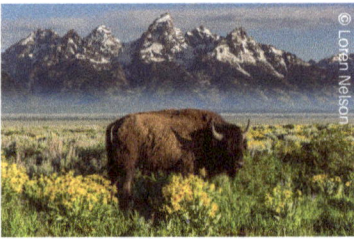

Bison migrate through the Triangle X property and can add drama to spring wildflower shots with mountain backgrounds.

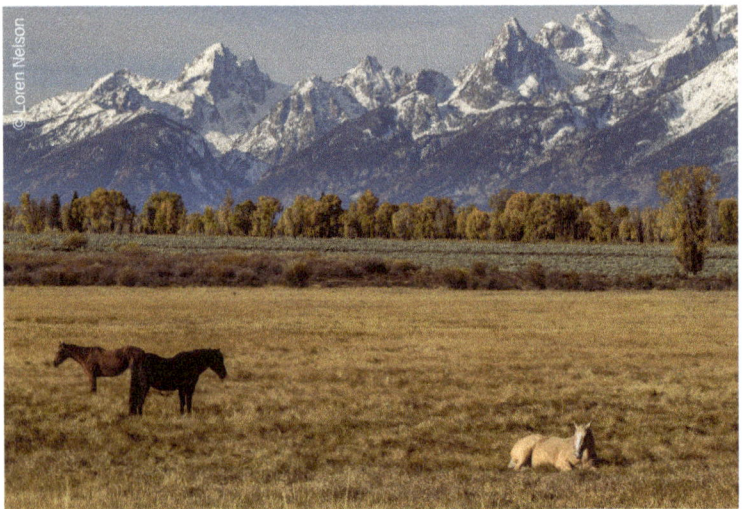

Canon 7D, 100-400mm, f/8, 1/320, ISO 100

The ranch's horses often add to the foreground and views of the Tetons. Finding them at the right distance can be a challenge.

Site Specifics:

Parking: Park on the west side of the highway (closest to the mountains) in the large dirt lot. Avoid blocking the roadway or the gate, as they are actively used by the ranch.

Access: The dirt turnout and parking lot are publicly accessible. Do not go through the wooden gate, as this is private property.

MAP 4

HOTSPOT #35

GPS coordinates
43.79504, -110.53726 /
43°47'42"N, 110°32'14"
W12T 0537227E
4849212N

HOT*SPOT* *#36*

Wolff Ranch Road / Elk Ranch Flats

DESCRIPTION:

The rough dirt road east of US191 and just north of Spread Creek is known as Wolff Ranch Road. It is a nearly unmarked ranch road that forms a loop with Elk Ranch Road to the north. It offers adventurous photographers a full day of unique photography. This road has few other visitors, even in the peak summer months.

The road requires a high clearance four-wheel-drive vehicle and will cross some rocky creeks. Crossings should never be attempted in early spring or high-water conditions. The road is closed by snow in winter. It leads to a turn-off to Uhl Hill which is a prime habitat for grizzlies and wolves. There are almost always deer and pronghorn and sometimes moose near the road.

There is an old farm reservoir with waterfowl and rocky hillsides worth photographing. Toward the north end of the loop is a photogenic stream and pond. Some abandoned ranch buildings and corrals make good foreground elements with the Tetons in the background.

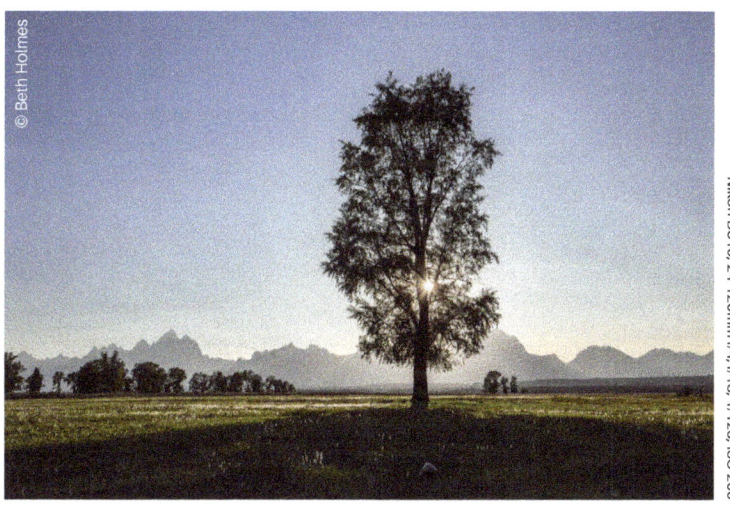

© Beth Holmes

Nikon D810, 24-120mm f/4, f/18, 1/125, ISO 200

MAP 4

DIRECTIONS

Distance from Town Square

Drive north from Jackson on US 191 for 26.6 miles (42.8 km) to reach Wolff Ranch Road.

📷 Site Specific Photography Tips

For landscapes, a wide to a slight telephoto zoom lens is most useful here. Anything in the 18-105mm range will yield effective results with the landscapes. For animals, the longer telephotos will be helpful. Often, animals are far in the distance. Note that during the middle of the day, atmospheric scintillation will distort far away objects and animals.

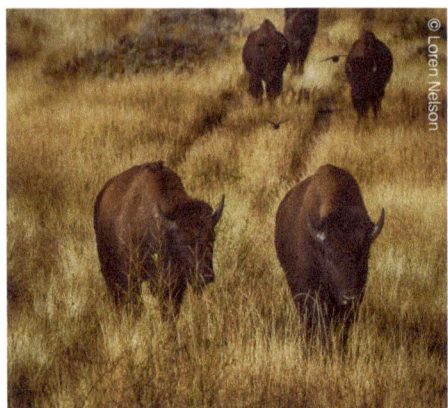

Canon 7D, 100-400mm, f/11, 1/250, ISO 100

Bison roam the woods and grasslands along Wolff Ranch Road. This is a prime birthing ground for bison in May and June. This high-contrast, high clarity shot was cropped from a long telephoto image.

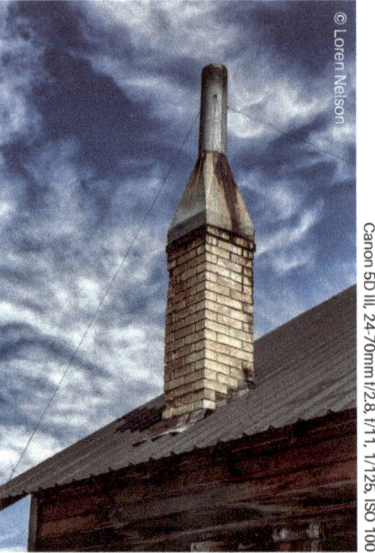

Canon 5D III, 24-70mm f/2.8, f/11, 1/125, ISO 100

Buildings and clouds always work well together and detailed shots can be attempted in the harsh mid-day sun.

Canon 5D III, 17-40mm, 1/160, f/14, ISO 100

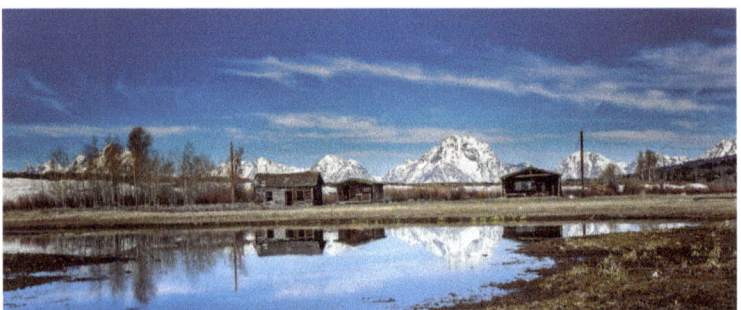

An 8-shot blended panorama image of the abandoned Elk Ranch and the reflecting pond in the foreground. Sometimes there is so much to see on the ground, a clear blue sky is boring. The multiple portrait-format images are easily combined in Adobe Lightroom or other editing software.

Site Specifics:

Parking: Pull off nearly anywhere alongside the road. As there is little traffic, this area is quite free of traffic issues.

Access: The entire area is accessible by car. During winter, the road is closed.

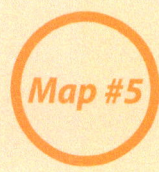

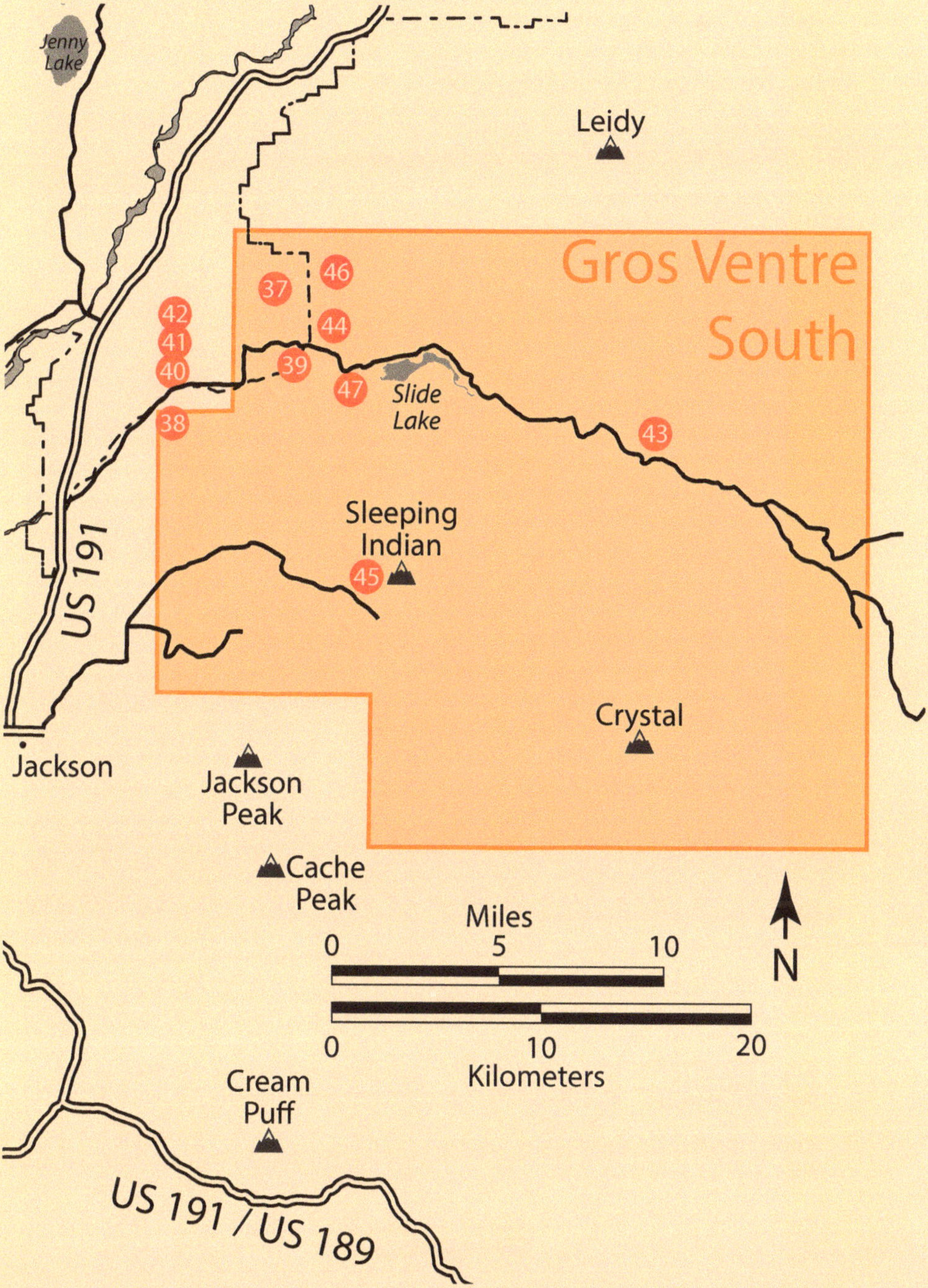

HOTSPOT #37

Antelope Flats Road

DESCRIPTION:

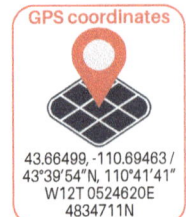

GPS coordinates
43.66499, -110.69463 /
43°39'54"N, 110°41'41"
W12T 0524620E
4834711N

Antelope Flats Road is the northern access point to many attractions in the eastern part of Jackson Hole. However, the roadway itself and the area it travels through have their photographic opportunities.

From spring to early summer, the wildflower bloom in this section of the valley is quite stunning. The best part is the unobstructed views of the Teton Range. Wildflower photography can range from macro and close-up flower portraits to using the flowers as a colorful foreground element for traditional landscapes.

The most important aspect of taking photos along Antelope Flats Road is safety. Pull completely off the road to take images. Distracted drivers are a concern in and around Jackson Hole.

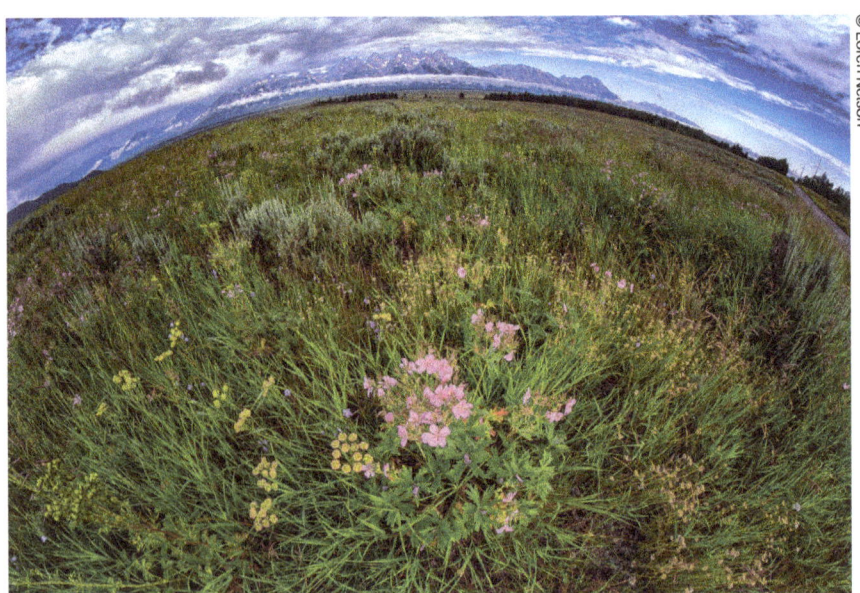

© Loren Nelson

Canon 5D III, 8mm, f/11, 1/30, ISO 100

MAP 5

Fish-eye lenses are a joy to shoot with. Another technique that allows very close-up shots of wildflowers and a wide shot of the surrounding landscape is to go ultra-wide with an 8mm focal length fish-eye lens. By adjusting where you place the horizon, you can create a very wide-angle but flat horizon or one that curves up or down to create a unique image.

DIRECTIONS

Distance from Town Square

Drive north from Jackson on Cache Street to US 191 for 13.6 miles (21.8 km) past Moose and turn right on Antelope Flats Road.

Site Specific Photography Tips

The best lenses to use for wildflower photographs along Antelope Flats Road are macro, wide-angle, and normal lenses. There are so many flowers in this area that the options can seem overwhelming. Macro lenses are quite useful here because they double as sharp landscape lenses.

The best and safest parking locations are located around the Mormon Row area. The dirt road is long, traveling from Antelope Flats Road to Gros Ventre Road. Blacktail Butte will obstruct Teton compositions. However, there is a good chance you'll be able to compose flowers with the large animals in this area. Make sure to maintain a safe distance as required by the Park Service.

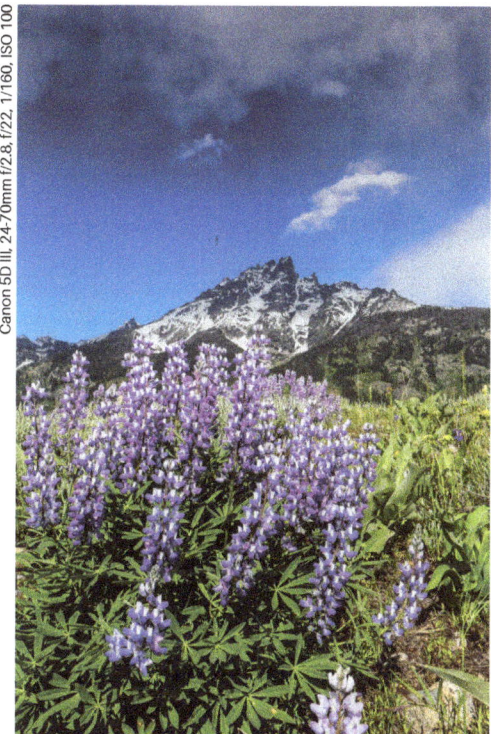

Canon 5D III, 24-70mm f/2.8, f/22, 1/160, ISO 100

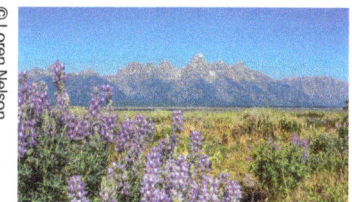

© Loren Nelson

From early June to mid-July, Antelope Flats is ablaze with wildflowers. A technique to consider to capture the flowers and a crisp background of the mountains is to use focus-stacking. Shooting multiple images with the camera on a steady tripod lets you focus on flowers two feet from the lens, through the mid-ground, and finally on the mountains. The images can be blended using Photoshop or other focus-stacking software to keep everything sharp.

A classic wildflower foreground with a mountain background is to close down your aperture. This lupine was captured by shooting at f/22 and manually focusing toward the far side of the plant. The great depth-of-field with the small aperture keeps everything in focus.

MAP 5

Site Specifics:

Parking: Parking is plentiful at designated locations, though in midday summer, it can be a challenge. Make sure to park safely when not parked in a designated turnout. The western section of the road is narrow and windy.

Access: As long as you can walk safely through the scraggly sagebrush in the area, access is not a problem. The area along Antelope Flats Road only has drainage ditches and badger holes to slow down a photographer.

HOTSPOT #37

HOTSPOT #38

Gros Ventre Road

GPS coordinates

43.57418, -110.73278 /
43°34'27"N, 110°43'58"
W12T 0521577E
4824614N

DESCRIPTION:

All along Gros Ventre Road past Kelly Warm Spring is a broad selection of vistas, aspen and cottonwood patches, lakes, overlooks, and old cabins. This road continues to Slide Lake, created by the earthquake and landslide of 1925. The lake is popular for boating and fishing and has areas of flood trees making interesting foregrounds. In the winter the lake is popular with skaters and skiers. Private ranches along the road bring the flare of the old West.

East of the Shane Cabins turnout is a long stretch of road that is aligned perfectly to Grand Teton. Although there is no parking or sidewalk along this section of the road, it is well worth visiting in the fall. The aspens with the road create the perfect leading line straight to the Cathedral Group. Either park at Shane Cabins and walk east or park east of this section and walk west for this view.

From the steel gate at the Atherton Creek Campground on Slide Lake, the road turns to dirt and continues 25 miles (40 km) deep into the Gros Ventre Range. The variety of landscapes, creeks, rivers, and seldom-visited lakes are well worth exploring. The 9.6-mile (15.4-km) round trip hike to the spring-fed Grizzly Lake takes the adventurous along a mild backcountry lake access trail that few visitors ever venture to.

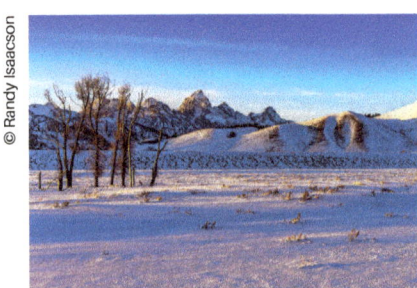
© Randy Isaacson

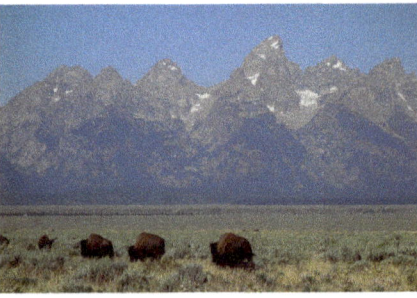

MAP 5

DIRECTIONS
Distance from Town Square

Drive north from the square on North Cache Street which turns into US 191 for 6.9 miles (11.1 km) to an intersection. Turn right on Gros Ventre Road and continue 7 miles (11.2 km) to the town of Kelly. Continue on the road as it turns left (N) at Kelly and drive 1.1 miles (1.8 km). Turn right on the Gros Ventre Road. From here, continue as far as 6 miles (9.6 km) to Atherton Creek Campground to explore the paved sections of Gros Ventre Road.

📷 Site Specific Photography Tips

Wide-angle and normal lenses are good choices along the Gros Ventre Road corridor. Many of the locations lend themselves to taking images with a foreground object with mountains in the background.

Photographing along the aspen tree tunnel on the straight section leading to Grand Teton works well with a moderately wide-angle lens, such as a 24mm lens. To compress the trees against the mountain, a normal to a slightly telephoto lens in the 50-85mm range will work well.

As Slide Lake is large and well below the road, using an 18-24mm lens range will allow for foreground objects to match the scale of the lake or make it look smaller than it is. As it is a long lake, using a telephoto to capture the lake will cause the water to dominate the image.

Farther along the road, the dry landscape lends itself to normal lens photography to keep the proportion of the eroded landscape in scale. Nearly all of the sites are best photographed early in the morning in the cool light. Once the land heats up, atmospheric scintillation will create fuzzier images.

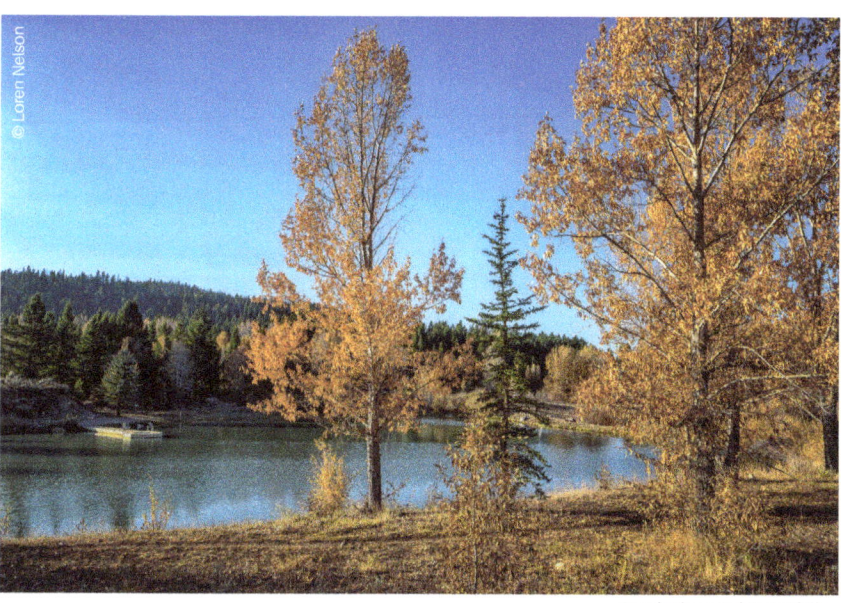

Roadside pond in the fall.

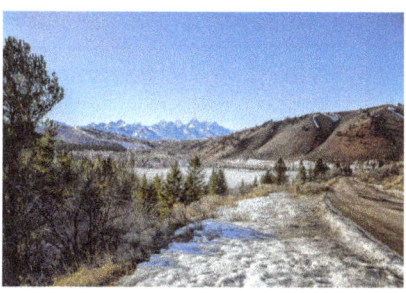

Melting snow in early spring view of the Tetons.

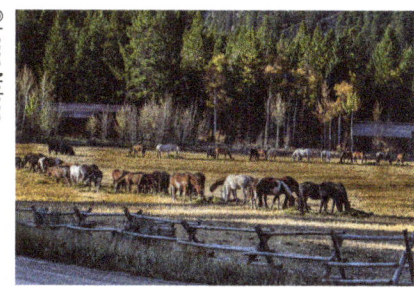

Working ranch and classic buck rail fence.

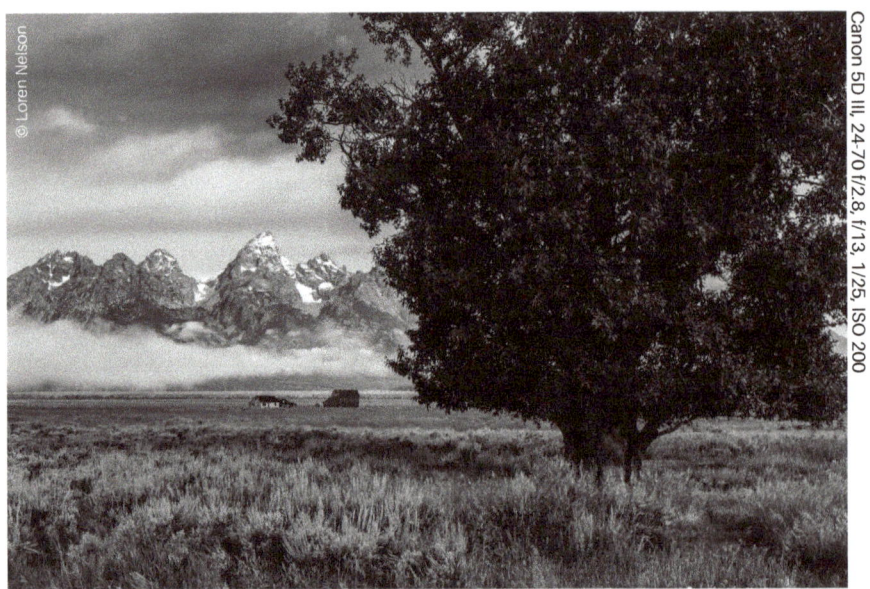

Monochrome view of a distant ranch.

Canon 5D III, 24-70 f/2.8, f/16, 1/80, ISO 200

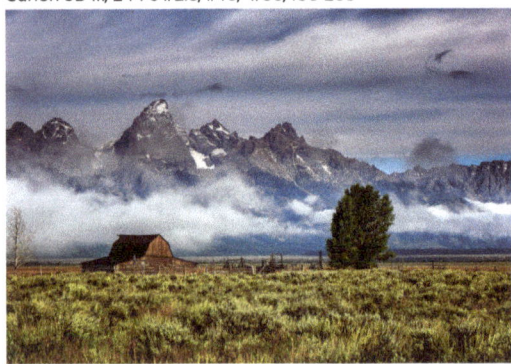

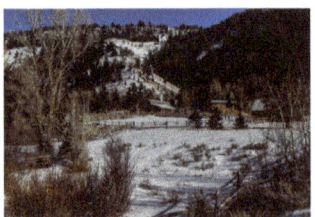

Pasture and barns with hay.

Distant Moulton Barn view.

Site Specifics:

Parking: Areas along Gros Ventre Road rarely are overloaded. The only busy site is Atherton Campground at Slide Lake. Campers are the dominant visitors here. If only stopping by for the day, parking is rarely, if ever, an issue.

Access: Some locations are drive-up like Slide Lake. Many views are along the roadside, making access easy. However, sites like the Slide Geology Walk, Grizzly Lake, and the like require hiking. The distances and elevation gain can be substantial for some sites, so be prepared.

GPS coordinates
43.63994, -110.61573 /
43°38'24"N, 110°36'57"
W12T 0530995E
4831955N

HOTSPOT #39

Kelly Warm Springs

DESCRIPTION:

Kelly Warm Springs is along the Gros Ventre Road just north of Kelly. The road and spring are accessible year-round on a well-maintained paved road. The parking area is large, and the walk to the springs is easy.

Steam from the springs attracts wildlife. This wildlife, in turn, makes this hot spring a desirable stop on any drive through the park. It is common to see waterfowl, bison, bear, moose, fox, coyote, bald eagles, elk, and deer around the spring.

Fog from the steaming water creates frost on the plants and animals here. The stream leading away from the spring is especially steamy in cold winter conditions. The water stays ice-free all year due to the thermal nature of the spring.

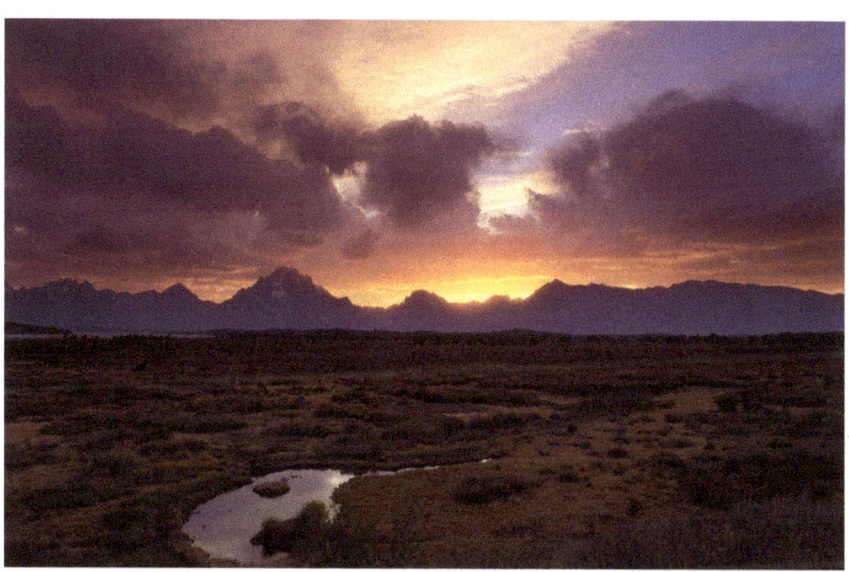

Nikon N80, 35mm f/2, f/11, 1/30, ISO 64

A vibrant sunset over the Tetons from Kelly Warm Springs.

MAP 5

DIRECTIONS

Distance from Town Square

Drive north from the square on North Cache Street which turns into US 191 for 6.9 miles (11.1 km) to an intersection. Turn right on Gros Ventre Road and continue 7 miles (11.2 km) to the town of Kelly. Continue on the road as it turns left (N) at Kelly and drive 1.1 miles (1.8 km). Turn right on the Gros Ventre Road, drive 0.4 mile (0.6 km), and park in the dirt lot.

HOTSPOT #39

📷 Site Specific Photography Tips

On occasion, bison will stand on the crest of the hill above the parking area. This is one location to capture a bison appearing to stand right in front of the summit of Grand Teton. Few other locations in the park afford this chance. A moderate telephoto is the best for this rare photograph.

Use a telephoto to capture animals here. Give them the space they need to survive in the harsh landscape.

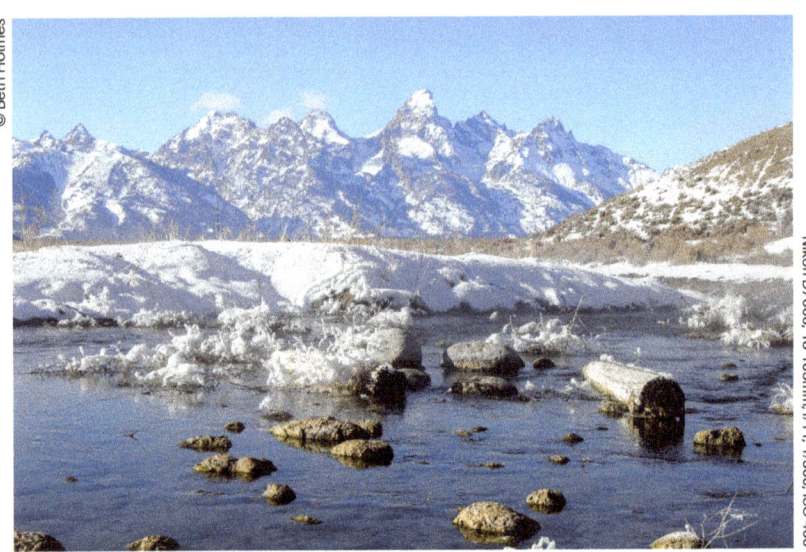

Canon 5D III, 24-70mm f/2.8, f/7.1, 1/200, ISO 400

Canon 7D, 100-400mm, f/5.6, 1/1000, ISO 100

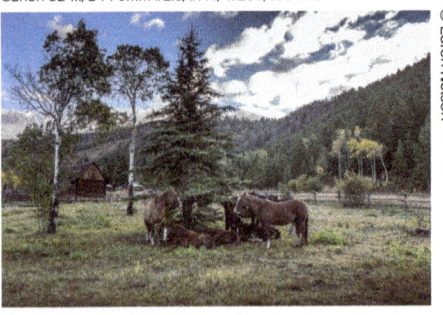

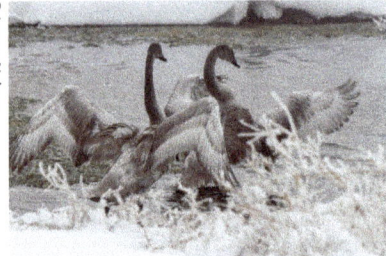

Along the paved Gros Ventre Road to the national forest area beyond the springs is a beautiful western ranch setting.

Young trumpeter swans frolic in the warm springs. The spring is ice-free in the coldest of the winter and attracts wildlife. Fog and the frost it creates add to the photo opportunities.

Site Specifics:

Parking: The parking area is large and rarely is busy. Note that the parking lot turns to mud during rainy or snowy conditions.

Access: This site has one of the few (pit) toilets open all year. It's a good point to turn to when in need.

HOTSPOT #40

Mormon Row

GPS coordinates

South Access
43.62460, -110.66395 /
43°37'29"N, 110°39'50"
W12T 0527111E
4830234N

North Access
43.66521, -110.66436 /
43°39'55"N, 110°39'52"
W12T 0527061E
4834745N

Photographing during afternoon rainy conditions can yield some of the most dramatic photographs. When looking for images to create, be mindful that not all of the best images are taken with the Tetons in the background. Be willing to adapt and shift around as conditions warrant.

Have a polarizer in your photographic kit that will fit all of you lenses. They can enhance or make rainbows visible. Use thread adapter rings to allow for only carrying one polarizer.

© Beth Holmes

Nikon D810, 150-600mm, f/9, 1/200, ISO 400

DESCRIPTION:

Mormon Row is the name given to the dirt road running from near the Gros Ventre Campground on the south to the Moulton Barns on the north. The road east of Blacktail Butte can be dry and dusty but can become impassable in a passenger car after a heavy rain.

The area is frequented by bison, pronghorn, and sometimes coyote, fox, and wolves. There are rustic fences dating to the last century and a couple of two-track side roads to Warm Springs Creek and Blacktail Butte. The road is gated and closed in the winter.

Many times, the Tetons are shrouded in clouds in unsettled weather. All is not lost. Look to the east, perhaps with one of the barns or other buildings in the foreground. So often, views looking east rather than west work quite well.

DIRECTIONS

Distance from Town Square

Drive north from Jackson on Cache Street to US 191 for 13.6 miles (21.8 km) past Moose and turn right on Antelope Flats Road. Drive 1.7 miles (2.7 km) to the Pink House parking area on the north side of the road.

MAP 5

📷 Site Specific Photography Tips

The wildlife photography at this location can be rather productive. Expect animals to be far away. Though, sometimes bison walk right by vehicles, affording photographers a chance to capture these animals up close. Stay well away from all animals, following the current Park Service regulations.

Blacktail Butte can be used as a foreground element with the Tetons in the background. For the enterprising photographer, the hike up the butte can yield some broad vistas and viewpoints. The parking lot at the north end of Mormon Row is a good starting point to access the butte's trail network.

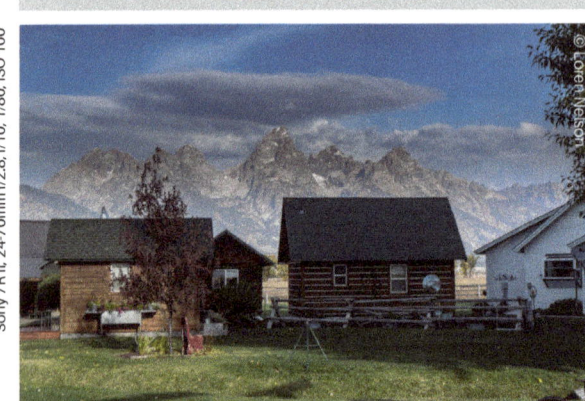

The Chambers Homestead has been used as a Bed and Breakfast lodge in the heart of Mormon Row for years. In 2019, it was purchased by the National Park Service for employee housing and is now closed to the public. This is a good spot for shooting the rustic cabins and outbuilding, a windmill, and a nice "leading line" stream. The Tetons are in the background and the best light is in the early morning for the cabins and late afternoon for the outbuildings and meadow.

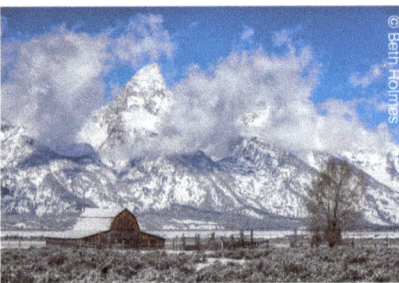

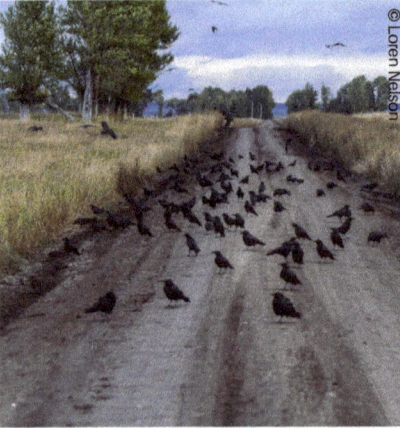

You never know what to expect on Mormon Row. Here a large murder of crows, not ravens, landed on the road.

Site Specifics:

Parking: When parking alongside the road, pull off as far as safely possible. Most of the road is along relatively flat sagebrush areas, so parking availability isn't an issue.

Access: The entire road is accessible by car in the summer. Expect crowds at the main interest points. Hiking up the butte takes some effort, as the trail gains moderate elevation when compared to other valley locations.

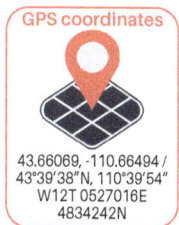

GPS coordinates
43.66069, -110.66494 /
43°39'38"N, 110°39'54"
W12T 0527016E
4834242N

HOTSPOT #41

Moulton Barn
(TA Moulton Barn)

DESCRIPTION:

Known locally as the Moulton barn, there are two famous barns. The John Moulton (north) and TA Moulton (south) barns, icons of Grand Teton National Park, were built by Mormon pioneers in the late 1800s that have been preserved by the Park Service. They are accessible by car from late spring to late fall and by skis or snowshoes in the winter months when the road is closed. The barns are frequented by bison and make wonderful foregrounds.

There is a parking area with a restroom building at the south barn. The short path allows visitors to walk on a separate path, off the main dirt road. This relatively new arrangement is designed to help prevent parking congestion. On fall mornings, the more photographed south barn can become quite busy. Photographers may be jockeying for the ideal tripod position.

Be aware that you and your tripod may cast a long shadow across the ground and even on the barn wall. Expect that there will be some visitors who will walk in front of a large crowd of waiting photographers. Due to the popular nature of this photographic opportunity, a little luck and a lot of patience will be required.

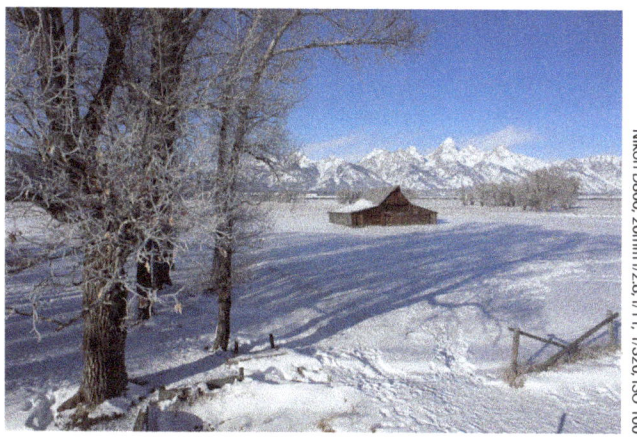

Nikon D800, 20mm f/2.8, f/11, 1/320, ISO 100

DIRECTIONS — Distance from Town Square

Drive north from Jackson on Cache Street to US 191 for 13.6 miles (21.8 km) past Moose and turn right on Antelope Flats Road. Drive 1.7 miles (2.7 km) to Mormon Row. Turn right and drive 0.2 mile (0.4 km) to the barn parking area.

📷 Site Specific Photography Tips

The best photography time is before sunrise. Arriving well before sunrise will ensure the best chance of catching alpenglow on the Cathedral Group. By the time the barn is lit by the sun, the desirable pink alpenglow will be completely gone from the mountains.

Once the sun rises above the eastern mountains and illuminates the barn, the contrast will increase in the shadows. Some photographers use high dynamic range imaging to capture detail in the shadows.

During May, June, and July, the sun rises north in the sky, increasing the chance photographer shadows will fall on the barn. There is a stand of cottonwood trees at the southern edge of the property. They are right in line with the barn to make compositions with. During the late spring and early summer, water runs through an irrigation and drainage ditch east of the barn. In fall, the cottonwoods northwest of the barn provide a colorful autumn backdrop.

The mountains east of the barn are not overly tall, so the actual sunrise happens only a few minutes after the official sunrise time. To capture untrampled snow at the barn, visit during or immediately after fresh snowfall. Visitors wander around the barn, leaving footprints. Expect people to wander around and in front of the barn at any time. The popularity of the location can make taking no-people photographs challenging.

Nikon D810, 24-120mm f/4, f/7.1, 1/500, ISO 140

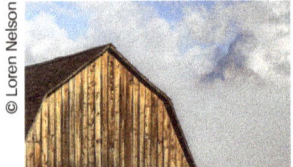
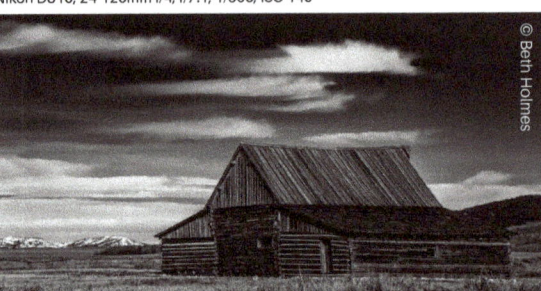

The north barn (John Moulton) with the Grand Teton poking through the clouds. Try a variety of compositions, positions, and telephoto lenses to capture something different than the classic shot.

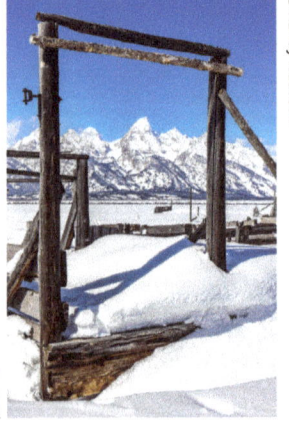
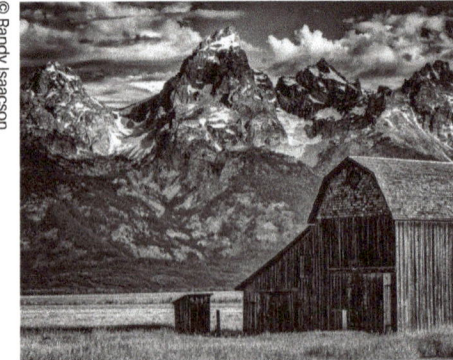

A Mormon farm in the winter.

Tom Murphy's homestead.

HOTSPOT #41

Nikon D810, 50mm f/1.4, f/2.8, 6 sec, ISO 400

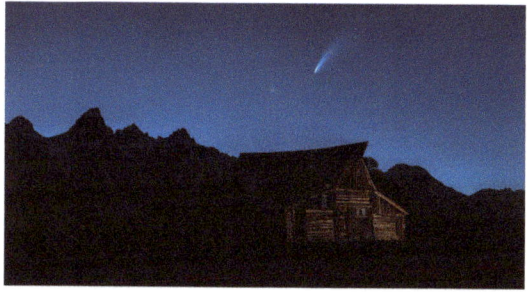

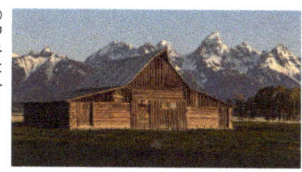

Comet NEOWISE made a photographic spectacle in July 2020 over the Tetons for enterprising photographers.

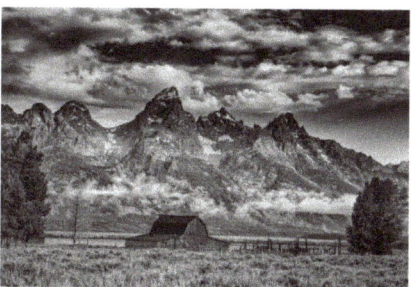

Monochrome version of the north barn on a cloudy day.

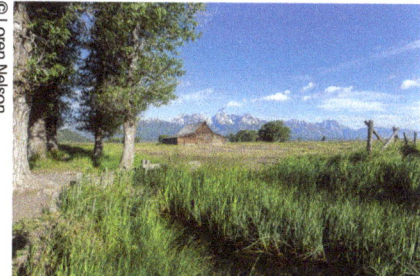

The south barn in summer.

Site Specifics:

Early morning photography is the best for capturing the light on the eastern side of the barn. The area around the barn is flat, but there are private buildings to the east, so creating a compressed shot with a telephoto lens is a challenge.

Groups of photographers may be at this site during the summer, jockeying for an optimal position along Mormon Row. Arrive very early to select a desired position. The creeks and water around the area can be quite useful to create a more complex composition.

Use a panoramic camera or wide-angle lens to capture a broad sweep of the land in and around the barn. Accessing the barn in the winter requires a ski or snowshoe walk through an exposed, snowy landscape. Be prepared for cold temperatures and strong winds in this area.

Parking: There is a parking area and restroom approximately 150 feet north of the barn. A separated pathway leads from the pathway to the front of the barn. There is a small amount of roadside parking by the barn, but it's limited.

Access: A small bridge crosses the irrigation ditch along the roadside, facilitating access to the barn. The barbed wire fence along the road limits photographers from walking around the fence or photographing over it.

This building is a protected historic structure and should not be disturbed in any way. Do not take samples or souvenirs per National Park regulations.

HOTSPOT #41

*HOT*SPOT *#42*

Pink House and John Moulton Barn

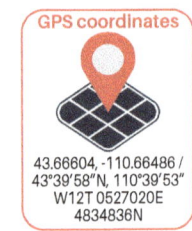

GPS coordinates
43.66604, -110.66486 /
43°39'58"N, 110°39'53"
W12T 0527020E
4834836N

DESCRIPTION:

The Pink House and John Moulton barn is an excellent location in all seasons. Guided tours and tour buses can make the location busy during the height of summer. It is difficult to take no-people photos, especially mid-day. As the sun rises early in June, there tend to be fewer crowds as visitors are busy eating breakfast in town.

The best photographic times are in the morning for sunlight on the east-facing buildings. When Alpenglow strikes the upper reaches of the Cathedral Group, the house and barn will be only lit by the sky. The blue skylight will dull and tint the pink color on the house until the sun rises above the eastern horizon.

During sunset, the east side of the house and barn will darken up and be backlit, adding exposure & dynamic range challenges. Once the sun drops below the mountains, the contrast will reduce, making it easier to select a correct exposure. High dynamic range images are a viable option for this site.

Be aware your shadow may be cast onto the buildings in the morning. If this is undesirable for your composition, mind where the sunrise will occur versus your position relative to the buildings. Use a sunrise/sunset table and a compass to determine the best place to avoid casting a shadow.

Access during the winter requires a hike/ski/snowshoe due to road closures. There is no shelter from wind and precipitation from the parking area to the buildings. Be prepared for harsh, cold conditions and deep snow.

Nikon D610, 24-120mm, f/8, 1/640, ISO 200

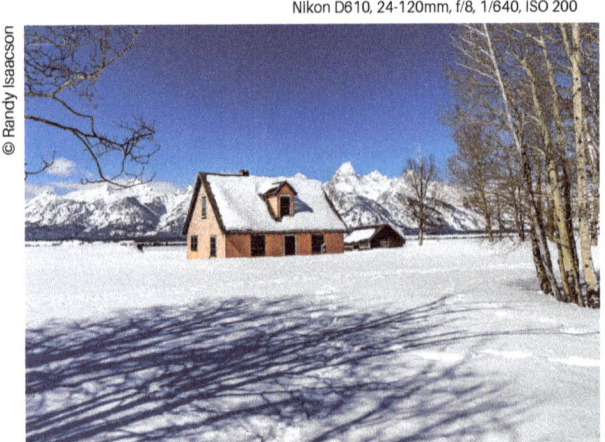

Access to the Pink House in the snow is done by foot, ski, or snowshoe. Be prepared for cold, exposed conditions in the winter.

DIRECTIONS

Distance from Town Square

Drive north from Jackson on Cache Street to US 191 for 13.6 miles (21.8 km) past Moose and turn right on Antelope Flats Road. Drive 1.7 miles (2.7 km) to the Pink House parking area on the north side of the road.

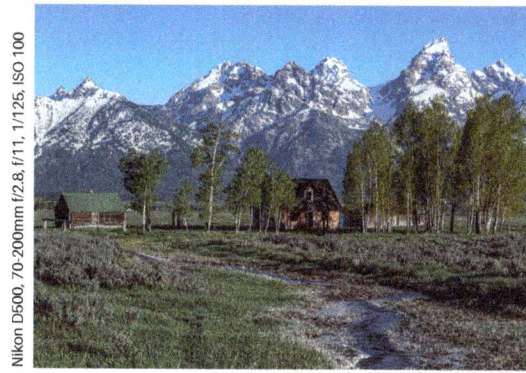

The stream leading to the Pink House along Mormon Row makes for a good leading line to guide the viewer's eye along a diagonal pathway.

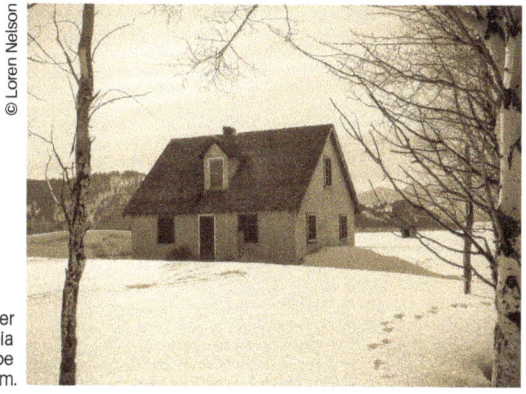

Late winter afternoon in sepia rendered in Adobe Lightroom.

Site Specifics:

Parking: There is a mid-sized parking lot for visitors. It does become busy during the mid-day in the summer. A bus and large vehicle turn-around is available 380 feet (116 m) east of the parking area.

Access: The access is drive-up during much of the year. The Park Service closes Antelope Flats Road during the winter. Accessing the barn during the winter requires a snowshoe or cross-country ski trip. The site is 0.9 mile (1.4 km) from the Antelope Flats Road gate parking area. There is no shelter along this route in the winter. Be prepared for cold, windy, and exposed conditions for winter photography.

The buildings are protected historic structures and should not be disturbed in any way. Do not take samples or souvenirs in accordance with National Park regulations.

📷 Site Specific Photography Tips

The classic composition for the barn is taken from the eastern side of the building, with the mountain range to the west in the background. The symmetric nature of the Pink House makes choosing interesting compositions easy. The biggest challenge is standing far enough from the house so it doesn't visually tower over the mountain range.

There is a line of trees along the eastern edge of the dirt road that leads to the barn. They make taking a telephoto image from the east of the house difficult. Once the leaves fall off, it is easier to see the house from the east.

The barn has no trees to the east, so taking telephoto images is easier than the house. The biggest challenge is finding a time when there are no people. The best time to avoid the crowds is to show up as early as possible. The sun rises early in June when there are fewer visitors. This is arguably the best time to photograph the house and barn.

The area around the buildings is flat and covered by sage. It is relatively easy to walk through the sage to find your ideal composition. There are a few minor ditches that run through the area but none are impassable.

There are options for taking both wide-angle and telephoto images from multiple angles. Since it is possible to stand farther away from the barn, it is possible to compress the mountains and make them look larger behind the building.

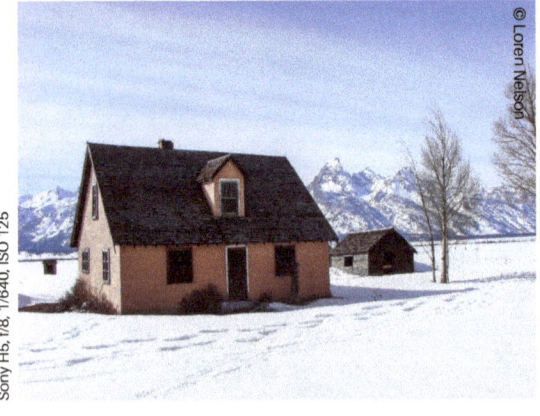

The color of the Pink House adds visual interest to an otherwise monochromatic landscape.

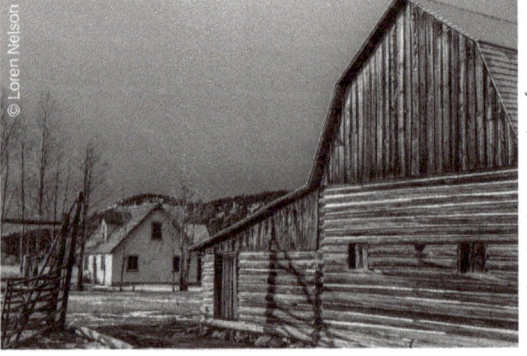

An autumn morning rendered to B&W in Adobe Lightroom.

GPS coordinates
43.61501, -110.46197 /
43°36'54"N, 110°27'43"
W12T 0543414E
4829255N

HOTSPOT #43

Red and Lavender Hills

DESCRIPTION:

Located deep in the Gros Ventre Range, the Red and Lavender Hills are unique landscape features of the Jackson Hole region. The hills themselves are eroded masses in the geologically active area that contains the Gros Ventre Slide.

The unique aspect of these hills is how they change color throughout the day when viewed from the road. These hills tower over the valley, creating an otherworldly badlands landscape. Directly across from this pair of hills is a large ranch with green grass in the spring and summer. The contrast of the rough landscape against the pastoral beauty of the ranch cannot be understated. It has to be seen and experienced first-hand.

The other photographic option is to hike to a few different viewpoints on the Red Hills. The Lavender Hills provides a gentle pastel backdrop over the landscape. The hike to the viewpoint is hot and dusty in the summer. The payoff is well worth the sweat and effort.

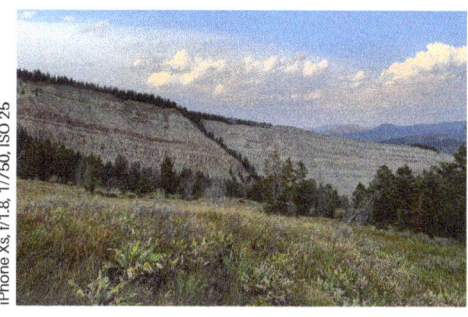
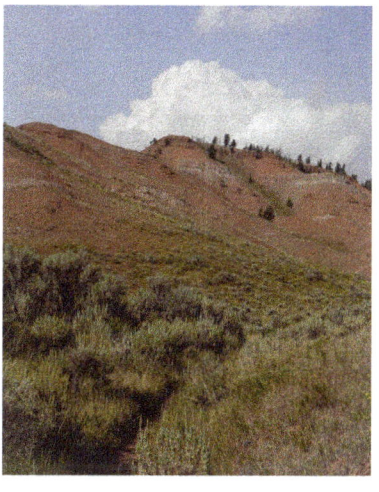

DIRECTIONS — Distance from Town Square

Drive north from the square on North Cache Street which turns into US 191 for 6.9 miles (11.1 km) to an intersection. Turn right on Gros Ventre Road and continue 7 miles (11.2 km) to the town of Kelly. At 1.1 miles (1.8 km) north of Kelly, turn right on Gros Ventre Road. Drive 10.2 miles (16.4 km) to a grass and dirt turnout on the south side of the road without blocking the steel gate.

📷 Site Specific Photography Tips

As with most landscapes, the hills are best photographed in the morning or afternoon. Midday sunlight tends to wash out the subtle hues of the Lavender Hills. Early morning light can turn the Red Hills brick red for an hour. By midday, the red will fade to a hazy, dusty southwestern red. The Lavender Hills area is pretty before or after sunrise. Make sure to shoot in raw for easier color correction to bring out the true lavender hues of the hills.

The early or late sunlight sculpts the hills with shadows, bringing out their undulating surface. A general wide-angle to a normal zoom lens is the most effective choice here. A 24-70mm or an 18-105mm lens will provide the best options.

Use a telephoto lens to create a panoramic image of the hills. At the summit and mid-hill viewpoint, a versatile zoom lens comes in handy. The distant Teton Range peaks of the Gros Ventre River valley are 19.6 miles (31.5 km) away at a bearing of 294° northwest.

A sweeping panoramic photo from the main viewpoint on the Red Hills is unmatched in Jackson Hole.

Using a color-calibrated chip card and a calibrated white balance card here is a wise choice. They can make all the difference in being able to extract the most pleasing colors from photographs.

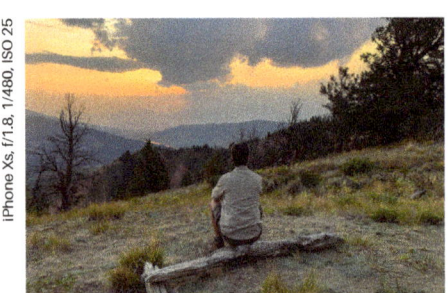

iPhone Xs, f/1.8, 1/480, ISO 25

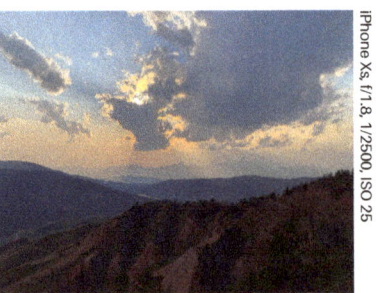

iPhone Xs, f/1.8, 1/2500, ISO 25

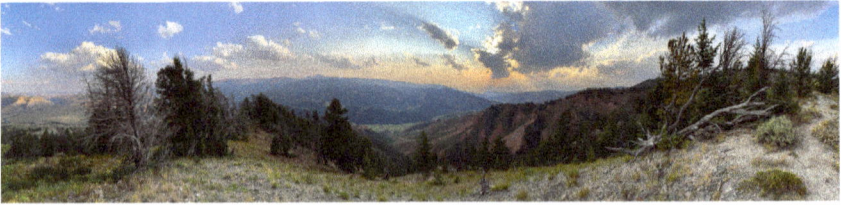

iPhone, f/1.8, 1/1000, ISO 32

Site Specifics:

Parking: Park off the dirt road on the south side of Gros Ventre Road, across from the hills. Ensure your vehicle is not blocking access to the private ranch.

Access: For general photos of the hills, photograph near the roadway. To photograph from the upper viewpoints, be prepared for a steep and strenuous hike.

HOTSPOT #44

Shane Cabins

GPS coordinates
43.64406, -110.60478 /
43°38'39"N, 110°36'17"
W12T 0531875E
4832416N

DESCRIPTION:

Officially known as the Luther Taylor Homestead, locals refer to these historic buildings as the Shane Cabins. The rustic wood buildings are at the site of the filming of *Shane*, the classic 1953 western movie. The deteriorating cabins provide contrasting texture and foreground elements for shots with the Tetons in the distance.

The old cabins are frequented by bison and other wildlife year-round. As the cabins are located in a depression, they do not have a broad expanse view of the area. Rather, they are situated to have a view of the Cathedral Group to the west and no long-range views east. The Gros Ventre Road is maintained through the winter so the area is accessible all year.

The National Park is allowing the buildings to naturally deteriorate. Over the years the cabins have slowly fallen apart. Be aware of the exposed nails and broken planking in the buildings.

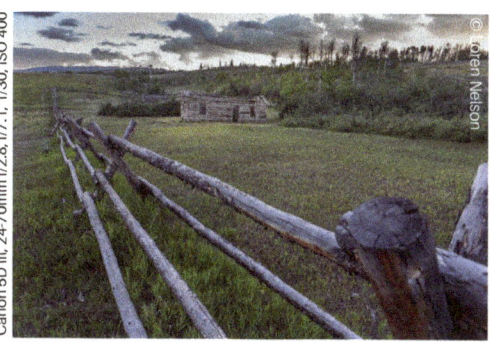

An early August morning yielded excellent photographic results.

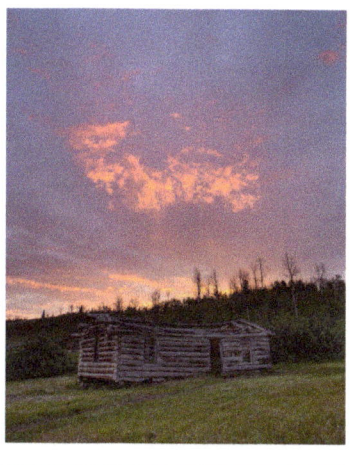

DIRECTIONS

Distance from Town Square

Drive north from the square on North Cache Street which turns into US 191 for 6.9 miles (11.1 km) to an intersection. Turn right on Gros Ventre Road and continue 7 miles (11.2 km) to the town of Kelly. Continue on the road as it turns left (N) at Kelly and drive 1.1 miles (1.8 km). Turn right on the Gros Ventre Road and continue 1.1 miles (1.7 km) to a small turnout on the north side of the road. From the turnout, walk 170 feet (52 m) north to reach an opening in the buck rail fence to access the cabins.

Site Specific Photography Tips

Wide-angle, normal, and slight telephoto lenses (12-80mm) tend to be the best options for capturing images at the Shane Cabins. There are a few remaining cabin window openings at the site, providing the opportunity to frame the Tetons through them. Using too wide of a lens for this image will cause the mountains to appear quite small.

The texture of the old wood matches the feeling of the landscape. Use a macro lens to capture the wood grain and the purple thistle that often dots the property.

Due to the nature of the topography around the cabins, creating telephoto compressed images of the cabins with the mountain range is difficult. The hill to the east is higher than the cabins and the shrubbery encroaches on the property edge.

The buildings are protected historic structures and should not be disturbed in any way. Do not take samples or souvenirs in accordance with National Park regulations.

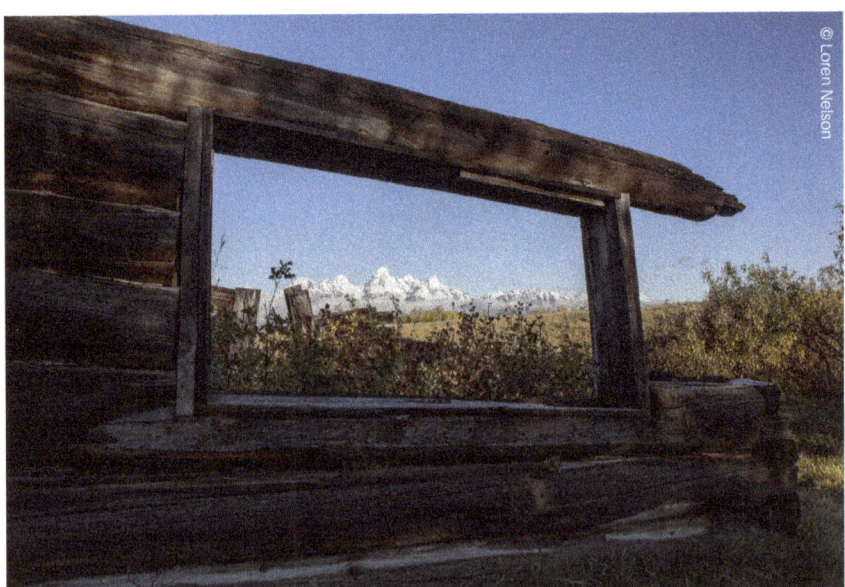

Using the remaining window frame on the north side of the large cabin to frame the Cathedral Group.

Site Specifics:

Parking: The roadside turnout is small and only accommodates a few vehicles. However, there are rarely more than a few visitors at any time at this site.

Access: The cabins are accessible all year. Walking to them requires a short stroll along a well-tracked trail. The cabins are visible from the roadway so there is no problem in finding them.

HOTSPOT #45
Sleeping Indian

GPS coordinates
43.55418, -110.60377 /
43°33'15"N, 110°36'14"
W12T 0532005E
4822435N

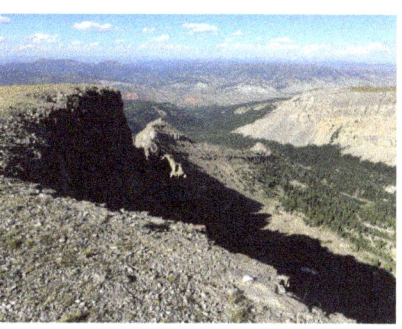

Blue Miner Lake viewed from Sleeping Indian.

iPhone 6, f/2.2, 1/1000, ISO 32

The hike to the summit of Sheep Mountain, locally known as "Sleeping Indian," is a worthwhile day hike. The non-technical trail provides the energetic with endless views to the summit.

DESCRIPTION:

Officially named Sheep Mountain, this iconic mountain is locally referred to as Sleeping Indian. This 11,239-feet (3,426-m) massive mountain rises high above the eastern edge of Jackson Hole and is immediately identifiable by its shape and height. The mountain has two summits. The northern highpoint is named the Belly. This is the summit most everyone hikes. The other highpoint is the Nose (11,106 feet / 3385 m) which is rarely climbed.

There are three possible options for photography involving Sleeping Indian. Each has its pros and cons.

The first option is shooting from the valley, from the Grand Teton park sign to the Jackson Hole airport, along Highway 89/191. These views are classic and are well-regarded. Be careful when parking off the side of the road if you are not using a turnout. The safest locations are at the Grand Teton park sign and the parking area at the Highway 89/191 and Gros Ventre Road roundabout.

The second option is from the Elk Refuge Road. Broad views are best from the largest parking area on the southeast side of the road near the broad Millers Butte. Farther along the Refuge Road, at Curtis Canyon Road, is another excellent photography point. Sleeping Indian becomes visible after cresting the rise past the Miller House near the Amphitheater where bighorn sheep are commonly seen.

The third option is to hike to the summit of Sleeping Indian. This hike is 5.3 miles (8.5 km) long and gains 4,217 feet (1,285 m) to reach the summit. Views of central Jackson Hole are unparalleled from this vantage point.

DIRECTIONS
Distance from Town Square

Drive north from Jackson on US 191 for 5 miles (8 km) to Grand Teton park sign turnout. This is where Sleeping Indian becomes visible.

Site Specific Photography Tips

From the viewpoint of the Grand Teton park sign 5 miles (8 km) north of the Town Square on Highway 89/191, a moderate telephoto lens will yield excellent results. Avoid standing too close to the elk fence to keep it out of the image. The same lens combination is useful at the parking area at the Highway 89/191 and Gros Ventre Road roundabout. This parking area offers clear views and trees for foreground objects.

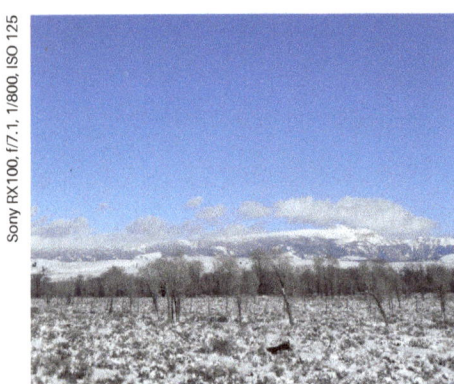

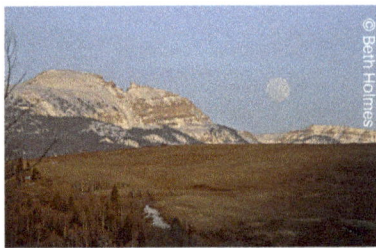

Using software to calculate the moon's position relative to the mountain, captivating photographs can be made.

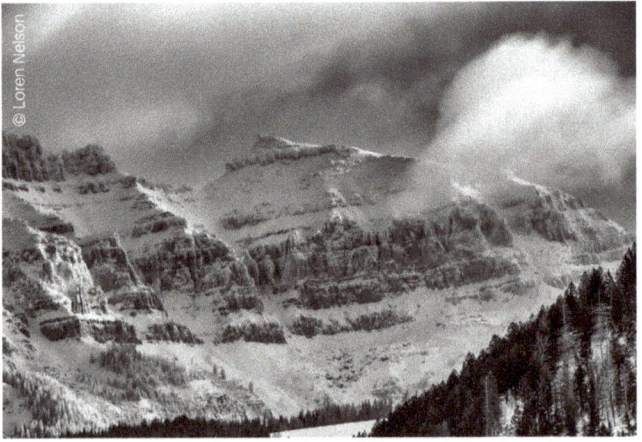

A monochrome rendition of Sleeping Indian in a winter storm.

Site Specifics:

Parking: Parking at the Grand Teton park sign is readily available. Parking at the Gros Ventre Road junction roundabout can be busy in the middle of summer. Parking along the Elk Refuge Road is always available. Only park in designated locations along the Refuge Road. Roadside parking is not allowed inside the Elk Refuge.

Access: Sleeping Indian is visible from any point described in this section. The summit hike is substantial and requires the better part of a day.

HOTSPOT #46

Teton Science School

GPS coordinates
43.66967, -110.59685 /
43°40'11"N, 110°35'49"
W12T 0532501E
4835264N

DESCRIPTION:

A unique school campus lies at the western edge of the Gros Ventre Range in Jackson Hole. The Teton Science School, a private school, is an excellent access point to forests in the eastern section of Jackson Hole.

The rustic campus hosts many educational activities and its wooded location makes it a great spot for wildlife. The open meadows to the west have ample wildflowers in the spring and early summer. Aspen groves to the south and east of the campus show wonderful examples of autumn color.

The Kelly campus of the Teton Science School is located about 1 mile (1.6 km) east of Elk Flats Road and about 1.5 miles (2.4 km) north of Kelly. The paved road is maintained year-round.

Creeks, hills, and groves of beautiful broadleaf trees dot the landscape around the school. When driving toward the school, the road appears to rise into the foothills. The campus sits at the very edge of the hills while the dirt road continues to make its way upward.

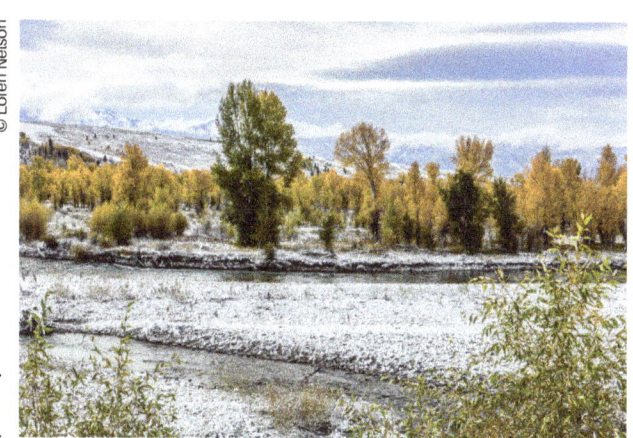

© Loren Nelson

Canon 5D III, 24-70mm f/2.8, f/22, 1/50, ISO 200

The meadow and woods are north of the road heading east to the Teton Science School Kelly campus. This area is frequented by moose in the late fall and winter.

MAP 5

DIRECTIONS

Distance from Town Square

Drive north from the square on North Cache Street which turns into US 191 for 6.9 miles (11.1 km) to an intersection. Turn right on Gros Ventre Road and continue 7 miles (11.2 km) to the town of Kelly. Continue on the road as it turns left (N) at Kelly and drive 2 miles (3.6 km) and turn right (E) on Ditch Creek Road. Continue 1.7 miles (2.7 km) to the campus.

Site Specific Photography Tips

The hiking trails around the school lend themselves to classic wide-angle images with the mountains in the distance.

Visiting in September when the aspen and cottonwood leaves change color is a prime photography time. Groves of aspen dot the landscape around the campus and are easy subjects to frame.

Canon 5D III, 24-70mm f/2.8, f/11, 1/80, ISO 100

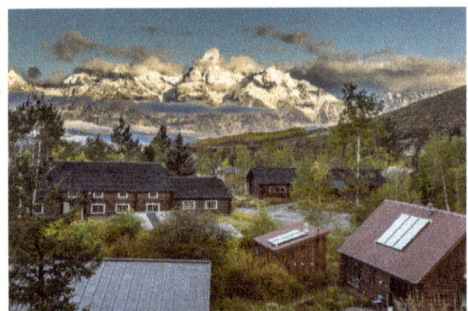

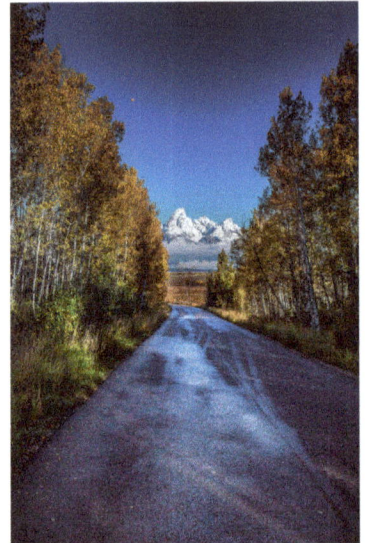

The Kelly campus of the Teton Science School overlooks Jackson Hole and the Tetons to the west. It is photogenic and accessible year-round.

The Gros Ventre Road south and east of the Teton Science School is a perfect spot for the aspen's autumn color. Natural frames for the Tetons are perfect in any season.

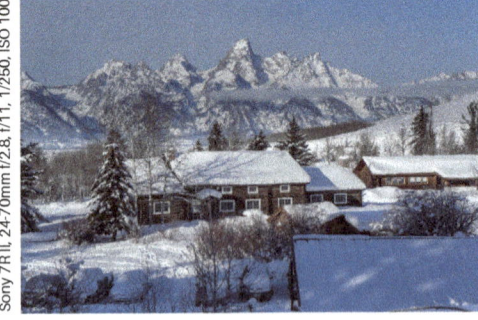

The historic main lodge of the Teton Science School with the Tetons and early morning lenticular clouds.

Site Specifics:

Parking: Parking is plentiful and available before or after school hours on the weekends. During the week, it is best to avoid school hours to respect the student and faculty privacy. The parking lots can fill up during school hours.

Access: Note that this is an active school campus. Respect any school hours and the restrictions that might be in place. The hiking trails adjacent to the campus are easy to moderate.

HOTSPOT #47

Wedding Tree

GPS coordinates
43.63194, -110.56653 /
43°37'55"N, 110°34'00"
W12T 0534967E
4831086N

DESCRIPTION:

Known by locals as the Wedding Tree, this particularly stately conifer, believed to be a white pine, offers a compelling composition. With the tree as a frame, it is a popular spot to photograph the Cathedral Group across the valley. The site is popular for weddings and engagement photos.

The hike to the tree is easy, covering 0.1 mile (0.2 km) from the trailhead to the best viewpoint. The path only gains 13 feet (4 m) of elevation over the whole walk. Although the path is not wheelchair accessible, mobility-challenged hikers should have little difficulty reaching this beautiful and unique spot. People of all ages and abilities have walked to this worthwhile photography spot.

Originally a popular campsite, the Forest Service has restricted overnight camping here. The popularity of the spot had a negative impact with waste and trash being strewn through the area. It has since been cleaned up and looked after by the Forest Service.

As the name implies, photographers use this spot for engagement photography. It is also popular with wedding parties. Although there are no restrictions for casual photography and videography, permits for events may be required. Check with the Forest Service for the latest information and regulations.

Interestingly, there are countless trees to use as a foreground with the Cathedral Group in the background across the valley. However, access can be difficult and there are few locations with a flat spot to stage an image. The combination of easy access and ideal framing makes the Wedding Tree location unique in the Jackson Hole area.

DIRECTIONS

Distance from Town Square

Drive north from the square on North Cache Street which turns into US 191 for 6.9 miles (11.1 km) to the roundabout intersection. Turn right on Gros Ventre Road and continue 7 miles (11.2 km) to the town of Kelly. Continue on the road as it turns left (N) at Kelly and drive 1.1 miles (1.8 km). Turn right on the Gros Ventre Road and continue 3.6 miles (5.8 km) to the small turnoff. If you see the large wooden Gros Ventre Slide Sign, you have driven too far.

HIKING DIRECTIONS

Begin at the west end of the turnout where the trail starts. From here, the trail meanders over a few rocks before leveling out. The trail then continues through sagebrush and conifers. If you are early in the season, there will be a cornucopia of flowers to make the hike more memorable. From the trailhead, the Wedding Tree will become visible in 250 feet (76 m). Once you arrive at the end of the trail, the tree is unmistakable. Enjoy taking photographs and respect this irreplaceable landmark.

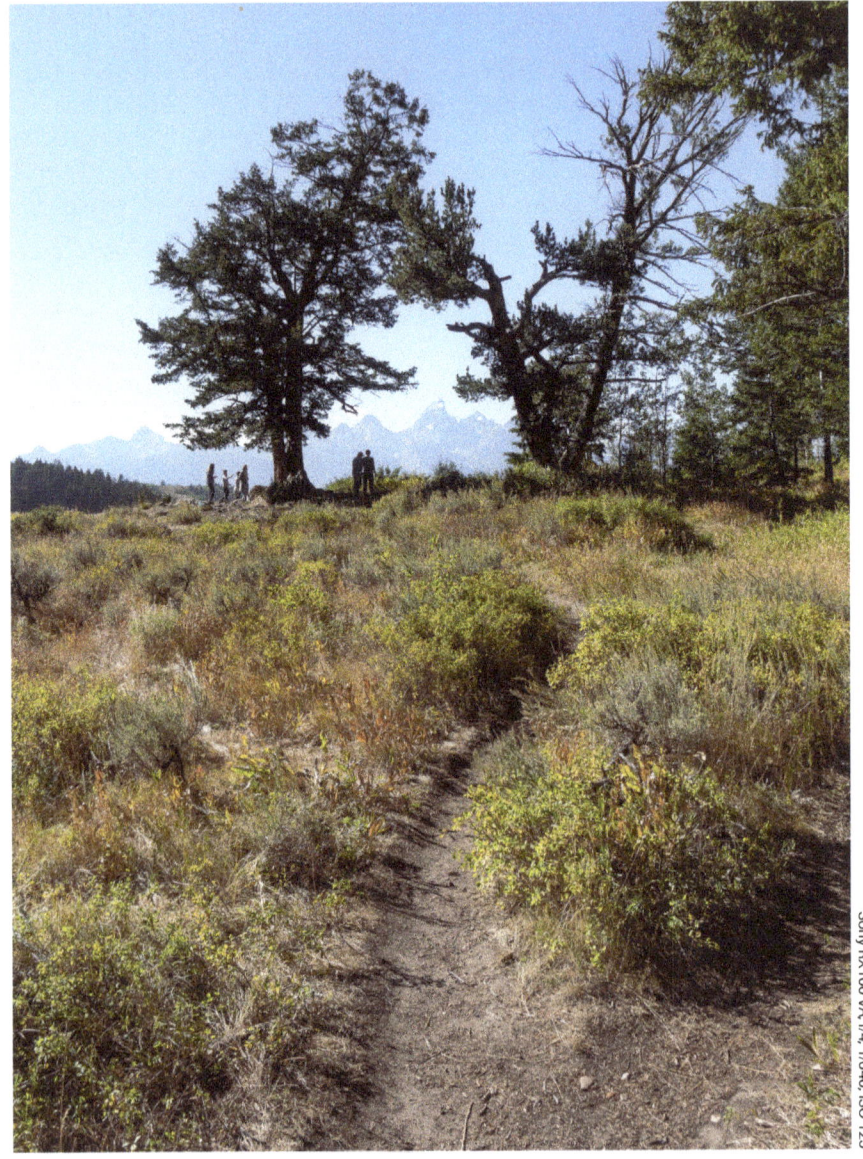

Sony RX100 VA, f/4, 1/640, ISO 125

MAP 5

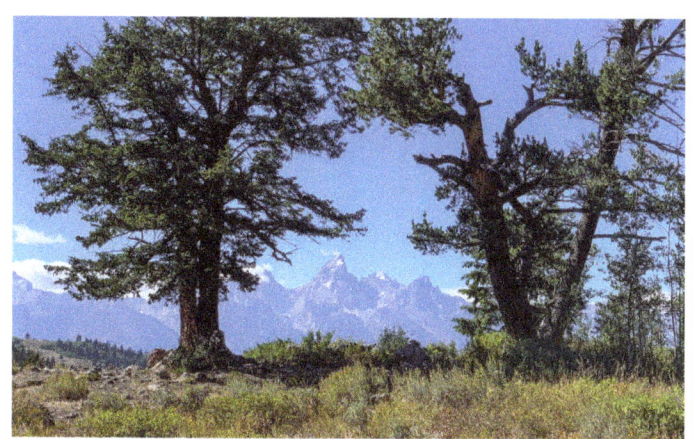

iPhone Xs, f/2.4, 1/800, ISO 16

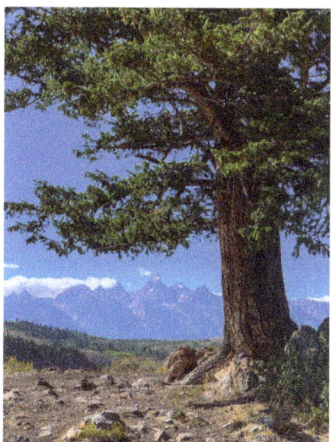
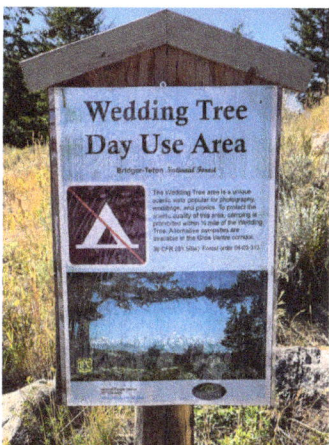

📷 Site Specific Photography Tips

The Wedding Tree cannot be seen from a significant distance to use a long telephoto. This makes creating compressed images difficult. The farthest distance the tree is visible is roughly 160 feet (49 m). To have the Cathedral Group and tree in a single frame forces the photographer to be even closer to the tree. In order to capture the tree without making the Cathedral Group look tiny, photograph the tree as far away as possible. Standing too close and using a wide-angle lens will make the mountains look small. They will lose their visual impact. The Cathedral Group is 14.1 miles (22.6 km) away at 302° west.

For portraits, many use a small portion of the tree's rough bark with the rocks at the base as compositional elements. There are multiple options for solo and group images. Bring a tripod with a remote release or timer to capture your whole group.

To have the tree lit, photograph this location early in the morning. Once the sun rises in the sky, the contrast on the tree will increase and the atmosphere will turn blue, making for a dull image. Near sunset, the tree and mountains will be in silhouette.

MAP 5

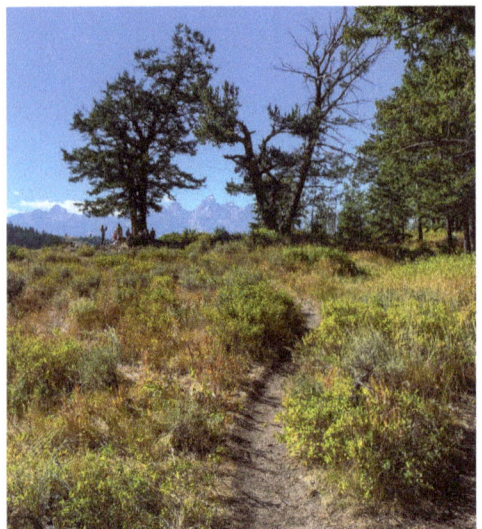

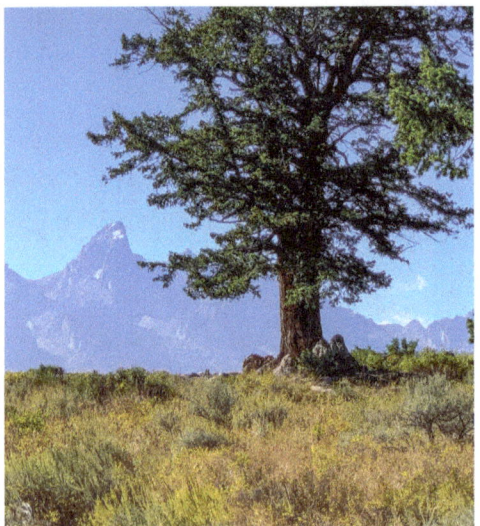

One of the interesting aspects of this tree is that it stands next to another gnarled pine which together creates a near-perfect frame for the Cathedral Group and Grand Teton in particular. This is why the site is so popular with photographers and event planners who are familiar with it.

The particular challenge with this site is that the photograph cannot be taken far away due to the surrounding trees. Not until the last short distance is the whole scene revealed. If an enterprising photographer figures out a method to take the photograph at a longer distance, a more dramatic scale of the mountains versus the trees can be taken.

As it is, the scene is difficult to match. There are few spots on the eastern side of Jackson Hole with a flat location and a weathered-looking old pine surrounded by open space that is also easily accessible. Countless other trees dot the eastern valley landscape but there are few if any like this with the right elements.

Site Specifics:

Parking: The paved parking area faces a steep ravine where the Gros Ventre River flows below the location. There is room for several vehicles, though the turnout has filled up in the busy summer season. During the winter, the trail is accessible. Snowshoes or skis are recommended to facilitate walking over uneven snow-covered ground.

Access: To view the Wedding Tree, a short 0.1-mile (0.2-km) hike along an easy trail is required.

Permit information: Bridger-Teton National Forest, 340 N. Cache, Jackson, WY 83001, (307) 739-5500

TETON VALLEY
COVERING HOTSPOTS #48-50

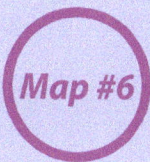

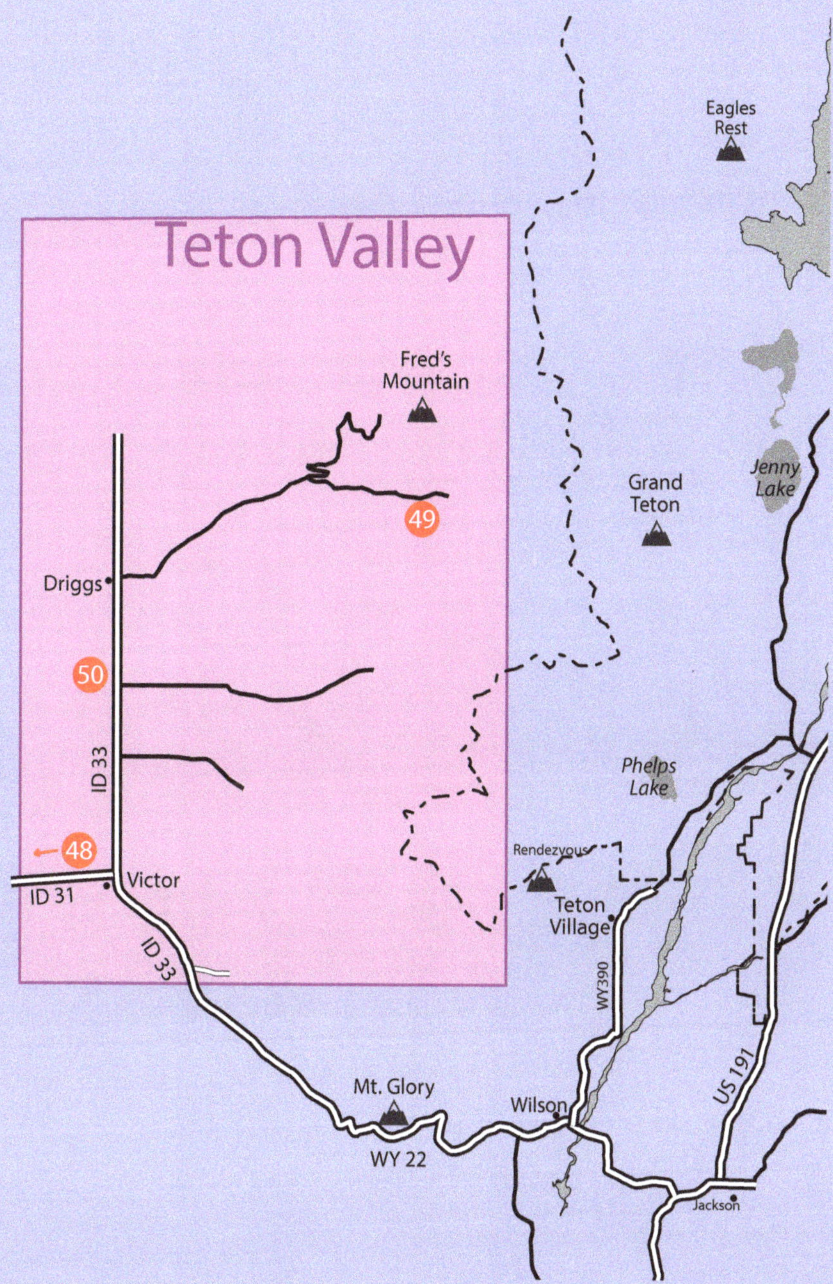

HOTSPOT #48

Pine Creek Pass

DESCRIPTION:

GPS coordinates
43.57139, -111.21570 /
43°34'17"N, 111°12'57"
W12T 0482582E
4824293N

Pine Creek Pass connects Teton Valley with Swan Valley at an elevation of 6,764 feet (2,062 m). This particular pass is not as treacherous compared to driving over Teton Pass in the winter. The vehicles passing through this area rarely stop because they are heading to or from somewhere. There are excellent photographic options on this pass because of the light visitation.

At the top of the pass is a parking lot with a dirt road to access camping areas. The camping area is 600 feet (183 m) above Teton Valley. The elevation difference is enough to provide a unique view of Victor, Idaho and the west side of the Teton Mountains.

Grand Teton and other summits rise out of the western foothills of Teton Valley. Viewed from this location, the Cathedral Group summits appear to be taking stealthy glances over the foothills. There is an air of mystery and drama when the Teton summits are viewed from this location.

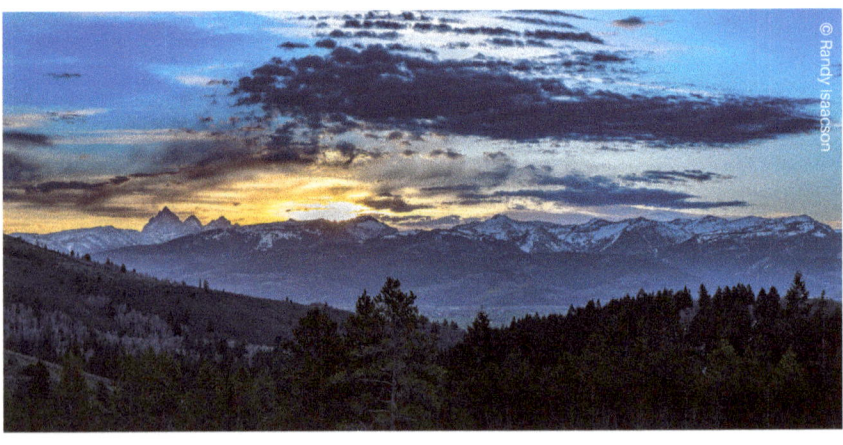

Nikon Z7, 24-70mm f/4, f/8, 100, ISO 100 © Randy Isaacson

DIRECTIONS

Distance from Town Square

Drive 1.5 miles (2.4 km) west from the Town Square on Broadway to Highway 22 and turn right (N). Continue 24.4 miles (39.3 km) to Victor, Idaho. Turn left (W) on ID 31 and continue 6.8 miles (10.9 km) to reach Pine Creek Pass.

📷 Site Specific Photography Tips

Longer lenses are useful here to capture the farther away summits in Grand Teton. Lenses with a 50mm – 105mm range are the most useful for this style of image. Wide-angle lenses will be good to capture local scenery, though they will make the faraway mountains appear small.

All along the roadway near the pass, the Cathedral Group summits appear and disappear from view. This allows the enterprising photographer the chance to select different foreground elements. Parts of the road have no safe roadside parking. Keep this in mind as you explore the area, looking for an ideal vantage point.

There is a Forest Service road that leads south at the top of Pine Creek Pass to camping areas. The dirt road that leads away southeast of the large parking area provides good viewpoints of Teton Valley and the distant Teton Range.

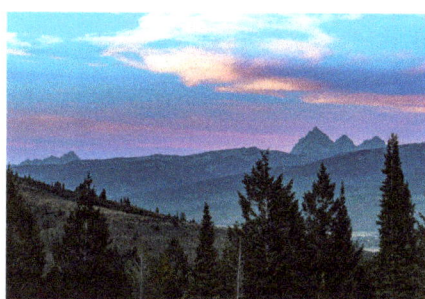
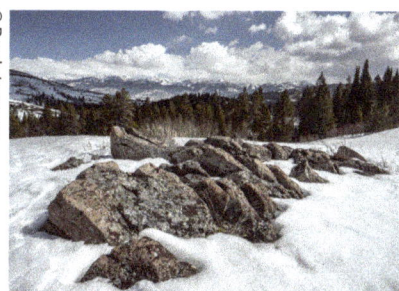

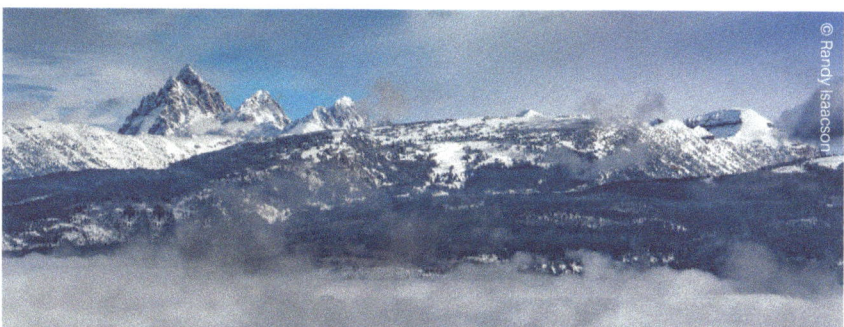

Nikon D500, 70-200mm f/2.8, f/8, 1/400, ISO 100

Site Specifics:

Parking: Pine Creek Pass has several turnouts for parking and one near the summit. Few stop at these viewpoints to take advantage of them. As a consequence, there is rarely if ever a shortage of parking.

Access: The summit and eastern side of Pine Creek Pass is all accessible by vehicle. There are a few turnouts and campgrounds to explore.

HOTSPOT #49

Teton Canyon Idaho

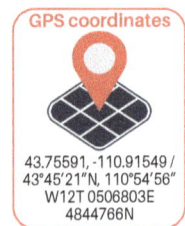

GPS coordinates
43.75591, -110.91549 /
43°45'21"N, 110°54'56"
W12T 0506803E
4844766N

DESCRIPTION:

Teton Canyon is the busiest destination in Teton Valley, Idaho. The multiple trailheads and attractions accessed by this canyon are only outmatched by Cascade and Paintbrush Canyons reached from the eastern side of the Tetons. Several popular destinations with excellent photo options are available from the Teton Canyon trailhead.

The one prime viewing point of the northeastern side of the Cathedral Group is from Table Mountain. This grueling 3.6-mile (5.8-km) hike with a 4,000-foot (1,219-m) elevation gain pays off at the summit. The Tetons come into full view from this vantage point. During the afternoon, sunlight plays off the northern faces of Grand Teton and Teewinot.

A long, 7.2-mile (11.7-km) hike to Alaska Basin, deep inside Grand Teton, is also best accessed from the western side of the park. The trail that leads into the mountains is gentle at first and eventually leads to either the Devil's Stairs or a steep climb. At the tops of either option, stunning views of Teton Canyon and the southern Cathedral Group can be enjoyed.

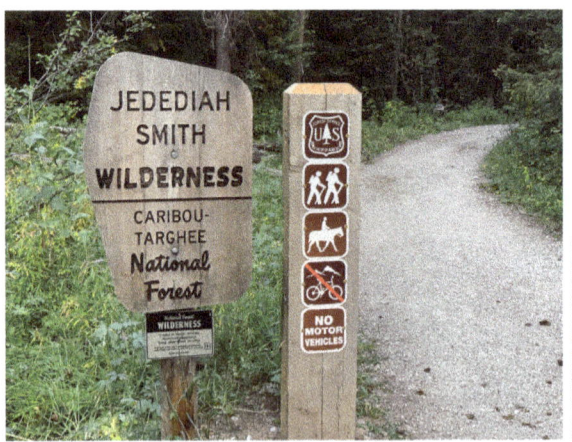

iPhone Xs, f/2.4, 1/90, ISO 125

DIRECTIONS

Distance from Town Square

Drive 1.5 miles (2.4 km) west from the Town Square on Broadway to Highway 22 and turn right (N). Continue 24.4 miles (39.3 km) to Victor, Idaho. Continue north on ID-33 for 8.3 miles (13.4 km) and turn right on Ski Hill Road. Drive 6.6 miles (10.6 km) and turn on Teton Canyon Road. Continue 4.4 miles (7.1 km) on the dirt road to the east parking lot.

📷 Site Specific Photography Tips

Longer lenses are useful at the summit of Table Mountain to bring in the Cathedral Group summits. Normal to moderate telephoto lenses are an excellent choice for some of the waterfalls and creeks in the area. Bring a neutral density filter for full daylight shots to feather out the water. A wide-angle or panoramic approach is best for Teton Shelf at the top of Devil's Stairs.

Be prepared with bear spray, as black bears and grizzly bears regularly wander through the area. Although the trails in the area are highly trafficked, that does not appear to deter the wildlife too much. The chance encounter with any animal is exciting and can make for good photography. Keep in mind that these animals are wild and should never be approached too closely.

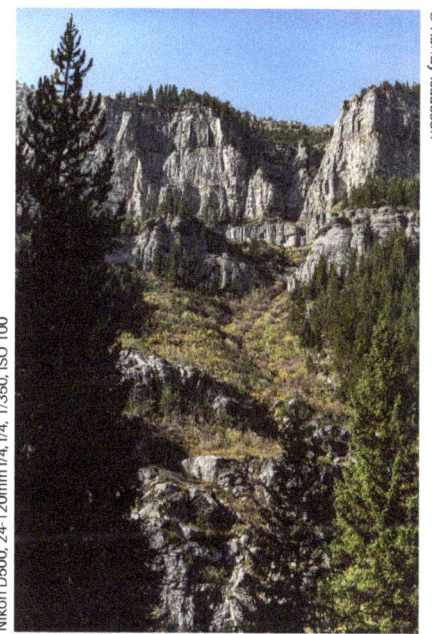
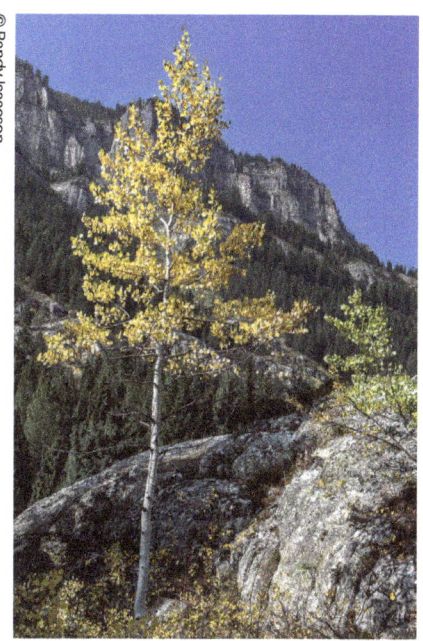

© Randy Isaacson

Nikon D500, 24-120mm f/4, f/4, 1/350, ISO 100

Nikon D500, 24-120mm f/4, f/5.6, 1/320, ISO 100

Site Specifics:

Parking: Parking in Teton Canyon is a real challenge in the middle of the day. Although there are multiple parking areas, they all fill up. Not until the late afternoon or early evening does the parking lot have regularly free parking spaces.

Access: The western part of the trail leading to Alaska Basin gains 30 feet (9 m) for the first 0.7 mile (1.1 km) up to Devil's Stairs. From there, it begins gaining elevation in earnest. The hike up the Face Trail to Table Mountain is steep and extremely strenuous.

HOTSPOT #50

Teton Valley

GPS coordinates

43.72293, -111.11087 /
43°43'23"N, 111°06'39"
W12T 0491070E
4841106N

DESCRIPTION:

There are many locations for viewing the west side of the Teton Mountains from Idaho. This is called the "backside" of the Teton Range by locals. Multiple viewpoint options are available in Teton Valley of the Cathedral Group. Along the Idaho-Wyoming state line, there are close-up views. This is especially true on Table Mountain.

Some views of the Tetons, like from Tetonia, place photographers nearly 10 miles (16 km) away. These perspectives provide a sense of place. Images taken from here provide a three-dimensionality not available from other viewpoints. The Tetons can be seen from Rexburg which is about 50 miles away. The atmosphere and mountains at this distance look different in the morning and evening for every season.

Grand Targhee is the ski resort on the western side of the Teton Range. At the top of Fred's Mountain, the jagged summits are visible, rising a short distance away. Many tourists never cross Teton Pass to photograph the mountains from the west. Residents of Jackson, Wyoming, rarely drive across the pass except to travel to Idaho Falls, Idaho. This side of the mountain range is referred to as, "the quiet side of the mountains." To take a particularly unique photo, try driving up to Grand Targhee and getting out after the last switchback at the "Targhee Peninsula."

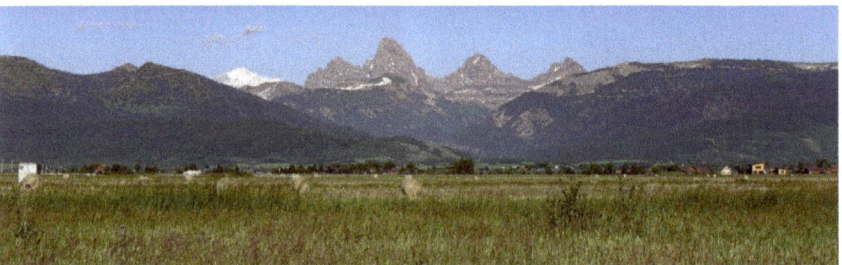
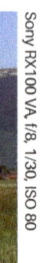

Sony RX100 VA, f/8, 1/30, ISO 80

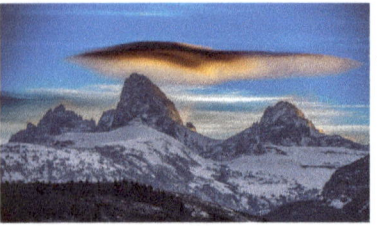

The morning perspective of the Teton Range makes for excellent photography from Teton Valley.

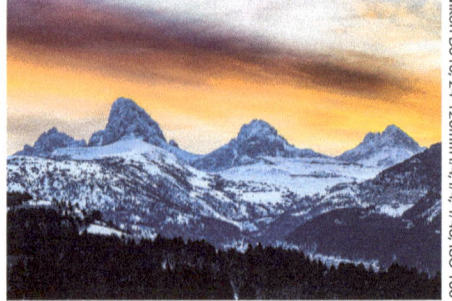

© Randy Isaacson

Nikon D610, 24-120mm f/4, f/4.5, ISO 100

DIRECTIONS
Distance from Town Square

Drive 1.5 miles (2.4 km) west from the Town Square on Broadway to Highway 22 and turn right (N). Drive 22.6 miles (36.4 km) to Victor, Idaho. From here, ID-33 continues 8.3 miles (13.3 km) north to Driggs.

Nikon D500, 70-200mm f/2.8, f/7.1, 1/320, ISO 100

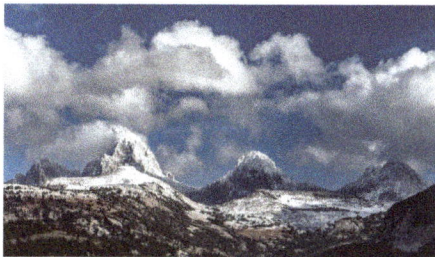
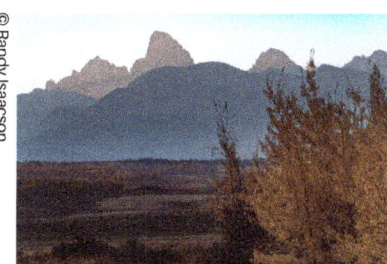

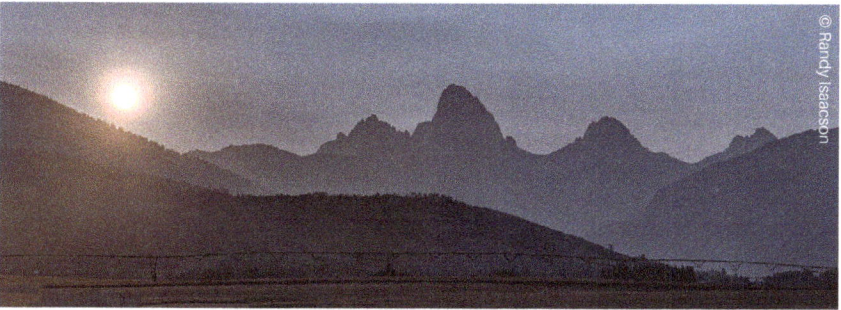

Nikon D500, 70-200 f/2.8, f/10, 1/800, ISO 100

📷 Site Specific Photography Tips

Normal to short telephoto lenses are most useful for capturing good landscapes and portraits of the Teton Range. The mountains appear farther away due to the slope of the foothills. However, this view from Teton Valley provides a better three-dimensional perspective of the range than from the eastern side.

The town of Tetonia, 8.4 miles (13.5 km) north of Driggs, offers a fine view of the summits. It is an excellent location to capture the winter sunrise over the Cathedral Group. Although farther away, a long telephoto lens in the 400-600mm range will provide a "sun enveloping the mountains" look that is not possible when photographing the range up close.

North of Driggs, several dirt roadways lead toward the foothills. Any one of these straight dirt tracks provides good views into Teton Canyon, perfectly framing the Cathedral Group. Interestingly, this is a better view of the summits than actually from Teton Canyon itself. Once you are too close to the canyon, the framing effect disappears and the mountains appear by themselves.

HOTSPOT #50

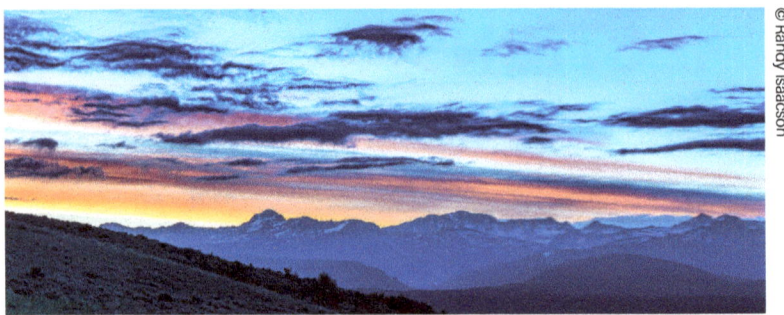

Nikon D500, 70-200mm f/2.8, f/9, 1/30, ISO 100

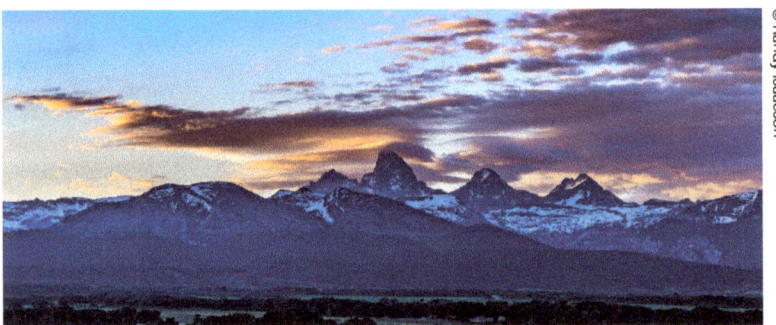

Nikon D500, 70-200mm f/2.8, f/6.3/ 1/250, ISO 100

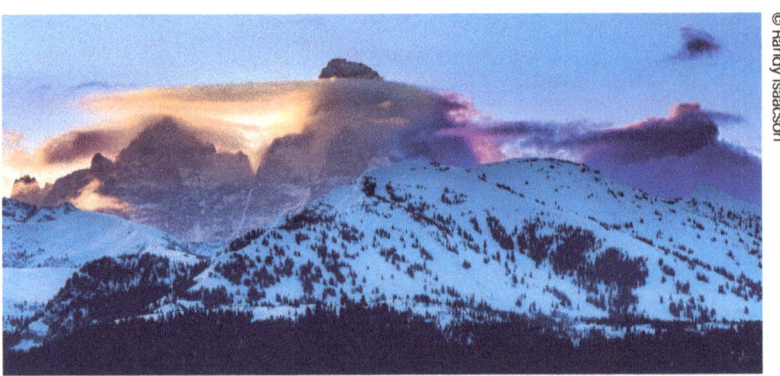

Nikon D500, 70-200mm f/2.8, f/8, 1/50, ISO 100

Site Specifics:

Parking: Most areas in Teton Valley have excellent parking and are rarely full. The only notable exceptions to this rule are the parking at Teton Canyon and Darby Canyon. These sites can be incredibly busy during the summer season.

Access: Most people are in a rush to reach Grand Teton, skipping the fine viewpoints available from Teton Valley. Views from Teton Valley of the Cathedral group are numerous and easy to explore.

About the Author

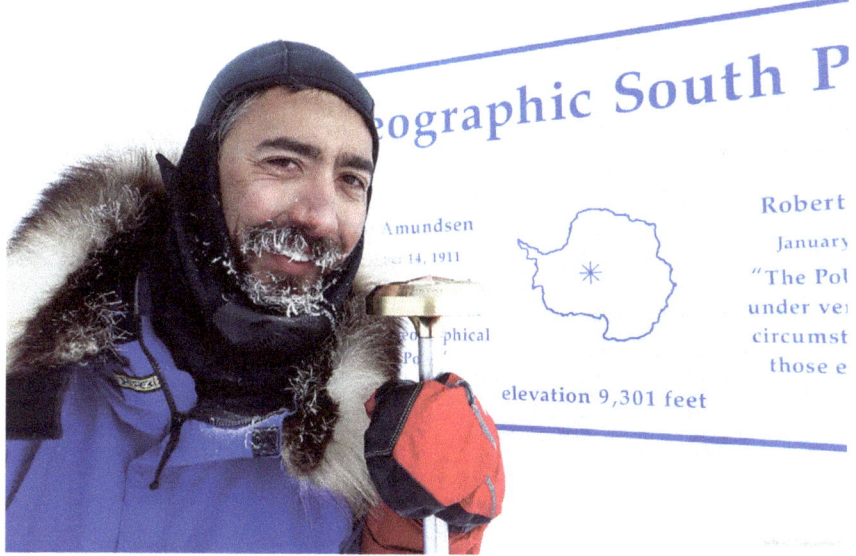

Aaron Linsdau is the second only American to ski alone from the coast of Antarctica to the South Pole, setting a world record for surviving the longest expedition ever for that trip. He has walked across Yellowstone National Park in winter, crossed the Greenland tundra alone, trekked through the Sahara desert, attempted to climb Denali solo, and successfully climbed Mt. Kilimanjaro and Mt. Elbrus in Russia.

He is an Eagle Scout and has received the Outstanding Eagle Scout Award. He holds a bachelor's degree in electrical engineering and a master's degree in computational science. Some of Aaron's books include *Antarctic Tears, Lost at Windy Corner, Adventure Expedition One, How to Keep Your Feet Warm in the Cold,* the *Jackson Hole Hiking Guide,* and *The Most Crucial Knots to Know.* He is also the author of the *2024 Total Eclipse Guide series*.

Aaron has been a professional photographer for over two decades. He has photographed millions of dollars in jewelry, fossilized dinosaurs, and artwork. His landscape photography work reflects his desire to help others appreciate nature in its rawest forms. He shares his photography with those who may never visit the inhospitable locations he explores.

Entertaining audiences around the world, Aaron's keynote speeches are engaging and memorable. Book Aaron as a keynote speaker for your next event.

**Visit Aaron's website at:
www.aaronlinsdau.com**

Additional Photographer Biographies

BETH HOLMES

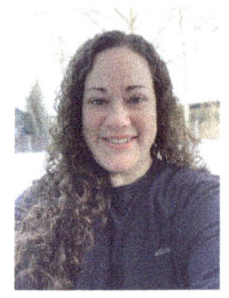

Beth Holmes, a Jackson, Wyoming resident, works full time. Landscape and wildlife photography has been her hobby for over 20 years. The last 9 years she has spent her spare time looking for unique and interesting perspectives to photograph in Jackson, Grand Teton National Park, and beyond. Her work has been published in Outdoor Photographer magazine. You can view her photos at: www.bethholmesphotography.com or follow her on Instagram at @bholmesphoto.

RANDY ISAACSON

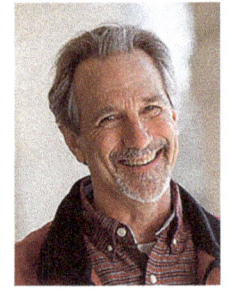

Randy Isaacson is a retired university professor who taught educational psychology and motivation to teachers at Indiana University for 37 years. Randy and his wife had vacationed in the Tetons since the early 1970s and retired to Teton Valley Idaho in 2012. In 2015, Randy launched his website (FirstAnAmateur.com) to share what he was learning in photography with other amateurs. And in 2016, he started a Peer Mentor Program in the Teton Photography Club (www.tetonphotographyclub.org/our-groups/peer-mentor-program/) to create a learning environment for beginner and intermediate photographers. The Peer Mentor Program continues to meet every month. Randy has always been a teacher and hopes to help advance others in their photography.

LOREN NELSON

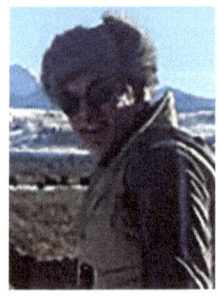

Loren Nelson is a retired inner-city trauma surgeon and medical educator who moved to Jackson, Wyoming after traveling the country visiting national parks and public lands for two years. His passion has always been wildlife and landscape photography and in 2010, he began his transition into serious digital photography. He continues to travel the world enjoying and photographing natural places. His home in Jackson is the perfect starting point to visit western public lands. He has spent extensive time in 42 of the US national parks and more than 28 national monuments.

Enjoy Other Books by Aaron Linsdau

50 Jackson Hole Photography Hotspots

This guide reveals the best Jackson Hole photography spots. Learn what locals and insiders know to find the most impressive and iconic photography locations in the United States. This is an excellent companion guide to the *Jackson Hole Hiking Guide*.

www.sastrugipress.com/books/50-jackson-hole-photography-hotspots/

Adventure Expedition One
by Aaron Linsdau M.S. & Terry Williams, M.D.

Create, finance, enjoy, and return safely from your first expedition. Learn the techniques explorers use to achieve their goals and have a good time doing it. Acquire the skills, find the equipment, and learn the planning necessary to pull off an expedition.

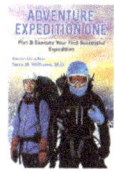

www.sastrugipress.com/books/adventure-expedition-one/

Antarctic Tears

Experience the honest story of solo polar exploration. This inspirational true book will make readers both cheer and cry. Coughing up blood and fighting skin-freezing temperatures were only a few of the perils Aaron Linsdau faced. Travel with him on a world-record expedition to the South Pole.

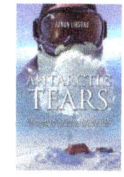

www.sastrugipress.com/books/antarctic-tears/

How to Keep Your Feet Warm in the Cold

Keep your feet warm in cold conditions on chilly adventures with techniques described in this book. Packed with dozens and dozens of ideas, learn how to avoid having cold feet ever again in your outdoor pursuits.

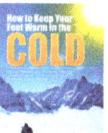

www.sastrugipress.com/books/how-to-keep-your-feet-warm-in-the-cold/

Jackson Hole Hiking Guide

Jackson Hole contains some of the most dramatic and iconic landscapes in the United States. The book shares everything you need to know to hike Jackson's classic trails with canyons, high mountains, and hidden alpine lakes. This book is an excellent companion guide to *50 Jackson Hole Photography Hotspots*.

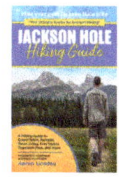

www.sastrugipress.com/books/jackson-hole-hiking-guide/

Subscribe to Aaron's YouTube channel at www.youtube.com/@alinsdau

If you enjoyed this book, please consider leaving a five-star review and a few words on what you liked about it at your favorite online retailer.

Lost at Windy Corner

Windy Corner on Denali has claimed fingers, toes, and even lives. What would make someone brave lethal weather, crevasses, and avalanches to attempt to summit North America's highest mountain? Aaron Linsdau shares the experience of climbing Denali alone and how you can apply the lessons to your life.

www.sastrugipress.com/books/lost-windy-corner/

The Motivated Amateur's Guide to Winter Camping

Winter camping is one of the most satisfying ways to experience the wilderness. It is also the most challenging style of overnighting in the outdoors. Learn 100+ tips from a professional polar explorer on how to winter camp safely and be comfortable in the cold.

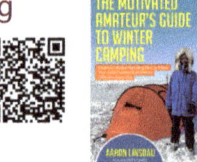

www.sastrugipress.com/books/the-motivated-amateurs-guide-to-winter-camping/

Two Friends and a Polar Bear
by Terry Williams, M.D. & Aaron Linsdau

Winter camping is one of the most satisfying ways to experience the wilderness. It is also the most challenging style of overnighting in the outdoors. Learn 100+ tips from a professional polar explorer on how to winter camp safely and be comfortable in the cold.

www.sastrugipress.com/books/two-friends-and-a-polar-bear/

About the Author

Aaron Linsdau is the second American to ski alone from the coast of Antarctica to the South Pole (730 miles / 1174 km), setting a world record for surviving the longest expedition ever for that trip. He lead a 310-mile (499 km) ski expedition across the Greenland icecap along the Arctic Circle. Aaron has climbed Denali solo, crossed the Greenland tundra alone, skied across Yellowstone National Park solo, trekked through the Sahara desert, and successfully climbed Mt. Kilimanjaro and Mt. Elbrus in Russia.

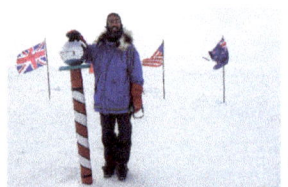

Aaron Linsdau at the South Pole.

Use your smart device to scan the QR codes for website links.

Visit www.aaronlinsdau.com/subscribe to learn more about the author. Receive updates when he releases new books and shows.

Visit Sastrugi Press on the web at www.sastrugipress.com to purchase the above titles in bulk. They are available in print, e-book, or audiobook form.

Thank you for choosing Sastrugi Press.

MY FIELD NOTES:

www.ingramcontent.com/pod-product-compliance
Lightning Source LLC
Chambersburg PA
CBHW040516220526
45473CB00012B/2883